Game Theory in Management

Game Theory in Management

Modelling Business Decisions and their Consequences

MICHAEL HATFIELD

GOWER

Published by
Gower Publishing Limited
Wey Court East
Union Road
Farnham
Surrey
GU9 7PT
England

Gower Publishing Company
Suite 420
101 Cherry Street
Burlington
VT 05401-4405
USA

www.gowerpublishing.com

Michael Hatfield has asserted his moral right under the Copyright, Designs and Patents Act, 1988, to be identified as the author of this work.

British Library Cataloguing in Publication Data
Hatfield, Michael, 1959-
  Game theory in management : modelling business decisions
  and their consequences.
  1. Game theory. 2. Decision making--Mathematical models.
  3. Management information systems.
  I. Title
  658.4'033-dc23

ISBN 978-1-4094-4241-7 (hbk)
ISBN 978-1-4094-4242-4 (ebk)

Library of Congress Cataloging-in-Publication Data
Hatfield, Michael, 1959-
  Game theory in management : modelling business decisions and their
consequences / by Michael Hatfield.
      p. cm.
  ISBN 978-1-4094-4241-7 (hbk) -- ISBN 978-1-4094-4242-4 (ebk)
1. Game theory. 2. Decision making. 3. Problem solving. 4.Management.
I. Title.
  HB144.H377 2011
  658.4'033--dc23

2011045652

Printed and bound in Great Britain by the
MPG Books Group, UK

Contents

List of Figures

List of Tables

About the Author

Michael Hatfield, MBA, PMP, CCC, EVP, belongs to an exclusive club: he is one of the few people who can legitimately claim to be an internationally-recognized expert in the field of Project Management, having received correspondence on his writings and presentations from every continent in the world, save Antarctica. He is the author of the long-running column in *PM®️ Network* magazine, "Variance Threshold," as well PMI®️ Publishing's 2008 title, *Things Your PMO Is Doing Wrong*. While he was blogging for the Project Management Institute, Nicole Adams named his one of the "Top 100 Project Management Blogs."

Michael's use of both logic and humour in his writings have earned him a reputation for clarity in style and insightfulness in content, both of which are abundant in *Game Theory in Management*. He is no stranger to exploring and testing the newest ideas in project management – his Project Management Professional®️ certification number is 1004 (out of more than 390,000 now), and his Earned Value Professional®️ certification number is 24. Michael was the youngest of those receiving invitations to become members of the faculty of the College of Performance Management for the 2004–2005 term, and was the keynote speaker for the Future of Project Management seminar, held in Silicon Valley, California, in 1999. He was also the Deputy Project Manager and contributing author of PMI®️'s *Practice Standard for Earned Value Management*.

In *Game Theory in Management*, he explores the methods through which managerial strategies may be tested for their effectiveness, and thereby confronts much of the conventional wisdom prevalent in traditional, project, and strategic management arenas. Never iconoclastic for its own sake, Michael nevertheless subjects what passes for current management science to the scrutiny of game theory, black swan theory, and traditional logic, and the results are ground-breaking.

While reading *Game Theory in Management*, the reader will immediately become aware that this is not your run-of-the-mill book on management science. Michael's writing is refreshingly free of the stodgy ponderousness that tends to afflict most books on the subject of management science. It's also fearless in its willingness to challenge and overturn much of what passes for conventional wisdom in the business world in general, and the project management arena in particular.

Michael lives in New Mexico with his wife, sons, collie, barn cat and goldfish, and can be reached at varthold@aol.com. The software tools based on the ideas in this book are available through austintechpubs.com.

Acknowledgements

I had a lot of help writing this book, and I want to thank some of those helpers. First and foremost, I want to thank my son Anderson Hatfield, currently a student at Notre Dame Law School, who set the whole project in motion when he recommended I read one of his textbooks from the University of New Mexico that dealt with Game Theory. Scientists and managers Ryan Maupin and Steve Renfro of Los Alamos National Laboratory also contributed profound insights and suggested paths of research, which I'm sure they will recognize once they get around to reading this book. My discussion on the epistemology of management information systems would have been far weaker if not for the insights of Charles ("Chip") Cooper, Bob Ryan, and Steve Reichelt, information technology specialists of the first order, all.

Dr Fred Tarantino, current head of the University Space Research Association, is both a friend and mentor, and taught me more than he realizes about strategic management. Professor William C. Dowling, currently of Rutgers University but formerly of the University of New Mexico, taught me how to research and write like a scholar, and will have a place in the acknowledgements section of every book I ever write. My middle older sister, a prominent psychologist, was invaluable in discussions on the practice of assigning psychological archetypes to people engaged in economic transactions, a topic few in the world are fluent, much less willing to share with an MBA author.

Award-winning author Marcia Daudistel (*Literary El Paso*, *Grace and Gumption*) just happens to be another one of my sisters, and contributed mightily to not only this book, but my previous one, *Things Your PMO Is Doing Wrong*. Jonathan Norman and Chris Muddiman of Gower Publishing have been professional and effective in the extreme, and it's been a joy to work with them.

Finally, I wish to thank those who got me past the difficult period in-between the time I finished the manuscript and the receipt of the e-mail from Jonathan Norman approving the publication. Author Neal Whitten was key, as were Raylyne Lujan, David Hampton, Alice Skehan, and Mary Kay and Troy Hatfield. All of you are dear to me, and it's important you know that I recognize how much you meant to the publication of this work.

1 *Win Using the Rules of the Game*

It's alright to disagree with me, because I've been disagreed with before, and you've been wrong before.

William F. Buckley

There's a certain arrogance involved in writing books on management. The starting point these authors are using assumes, at some level or in some area of expertise, that the reader isn't as good at managing their affairs as is the author. It only gets worse when epistemology – the study of knowledge and its limits – is thrown into the mix, because now we're not just talking about a supposedly superior way to manage, we're pushing forward a supposedly superior way to think!

That having been admitted, I kept coming across what Nassim Taleb calls "flawed tools of inference"[1] while I was researching my previous book, *Things Your PMO Is Doing Wrong*.[2] In fact, the entire first part of that book deals with commonly-used, but ultimately futile, tactics in setting up a Project Management Office (PMO) and attempting to further project management expertise within the macro organization. And the use of those flawed tactics lead to more than your garden-variety frustration in setting up a functional PMO: without a sufficient project management capability, projects come in late, over cost, wasting time and money, and ruining careers.

I observed something I thought was very interesting among my classmates while I was pursuing my MBA. We were subdivided into teams, and these teams stayed pretty much intact throughout the two years it took for us to graduate, except when members left the program. We were told on the first day of the first class that fewer than half of us would make it all the way to graduation, and I remember summoning a resolve to graduate on time, while fully executing my duties to my young family and full-time job. But it wasn't a conflict of duty or time that led to many of my classmates leaving the program. After a couple of introductory classes on Strategic Management and Organization Behavior and Performance, we got into the thick of the curriculum, with two classes each of Accounting and Finance. Graduate Statistics was next up for the MBA candidates, but a member from my team decided to leave at this point, not because she couldn't keep up, but because she believed that the most important aspects of management were in the realms of Finance

---

1   TBS, p. 210.

2   PMI Publishing, 2008.

and Accounting. She was going to change her coursework so that she could become a Certified Public Accountant rather than an MBA. We were sorry to see her go, but the rest of us hunkered down for Statistics.

After Statistics was Business Law, and the same thing happened again. A member of one of the other teams felt that protecting the organization's assets from liability was the most important aspect of management, and left to study the law. I don't know if he would end up as a lawyer, or if he even got into law school, but a definite trend was emerging. Two students left after the Management Information System course, to pursue careers as either programmers or system administrators. Each class instructor, being both highly educated and a practicing professional in their subject areas, had imparted to some students the notion that their take on their subject areas was the most important and, by extension, probably the most lucrative, even if this wasn't provably apparent at that particular time. This competition of perspectives would claim easily as many dropouts as all of the other causes combined, and at our graduation ceremony, just as predicted, there were fewer than half of the people there than had been present at that first class.

I was no stranger to the battle of perspectives in the management theory world. I was working at the time for a contractor for a United States Government agency as a project control specialist, which involved setting up the cost and schedule performance information systems used to manage projects. At that time this particular agency granted their contractors some latitude in complying with the requirements on how these systems ought to be set up and maintained, and what the output of these systems should look like. By contrast, the requirements on how the accounting system should be set up and maintained were highly rigid and consistently enforced, and so the company's accountants' decisions always received deferential treatment on matters of how costs should be collected, how cost performance should be analyzed and reported, and a whole range of matters where clearly Generally Accepted Accounting Principles had no sway. The Project Management Institute® had been founded in 1969, and had created its first professional certification, the Project Management Professional (PMP®), in 1984 – two years after Tom Peters and Robert H. Waterman, Jr. released *In Search of Excellence*. Up until this point there was really no effective counter to the notion that the perspective of the accountants ought to dominate the realm of business decisions. But when I saw a tape of Tom Peters discussing the folly of myopically pursuing bottom-line strategies while ignoring even the slightest of customer-oriented actions, I realized that a massive change was underway. Here was Professor Peters mocking Sloan School MBAs, *to their faces*, for having adopted the very notions and perspectives they had learned from the most prominent business teachers in the land, and he was receiving standing ovations for it. Having received some weeks of training in project management information systems, I knew that I was on the right side of the coming sea-change, but I was still frustrated and stymied in my attempts to advance project management maturity within my organization. The accountants held all the cards. So, I decided if I was going to have any chance at all in the coming conflict of perspectives, I had to know what my opponents knew. With the company's generous tuition reimbursement program, I signed up for the entrance examination to graduate business school, and pursued my MBA.

After graduating, I felt I had to be stronger in the project management realm, and so worked for and achieved my very own Project Management Professional certification,[3] in

---

3   This may have been one of the very earliest PMP®s that PMI® granted – its number is 1004.

1992, followed quickly by a Certified Cost Consultant certification from what was then known as the American Association of Cost Engineers, or AACE (now the Association for the Advancement of Cost Engineering, International. I guess they wanted to be more cosmopolitan). Within a few years I was writing a monthly column for PMI's trade magazine, *PM® Network*. The name of the column was "The Variance Threshold," and they put me on the back page where I had remarkable latitude to make fun of anything I wanted in the management realm, and, brother, was there a mother lode of material for the taking. From early on, though, I was poking fun at the narrowness of vision exhibited by "our friends, the accountants" (as I often described them). But I'll never forget an exchange I had with my wife (who also holds an MBA, though from a different school) leading up to one of my columns:

Hey, babe, in my next piece I'm going to advance the idea that the overall goal of management is NOT "maximizing shareholder wealth."

What?

Yeah, if there was one common theme that all my professors were comfortable with retreating to, it was those three words. But I'm beginning to think they're not valid.

If you assert that, or anything like it, you'll lose all credibility, and PMI will drop your column.

Yeah, maybe. But I think I can make it entertaining enough so they'll print it.

Good luck.

As it turned out, "The Variance Threshold" was a pretty successful column over its 11-year run. Some of that success had to do with my being irreverent, or turning the occasional phrase. But I'm also pretty sure that much of the column's success had to do with my asserting unequivocally that there is a fundamental difference between asset management and project management, and that recognizing these differences was crucial to the ability of managers within the organization to make informed decisions.

Flash forward to the spring of 2010. My older son invited me to read one of his textbooks, *A Beautiful Math*, by Tom Siegfried. Its subtitle is *John Nash, Game Theory, and the Modern Quest for a Code of Nature*. *A Beautiful Math* draws heavily from John Von Neumann and Oskar Morgansters' book, *Theory of Games and Economic Behavior*, which was published in 1944. Von Neumann is considered one of the most brilliant thinkers of the twentieth century, and *Theory of Games* is the starting point for virtually all of the ensuing work in the field. A profound refinement in Game Theory was introduced in 1950, by the aforementioned John Nash. In *Equilibrium Points in N-Person Games*, an essay in the Proceedings for the National Academy of Sciences, Nash introduced what would later be named the Nash Equilibrium (I will cover the basics and nuances of these terms and ideas in Part 1 of this book). With the introduction of the Nash Equilibrium, Game Theory began to find applications in a wide variety of disciplines, including medicine, traffic control, economics … and business and management. As referenced in the subtitle, Siegfried not-so-subtly asserts that Game Theory, when combined with Network Theory and the statistical analysis techniques that support modern Risk Management Theory, might actually be able to produce at some point in the future a Code of Nature. This Code of Nature is essentially an overarching theoretical structure that can explain not only how current processes produce current events and phenomena, but can predict future events and phenomena, similar to the psychohistory concept introduced by Isaac Asimov in the *Foundation* series in (coincidentally?) 1951.

For those of you who are not partakers of science fiction, *Foundation* takes place in a future where the Milky Way galaxy has been colonized by humans. A scientist name Hari Seldon develops the concept of psychohistory, a highly-advanced mathematical structure which can predict the future, but only in very large populations. The most common analogy used is that of the impossibility of predicting the behavior of a single molecule of a given gas; but, given a sufficiently large sample, predicting the gas' behavior becomes simpler and easier. In the series, Seldon predicts/calculates that a civilizational collapse will come about, and hopes that the ensuing 30,000 years of Dark Ages and barbarism can be reduced to a single millennium by sequestering away knowledge and technology in a safe haven, to have it re-introduced at an appropriate time. One additional critical aspect of the story in the *Foundation* series that the Game Theory practitioner will need to know is that the Seldon plan is almost completely undone by the unexpected appearance of a character named The Mule, who has mutant powers of mental persuasion. Since The Mule is a mutant, his sudden appearance and success in conquering the galaxy could not have been predicted or calculated using psychohistory.

The essence of Game Theory is to evaluate which set of canned strategies are most likely to be used by participants in some form of interaction (or game) in a common environment, which is why, no doubt, it is so attractive to those seeking a Code of Nature. Sitting as it does on the cusp of explaining why things are the way they are (Game Theory is very popular among Darwinists) and predicting how things will be in the future, it does present as an overarching structure that explains and predicts all things, or at least those things that come about (or will come about) when the interactions are economic in nature, and the common environment is the free market. This is also why Game Theory so readily incorporates current Risk Management Theory, since Game Theory evaluates which set of canned strategies *is most likely* to be employed.

But then a funny thing happened on the way to the successful implementation of the Seldon Plan. Nassim Taleb wrote *The Black Swan: The Impact of the Highly Improbable*, and it became a *New York Times* best seller. In *The Black Swan*, Taleb doesn't merely overturn the notions of some confab of Game Theory, Risk Management Theory, and Network Theory coming together for some usable Code of Nature; he thoroughly deconstructs them, and reveals the illogical underpinnings of the lot. I will cover Taleb's counterpoints, ripostes, and assertions in detail in Part 2 of this book; for now, suffice to say that *The Black Swan* provides a clear upper-boundary to the limits of the utility of Game Theory and current Risk Management Theory, and these limits are far, far lower than current practitioners realize. Indeed, if a simple majority of the assertions contained in *The Black Swan* are valid (and I believe that a vast majority of them are), then the entire section on Risk Management in *A Guide to the Project Management Body of Knowledge*®, and any and all of the literature that agrees with it, is almost certainly suspect, at the very least.

So, in writing a book on the theory of games and management behavior, my goal was made clear for me early: define those circumstances and environs where modeling behavior and events, calculating Nash equilibriums, and evoking a particular set of canned strategies was appropriate, and asserting a clearly articulable acid-test that could show where these types of analyses are a complete waste of time and money. Similar to the structure in *Things Your PMO Is Doing Wrong*, this book is divided into three parts: Part 1 will cover the basics of Game Theory, as well as accompanying tangential Risk Management and Network Theory ideas, and will make the case for those times and places where they can lead to informed managerial decision-making. Part 2 will review Black Swan theory, and show exactly where Game Theory's limits are, and how current practitioners of both Game Theory and Risk Management have advanced their notions so far beyond their appropriate application domain that they are threatening to becoming utterly fraudulent as currently practiced. Part 3 will thread the theoretical needle, and offer a testable structure for correctly using Game Theory in management to deliver better informed (and, one would hope, more insightful) managerial decisions.

And with that, let's tackle game theory in management.

CHAPTER

1 *Chess Openings and Risk Management*

He attacked everything in life with a mix of extraordinary genius and naive incompetence, and it was often difficult to tell which was which.

Douglas Adams

The Western Roman Empire fell at about the same time as the game of chess was introduced in Western India – around the fifth and sixth centuries. This, perhaps the earliest game that pretended to represent elements from real-life conflict, and where canned strategies and tactics could be compared, or tested empirically, came to Europe in the ninth century. As a young man, I spent a great deal of time studying, practicing, and playing chess in order to become a proficient tournament player of the game. This experience taught me a great deal about chess, life, and, though I didn't know it at the time, Game Theory and its possible applications to real-life situations.

When I joined my first competitive chess team in high school, I hadn't spent a lot of time studying the game; I just had a pretty canny sense of how to win. It didn't take long for inferior players who had done just a bit of studying to wipe me and my canny sense all over the chessboard and take my United States Chess Federation points away. The studying they had done that enabled them to do this centered on chess openings.

Chess openings are an orchestrated set of moves – canned strategies, or a list of specific tactics, if you will – that are used in the first (up to 30) moves of a game. These sets of orchestrated moves have names, such as Ruy Lopez, or the Catalan, for the basic (first 4–9 moves) version of the opening, and then names for their variants (the versions that manifest after the initial set of moves). It is a very rare tournament player who has any chance at all without complete familiarity with at least four openings, with their attendant variants: one for when the player is playing white, and black's first move is the one expected; one for when the player is playing white, and black's first move is other than the one expected; one for playing black against 1. P-K4, and one for playing black against 1. P-Q4. Since each opening usually has at least three key variants, the tournament player needs to memorize *at least* 12 games through the 20-somethingth move, and know how to punish a player who does not have the same knowledge. This is a key element: in an environment where people are executing canned strategies, the ability to recognize which strategy is being employed, and to counter it effectively, is the difference between winning and losing the "game."

So, how did I move from chess team punching bag to the number one player on the team? By employing something that Von Neumann had described 45 years earlier as a "mixed strategy."

The Queen's Gambit was very popular at Eldorado High School's Chess Club at the time I joined. The opening moves are:

	White	Black
1.	P-Q4	P-Q4
2.	P-QB4	......

Black now has a dilemma. If he takes the (apparently) unguarded pawn, he opens himself up to a variety of traps and setbacks in space, time, and pawn structure (more on leveraging advantages in one theater into another, seemingly unrelated one in Part III). But if he declines to capture the pawn, his own pawn is under attack, and deploying the defending Queen to the middle of the board all by her lonesome is an unattractive prospect, at best. My new teammates knew what to do in either case, and could very effectively outplay the opponent who did not know how to execute sufficiently to reach the middle game without a significant disadvantage.

My solution? Don't answer P-Q4 with P-Q4. I studied the variations of Bobby Fischer's favorite response to the Queen's Gambit, the King's Indian Defense. It answered 1. P-Q4 with N-KB3, followed by 2. P-QB4 P-KN3. For those of you who are reading this book without a chess board nearby, suffice to say that this opening looks nothing like the scenario the Queen's Gambit lovers were used to seeing. And with copies of the way Fischer played this opening right there in my copies of *Chess Life & Review*, I was suddenly in a position to punish the Gambit players who weren't familiar with *this* opening through the 20-somethingth move. In short, I knew beforehand what their canned strategy was, recognized it when it first manifest, and was ready with a thoroughly robust response.

After memorizing the opening sequences I needed to survive the first 20-something moves, I moved up, but it wasn't long until I hit another wall. The next set of canned strategies I needed to get ahead was contained in the book *My System*, by Aron Nimzovich.[1] This book is an extraordinary aid to any chess player seeking to improve their game dramatically and quickly. Nimzovich lays out nine elements:

- On the center, and development.
- On open files (files are the up-and-down rows on a chess board).
- The seventh and eighth ranks (ranks are the across rows).
- The passed pawn.
- On exchanging.
- The elements of end game strategy.
- The pin.
- Discovered check.
- The pawn chain.

I quickly discovered that the tournament player who had done her homework with respect to the openings, and had read Nimzovich's treatment of these mid-game canned strategies, was very difficult to defeat, even in the upper levels of tournament play. I would encounter players whose only influence was *My System*, and they were tough to

---

1   Nimzovich, Aron, *My System*, McCay Chess Library, 1947.

beat. It was proving very easy to associate the ability to select the most appropriate set of canned strategies in a given situation with ultimate success – and not just in the world of chess.

In several ways chess represents a superior real-life modeling game over the ones introduced by Von Neumann because of something the game theorists refer to as utility. Utility is essentially the payoff(s) the games' participants receive, or are expecting to receive, and profoundly influences the selection of strategies. The reason chess may prove superior to the games reviewed by Von Neumann is that, with very few exceptions, the utility offered by the Von Neumann games was one-dimensional. For example, in the Prisoner's Dilemma, the utility involves minimizing or eliminating the amount of time each player must remain in prison. In the Ultimatum Game (and most of the others), the payoff is the amount of money that the participants stand to gain out of a fixed amount.

But chess is different in that, not only are there multiple payoffs that can be pursued by engaging different strategies, those payoffs can be leveraged to attain other types of payoffs. In *New Ideas in Chess*,[2] Grandmaster Larry Evans argues that there are four main elements in chess: pawn structure, force, time, and space. Certain openings, or set strategies, can obtain advantages, say, in time and space, while (temporarily) giving up an advantage in force, which is what happens in the Queen's Gambit Accepted. Chess comes closer to modeling real life than the single-utility games because it's not always readily apparent which strategy the other player(s) will adopt, because it's not always readily apparent which payoff they are seeking to attain.

Indeed, having the experience of learning to play tournament chess at a fairly competent level ingrained in my head the idea that life was like a great game of chess. Tournament chess teams are arranged by "boards," or one's relative position on the team. The first-best player is "First Board," the second-best player is "Second Board," and so forth. Your team's First Board plays your opponent's First Board, Second Boards play Second Boards, and so on, usually to Seventh Boards.[3] As First Board, I was expected to fulfill the role of Head Coach (to a certain extent), and my favorite piece of advice was "If you can foresee your opponent's next move, you will almost never lose."

Acting as if life was a chess game writ large, I was continually trying to anticipate that "next move" that life was going to throw my way. Sometimes I was right, but often enough I had no clue. The Behaviorism School of Psychological Thought teaches that a variable rate of reinforcement tends to guarantee the behavior; hence the number of people who are addicted to gambling. The notion that expertise in chess could lead to an advanced ability to anticipate events, and thereby to respond more quickly and with a superior set of response strategies, was one that did not die easily.

Risk Management, as Currently Practiced

If patterns of strategy-consistent behavior couldn't be reflexively recognized, leading to the most appropriate response on a consistent basis, could the *odds* of a certain strategy

---

2   Evans, Larry, *New Ideas in Chess*, Cornerstone Library Publications, Reprinted 1973.

3   Even here, there was some Game Theory working itself out. If a chess team perceived it was overmatched, it would occasionally deliberately assign its first-best player down to third board, second to fourth, and so on. They would lose their top two board's games, but could be expected to run the table otherwise. This canned strategy was known as "stacking the boards."

being implemented be evaluated? And could *that* lead to the adoption of the most appropriate response?

In project management circles risk management is a big deal. The 1996 edition of *A Guide to the Project Management Body of Knowledge® (PMBOK® Guide)*[4] states:

> *Project Risk Management includes the processes concerned with identifying, analyzing, and responding to project risk. It includes maximizing the results of positive events and minimizing the consequences of adverse events.*

The *PMBOK® Guide* then goes on to lay out four "major processes" of risk management:

1. Risk identification;
2. Risk quantification;
3. Risk response development; and
4. Risk response control.

Current (2011) risk management software tools primarily deal with the first two of these major processes: risk identification and quantification. The reason risk management is applicable to project management and project management alone is that the identification and quantification of risk events is predicated on project work that has been decomposed using a Work Breakdown Structure (WBS). The risk identification and quantification processes can then be used at the lowest level of the WBS. Once each of the lowest WBS elements has been so evaluated, the quantification of the risks are summed for a value of overall project risk, which can then be used to approximate cost and schedule contingency reserve amounts.

Risk events are categorized as *known-unknowns*, and *unknown-unknowns*. Known-unknowns are risk events that have some level of predictability and, presumably, quantification. Known-unknowns are often further subdivided into categories such as internal and external, or technical, internal non-technical, insurable, and legal.

The identification and quantification processes generally use one of three techniques, which provide successive levels of detail and complexity while requiring more effort in data gathering. The first (and most basic) of these techniques is *Risk Categorization Bracketing*, or just Bracketing. This involves the establishment of three risk brackets, low, medium, and high, and their associated percentage categories. For example, a given project may assign a 5% risk bracket to low-risk activities, a 25% risk bracket to medium-risk activities, and a 100% risk bracket to high-risk activities (meaning that, say, if something were to go catastrophically wrong with a high-risk activity, it could double the amount of time and resources needed to complete the scope of that activity).

Once these brackets are established, the risk management analyst would then go through the WBS at its lowest level and determine whether each of the elements represented a low, medium, or high risk, and assign them an "L," "M," or "H." After these assignments have been made, the analyst will again go through the WBS at the lowest level and multiply the duration and the budget for the activity by the percentage associated with its classification. These calculations are "rolled up" through the WBS and

---

4   Duncan, William R., *A Guide to the Project Management Body of Knowledge*, Project Management Institute, 1996.

Table 1.1   Risk Quantification Example

WBS Element/Task	Budget ($K) Duration (days)	Risk Category	Risk %	Budget/Schedule Contingency
1.1 Project Management	$98 210d	Low	5%	$4.9 10.5d
1.2 Project Controls	$78 210d	Low	5%	$3.9 10.5d
2.1 Design Creation	$55 40d	Low	5%	$2.7 2d
2.2 Design Validation	$32 15d	Medium	25%	$8.0 3.7d
3.1 Construct Foundation	$340 34d	Medium	25%	$85 8.5d
3.2 Utilities	$46 65d	Medium	25%	$11.5 16.2d
3.3 Structure	$120 52d	High	100%	$120 52d
3.4 HVAC	$54 37d	Medium	25%	$13.5 9.2
3.5 Interior	$103 68d	Medium	25%	$25.7 17d
3.6 Roof/Ceiling	$98 82d	Medium	25%	$24.5 20.5d
3.7 Landscaping	$19 14d	Low	5%	$0.9 0.7d
Total Project	$1,043 210d			$300.7 86.7d

summed for an approximation of the overall project's contingency budget and schedule. An example is shown in Table 1.1.

While this is admittedly a crude method for evaluating project risk, it does have two advantages: it's quick, and it's (relatively) easy. It also has the added benefit of allowing you to tell your customer that you have performed a risk analysis on your baseline, and are using that analysis as the basis for establishing cost and schedule contingency reserves, without being dishonest.

The next most sophisticated commonly-used technique in risk identification and quantification is the Decision Tree analysis, which will come up again in the discussions on Game Theory. As with Risk Bracketing, Decision Tree analysis is usually performed at the lowest level of the WBS, though it does not have to be. It's also similar to Risk Bracketing in that it assigns odds of risk events occurring and calculates an impact, but does so in significantly more detail and with, presumably, more accuracy.

---

5   The reason that the total amount of schedule contingency is not the sum of the WBS element's schedule contingency amount is that total project schedule contingency is only affected by activities on the critical path, or activities with contingency duration that is in excess of float.

For each activity or task being evaluated in a Decision Tree Analysis, the person performing the analysis attempts to quantify the odds of an identified risk event occurring, and its impact in terms of cost and schedule. For example, from Table 1.1, WBS 3.3, Structure, is considered a high-risk activity. Its budget is $120,000 and it is scheduled to last 52 days. However, our fictitious task leader for WBS 3.3 is worried about several potential risk events, not the least of which is that the Design Validation (WBS 2.2) guys have no idea what they're doing, and a design flaw may not become apparent until significant progress has already been made. He's also concerned about the availability of steel workers with the necessary level of expertise, as well as the impacts of weather. These identified risk events laid out as follows (Figure 1.1):

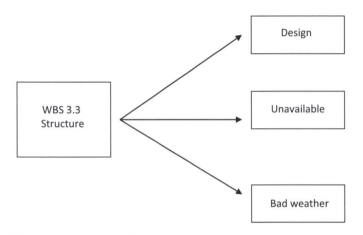

Figure 1.1   WBS 3.3 Structure (Part 1)

Our manager then proceeds to assign what he believes are the odds of each of his concerns coming about, and what impact it would have (Figure 1.2):

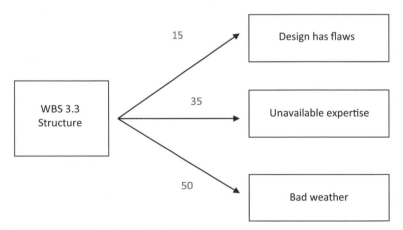

Figure 1.2   WBS 3.3 Structure (Part 2)

With these data elements in place, the calculation proceeds as follows:

Table 1.2   Decision Tree Analysis Calculation

Risk Event	Odds of Occurrence	Cost Impact Schedule Impact	Cost Contingency Schedule Contingency
Design Flaw	15%	$80K 35 days	$12K 5.25 days
Unavailable Expertise	35%	$40K 20 days	$14K 7 days
Bad Weather	50%	$15K 10 days	$7.5K 5 days
Task Total		$135K 65 days	$33.5K 17.25 days

A couple of things to note about this example. It's known as a *single-tier* Decision Tree, because we only evaluated one set of non-mutually-exclusive risk events. If we were to evaluate the odds and impacts, say, of the design flaw being recognized early or late in the task, the extra effort involved in recruiting versus a full-up strike from the union, and the disparate impacts of snow versus rain, that would require a quantification of the risk events that are subordinate to the events we've already quantified, and that would require another tier. Also, when Decision Tree analysis comes up in later chapters on Game Theory, each alternative in a Decision Tree is considered to be mutually exclusive, meaning that you can only select one decision or path from the alternatives. Because of this exclusivity, the sum of the odds of each tier in a Decision Tree must add up to 100%. Note that the fact that each tier's odds sum to 100% does not imply an awareness of any and all possible risk event that could occur. Those who maintain to the contrary are failing to make the distinction between known-unknowns and unknown-unknowns. For example, if the sum of the odds of a given tier in a Decision Tree were to total, say, 83%, wouldn't that indicate that there is an estimated chance of 17% of an unknown-unknown risk event occurring? And, if any event has a 17% chance of occurring, isn't it now a (somewhat) *known*-unknown? No, the individual tiers adding to 100% simply implies that those are all of the known-unknowns being evaluated by the analysis. But the fact that the tiers sum to 100% without strict exclusivity being observed among the quantified risk events does introduce a level of error into the analysis, which I will address more fully in Part 2.

The third and most sophisticated of the commonly-used risk analysis techniques is Simulation, most often performed via Monte Carlo analysis. Monte Carlo simulations require the existence not only of a project WBS, but all of the project's activities captured in a Critical Path Method (CPM) – capable software package in order for its analysis to maximize usefulness. Monte Carlo simulators are often sold and installed in conjunction with CPM software for this purpose.

Each activity is evaluated for identification and quantification of risk events, and this data is entered into the Monte Carlo engine. The bare minimum data needed includes activity I.D., duration, budget, worst-case scenario cost and schedule impact, and best-case scenario cost and schedule impact, with the original budget and durations taken to be the most likely. The software then calculates a series of performed projects modeled on the version captured in the CPM software, using a random number generator to create multiple different outcomes for each activity. Monte Carlo simulations are vastly superior to other risk analysis techniques for capturing the total impact of risk events that cascade, or affect activities that, in turn, delay or otherwise negatively affect the risk-encountering activity's successors, and those activities' successors, and so forth throughout the CPM network.

For example, in an article appearing in the *Wall Street Journal* on December 20, 1999, John J. Fialka describes how the National Ignition Facility (NIF) project experienced its massive cost and schedule overruns.[6] The NIF was a project designed to help researchers answer questions surrounding nuclear fusion. The concept was to surround a pellet of a hydrogen isotope with 192 high-powered lasers that could deliver sufficient energy to the target quickly enough to induce nuclear fusion, the same type of reaction that the Sun uses. The project was spearheaded by a scientist, who swore to Senate Appropriations Committee staffers that if Lawrence Livermore National Laboratory was selected to build the project, he would make sure it stayed on budget.

Unfortunately, cascading risk events rendered that promise impossible to keep. Work began in 1997 with an estimated budget of $1.1 billion. The final price was nearly quadruple that amount. The Wikipedia article on NIF states:

> *The Pulsed Power Conditioning Modules (PCMs) suffered capacitor failures, which in turn caused explosions. This required a redesign of the module to contain the debris, but since the concrete structure of the buildings holding them had already been poured, this left the new modules so tightly packed that there was no way to do maintenance in-place. Yet another redesign followed, this time allowing the modules to be removed from the bays for servicing. Continuing problems of this sort further delayed the operational start of the project, and in September 1999 an updated DOE report stated that NIF would require up to $350 million more and completion would be pushed back to 2006.[7]*

More problems like this manifested, but perhaps the most damaging risk event had to do with dust. High-energy lasers do not react well to dust: if the various mirrors and lenses used to aim and manipulate the beams have so much as a speck on them, the damage can be explosive, immediate, and expensive. Insufficient consideration was given to the difficulties of performing an extremely large construction effort, with new technology and large, heavy, and expensive components, all in a clean room environment. The early problems with design, construction, and dust cascaded to the point that NIF became the poster child for the perils of failing to perform the project management function adequately. I do not claim that a complete Monte Carlo analysis on this project could have predicted or prevented what happened from happening; rather, I am using the example of NIF to demonstrate what can happen in cascading risk event scenarios, the same type of scenarios that Monte Carlo analysis is far more adept at predicting and capturing than other risk analysis techniques.

---

6   Fialka, John J., "Dust Storm: Fear of a Different Sort of Infiltrator Paralyzes US Nuclear Project," *The Wall Street Journal*, December 20, 1999.

7   National Ignition Facility (2010, July 8). In *Wikipedia, The Free Encyclopedia*. Retrieved 21:27, July 16, 2010, from http://en.wikipedia.org/w/index.php?title=National_Ignition_Facility&oldid=372355449

What Comes Next?

Once risk events have been identified and quantified, they are assigned to one of four categories (according to the Defense Acquisition University):

1. Avoid;
2. Control;
3. Accept; or
4. Transfer.

These assignments, along with the task's risks' identification and quantification, are entered into a risk management plan. The risk management plan is updated as the project progresses. The more advanced risk management systems will recognize contingency release points for those projects that have a contingency budget generated from the risk identification and qualification. For example, in the example we have been using so far in this chapter, once the task manager for the utility activity (WBS 3.2) has successfully completed his task on-budget, the amount of contingency that had been set aside for that activity ($11,500) can be released to another reserve, added to the baseline for accomplishing additional work, or kept in the contingency reserve in the event that another activity is expected to draw down more funds than the risk identification and quantification had originally estimated.

Another major function of the risk identification and quantification phases in current practice is to provide a confidence interval for the bases of estimate that serve as the underpinnings of original budgets. The aforementioned National Ignition Facility was by no means the first major overrun the United States Government has encountered in dealing with the contractors who provide vital goods and services to them. Management practices were developed to avoid finding themselves in a situation where a project that had been originally estimated to cost, say, $1.1 billion would be so far along in the project work that, should the real price tag be revealed to be far higher, the Government would not have to choose between walking away from the already-sunk costs and the equally distasteful choice of scraping together the funds to cover the higher estimate. One of these techniques involves performing a Monte Carlo simulation with enough iterated modeled project performances so that a contingency budget can be declared that would cover 80% of those modeled performances. If the proposed budget plus estimated contingency is considered too high a price, the project is not authorized.

The second way of reducing the risk of being committed to an overrunning project is to divide the project lifecycle into phases, separated by Critical Decision Points, also known as just Critical Decisions, or CDs. These points are:

- CD-0, Identification of Mission Need.
- CD-1, Initial Estimates and Baseline Creation.
- CD-2, Approve Cost and Schedule Baselines.
- CD-3, Approve Start of Construction.
- CD-4, Completion of Construction, Turn Over to Customer.

At any one of these points the Government can cancel the project and reclaim any funds that had been previously committed but not yet spent.

This section of the book was not intended as a comprehensive assessment of the available risk management techniques or an in-depth analysis of the utility of using them; rather, it was intended as an overview of the common practices associated with risk management today, and to provide enough of a primer for when the discussion turns to the conflation of risk management theory with Game Theory, and the limits of risk management as an aid to informed decision-making (which will happen in Part 2). As we will see, these limits are far more confining than many risk management practitioners are prepared to recognize, much less admit.

2 Introduction to Game Theory, and a Code of Nature

There can be as much value in the blink of an eye as in months of rational analysis.

Malcolm Gladwell, *Blink: The Power of Thinking Without Thinking*, 2005

Never try to draw to an inside straight.

After learning the basics of poker, this is probably the first piece of advice the person who taught you gave you – that is, if the person who taught you actually won hands of poker from time to time. It's good advice – the odds of holding, say, a nine, queen, and king, and drawing two cards in anticipation of getting a ten and a jack and actually *getting* a ten and a jack are fairly remote. Problem is, depending on how young you were when you learned poker, this may have instilled two notions:

1. Knowledge of canned strategies, as well as having a certain ability to compute the odds of something happening in the future, was endemic to winning; and
2. Perhaps not just at poker.

While attempts to reduce real-life situations and events into an environ where boundary parameters were known (or could be known), and certain rules of interaction between players could also be known and observed, have been around in some form since the dawn of civilization, the idea that such a reduction could retain sufficient complexity to explain observed phenomena, perhaps predict a very near-term future, and then go on to predict a long-term future, gained prominence with John Von Neumann and Oskar Moregenstern's *Theory of Games and Economic Behavior*, in 1944. Baseball, bridge, poker … all were reduced to mathematical quantifications and predictable strategies undertaken by the players. If concepts such as "utility" could be sufficiently captured and evaluated mathematically, and the parameters of the games used to describe larger reality, then a Code of Nature (see the Introduction for a discussion of a Code of Nature) could actually be within mankind's grasp.

There are some key concepts the reader needs to know going forward. Wikipedia's definition of Game Theory is similar to Von Neumann's and Tom Siegfried's, and reads: "Game theory attempts to mathematically capture behavior in *strategic situations*, in which an individual's success in making choices depends on the choices of others."[1] As we proceed, we will be adding to and refining this definition, but for now it suffices.

The most common game referenced, and perhaps the most famous, is The Prisoner's Dilemma. I actually used this game extensively in my first book, *Things Your PMO Is Doing Wrong*, because it does a nice job of quantifying cooperation and defection among non-related biological units in a common environment – very much like the workplace. Though the numbers vary depending on the version, the essence is that you are a prisoner, and your guard comes to you with a proposal: if you rat out (tell on, or reveal evidence about) your cellmate, the jailer will reduce your sentence. Problem is, you know the same offer is being made to your cellmate. There are four possible outcomes:

- You cooperate (with your cellmate, i.e., you don't tell), but your cellmate rats. Result, you get 10 years, and your cellmate walks free (this is known as the "sucker's payoff").
- You rat, but your cellmate doesn't, resulting in the opposite of the above bullet. You walk, but the cellmate gets 10 years.
- You both cooperate, or refuse to divulge information on the other. You both get six months.
- You both rat, and both get five years.

In evaluating possible outcomes and solutions, game theorists set up a grid, called a *payoff matrix*, which looks like this (Table 2.1):

Table 2.1   The Payoff Matrix

	Cooperate	Defect
Cooperate	6 months, 6 months	10 years, walks
Defect	Walks, 10 years	5 years, 5 years

Another way of expressing this payoff matrix is (Table 2.2):

Table 2.2   The Payoff Matrix (Alternative Version)

	Cooperate	Defect
Cooperate	Lose little, Lose little	Lose Big, Win
Defect	Win, Lose Big	Lose Medium, Lose Medium

Still another way of expressing this mathematically is to say, if you defect, and your cellmate cooperates (scenario *D*), it is better for you than if you both cooperate (scenario

---

1   Game theory (July 8, 2010). In *Wikipedia, The Free Encyclopedia*. Retrieved 19:12, July 11, 2010, from http://en.wikipedia.org/w/index.php?title=Game_theory&oldid=372467612

C), which is better than if you both defect (*2D*), which is better than being at the receiving end of the Sucker's Payoff (scenario *S*). In other words:

$$D > C > 2D > S$$

Based on this formula, it becomes apparent that, in order to avail yourself of the best possible outcome, or *utility*, as well as to avoid the worst possible outcome, the logical choice is to always defect. The efficacy of this strategy will be evaluated in subsequent chapters.

When a game such as the Prisoner's Dilemma is played multiple times, it's said to be an *iterative* game. Since you don't know what your cellmate is going to do, you are said to have *incomplete information*. Also, since you can't communicate with the other player, the Prisoner's Dilemma is also a *non-cooperative* game. Games where communication is possible are said to be *cooperative*.

After the Prisoner's Dilemma, probably the best-known game is Chicken, thanks to that iconic scene in *Rebel Without a Cause* where James Dean's character's antagonist stays in his car headed for the cliff as it careens over. Whether the cars are driving towards each other or simultaneously towards a cliff, the payoff matrix is the same. The cars are headed towards a crash, unless one of the drivers swerves. The driver that swerves is considered to be cowardly, or "chicken." Here's the payoff matrix (Table 2.3):

Table 2.3   The Payoff Matrix for Chicken

	Swerve	Don't Swerve
Swerve	Both considered chicken	Considered chicken, Wins
Don't Swerve	Wins, Considered chicken	Both idiots die in a fiery crash

Put another way (Table 2.4):

Table 2.4   The Payoff Matrix for Chicken (Alternative Version)

	Swerve	Don't Swerve
Swerve	Lose, Lose	Lose, Wins
Don't Swerve	Wins, Lose	Both Lose Catastrophically

Now, if a young tough in blue jeans and a pack of cigarettes rolled up his T-shirt sleeve is going to establish his level of physical courage among his peers by playing Chicken, just one iteration won't do. Such a one would be smart (well, as smart as anyone playing Chicken could be) to employ a *mixed strategy*. This is because employing the same strategy over and over would be foolish: always swerving means always losing (though not catastrophically), and always failing to swerve means that you will die, and probably pretty quickly. But which mixed strategy should the player adopt? Here's where an information exchange can make a big difference. In *Rebel Without a Cause* (and, I suppose, in real life) there was an opportunity for the players to communicate with each other prior to the cars actually speeding off. In this communication, if you were to convince your opponent that you would not swerve, even if that meant fiery death, then you have increased your chances of selecting the don't-swerve strategy and living to tell of it. If, however, your opponent presents as being equally as fearless, then you might want to reconsider the no-swerve strategy.

Chicken is also said to be a *symmetric* game, since it's the strategy the other player employs that's key, not the player himself, and the players have identical strategies available to them. An example of an *asymmetrical* game is the Ultimatum Game. Here you have two participants – we'll call them A and B. Person A is told that he has access to 100 gold coins, to be split between him and Person B. Person A is to submit how these coins should be divided, and communicates the plan to Person B. Person B has two choices: if Person B approves Person A's plan, then the coins are distributed according to the plan. If Person B disapproves of Person A's plan, then neither of them receive anything. The Ultimatum Game is *non-iterative*, as well as being asymmetrical.

A game similar to the Ultimatum Game is the Pirate's Game. Here, we have five pirates – we'll call them A, B, C, D, and E. Let's also posit that Pirate A outranks Pirate B, who outranks C, and so forth. The lot of them have acquired a chest of 100 gold coins. As the ranking pirate, A's role is to put forth a plan for distributing the gold among the five of them. If half or a majority of the pirates agree to the plan, the gold is distributed according to plan. However, if Pirate A fails to gain at least half of the others' votes, then Pirate A gets thrown overboard, and Pirate B is allowed to submit a plan for distributing the gold. If Pirate B's plan fails to garner at least 50% approval, then he is thrown overboard, and Pirate C proposes a plan, and so on.

The Pirate's Game is asymmetrical, since the available strategies change between voting and laying out a distribution scheme. It is also considered a *zero-sum* game, since the players' strategies cannot increase or decrease the total payout.

Now, the uninitiated may be inclined to believe that Pirate A's best strategy is to propose a distribution scheme that would strike a simple majority of the other pirates as being fair, but this is not the case (at least according to basic Game Theory). Consider what would happen if Pirates A, B, and C were to be thrown overboard due to their distribution schemes being rejected. Pirate D could declare a solution where he got all of the coins, and Pirate E received none. Since Pirate D's plan would receive half of the available votes, it would be enacted. Therefore, it's reasonable to assume that any solution that paid Pirate E anything at all would receive Pirate E's vote.

Pirate C knows this. So, if it gets all the way to him, he can maximize his utility, or payoff, by proposing that C gets 99, D gets nothing, and E gets one coin.

Okay, now we're getting kind of complex. Pirate B knows all of this, so he knows that any solution where D gets anything will gain his vote. Therefore, he maximizes his utility by proposing B gets 99, C gets nothing, D gets one coin, and E gets nothing. With his and D's vote, the half-of-the-vote condition has been met.

Finally, A knows all of this. So, he maximizes his utility by proposing A gets 98, B zero, C one, D nothing, and E one. And this is the essence of the use of Game Theory in situations that can present as being singularly non-game-like: when presented with the initial rules of the Pirate Game, Everyman would have probably not selected the solution that maximizes his payoff, or utility. But by evaluating:

- The potential payoffs of the various players;
- And which strategy they would likely employ;
- Based on which strategies the other participants would likely employ;
- As the game progressed.

We could arrive at the most logical strategy available to us, or at least the strategy that has the best odds of delivering an acceptable outcome. And, unless I'm mistaken, I've just described the job of a manager: to evaluate the parameters before us, and arrive at the most logical strategy available to us, or at least the strategy that has the best odds of delivering an acceptable outcome.

More Game Theory

Von Neumann theorized that in multiple-player, zero-sum games that do not include an element of chance, a set strategy can be ascertained and employed that maximized payoff, or utility, or, at the very least, minimized losses. This theory is called *minimax*, or sometimes *minmax*.

Sometimes the minimax strategy isn't just one strategy, but a combination of strategies. Consider the Matching Pennies game. It's a two-player zero-sum game, where each player has a penny in their hand. They secretly select which side of the coin faces up and, at a set signal, reveal their coin to the other player. If both pennies have the same side of the coin showing, player A receives $1 from Player B. If, however, the coins revealed have one heads side up, and the other tails side up, Player A pays $1 to Player B. Here's the payoff matrix (Table 2.5):

Table 2.5   The Payoff Matrix for Matching Pennies

	Heads	Tails
Heads	A wins, B loses	B wins, A loses
Tails	B wins, A loses	A wins, B loses

Put another way (Table 2.6):

Table 2.6   The Payoff Matrix for Matching Pennies (Alternative Version)

	Heads	Tails
Heads	+1, -1	-1, +1
Tails	-1, +1	+1, -1

If this game is played only once between any two players, the only "strategy" that would be of any use would be to make sure your opponent has no foreknowledge of which side of the coin you are likely to have face up. But if there are to be multiple iterations, just one set strategy would not be the minimax, since your opponent would probably catch on pretty quickly if you were to have face-up nothing but heads over multiple iterations. What's needed here is a mixed strategy, or an approach that includes changing strategies in such a way as to present as unpredictable.

A more lifelike example of an appropriateness of mixed strategies can be seen in a derivative of Chicken, the Hawk and Dove Game. The earliest presentation of this game was by John Maynard Smith and George Price in their 1973 *Nature* paper, "The Logic of Animal Conflict."[2] Imagine two birds in a common environment, with a certain amount of available food, expressed as V (the value of the available food). If these two birds cooperate, or passively forage for themselves, their payoff is $V / 2$, or ½ V. If, however, Bird A decides to act aggressively, and actually excludes Bird B's access to the food, then Bird A's payoff is all of the food (V), minus whatever cost (C) incurred in excluding Bird B from accessing V, or $V - C$. If, however, Bird B also elects to act aggressively to shut off Bird A's access to the food, and neither bird excludes the other's access, then they each receive half the food (as they did before), only less the cost (C) of attempting to prevent access to the other. The payoff matrix looks like this (Table 2.7):

Table 2.7   The Payoff Matrix for Hawk and Dove

	Hawk	Dove
Hawk	(V-C) / 2, (V-C) / 2	V, 0
Dove	0, V	V / 2, V / 2

One of the interesting things about the Hawk–Dove game is that, while consistently adopting Dove strategies in multiple iterations results in the largest payoff for the overall bird population, always choosing that strategy against a Hawk will result in starvation for the individual Dove.

Also consider a variant of Hawk–Dove where Bird B decides to employ a Hawk strategy, but is unable to implement it. In other words, Bird B attempts to prevent Bird A from accessing the available food (V), and not only fails, but falls victim to Bird A's successful Hawk strategy. Bird A would then receive all of the food (V), minus the cost (C) of successfully preventing Bird B from accessing it, while Bird B would endure the cost of attempting to employ the Hawk strategy while receiving no food. Also, the costs (C) have increased, since Bird B is not only preventing a Dove from accessing the food – Bird B must also attempt to counteract the aggressive strategy of Bird A. This payoff matrix looks like this (Table 2.8):

Table 2.8   The Payoff Matrix – Successful Hawk/Unsuccessful Hawk

	Successful Hawk	Unsuccessful Hawk
Successful Hawk	(0-2C), (0-2C)	V – 2C, 0 – 2C
Unsuccessful Hawk	0 – 2C, V – 2C	(V – 2C) / 2, (V – 2C) / 2

2   Chicken (game) (June 16, 2010). In *Wikipedia, The Free Encyclopedia*. Retrieved 19:26, July 11, 2010, from http://en.wikipedia.org/w/index.php?title=Chicken_(game)&oldid=368382918

Note that in those instances where C is greater than ½ V, each of these payoffs leaves both birds less well off than they were before.

Adding in the success–failure factor in selecting a strategy allows the Hawk–Dove game to more closely simulate warfare among humans or strategic corporate behavior in the free market. Imperial Japan of the 1930s was extremely successful in expanding its land holdings until it attacked a technologically and industrially superior United States, with the final result $0 - 2C$, leaving Honshu devastated.

I chose the example of Imperial Japan for an additional reason. Recall the discussion of the Chicken Game where communication about the other player's intended strategy could influence the odds of successfully implementing a don't-swerve approach, or, for this example, a Dove strategy. In the years prior to December 7, 1941, Japan had been consistently signaling a Dove strategy with respect to the United States, even as it carried out Hawk strategies in China, Taiwan, and the Dutch East Indies. Admiral Isokuru Yamamoto had studied at Harvard, and knew of American industrial might first-hand. Yamamoto used his influence to try to prevent his nation from adopting a Hawk strategy towards the United States, for he was fairly certain that, should the United States be roused to employ a Hawk strategy, the eventual outcome would be both devastating and unavoidable. He may not have employed game theory terms in evaluating the potential conflict, but he knew what happens when an Unsuccessful Hawk takes on a Successful one.

When Secretary of State Cordell Hull reinstated the embargo of tin, rubber, and (most importantly) oil to Japan in the summer of 1941, the Japanese War Cabinet felt they had little choice, and made the decision to go to war with the United States. Yamamoto had lost that fight, but there was still some hope: if Japan could adopt a Hawk strategy without inducing the United States to do the same, there would still be the possibility of an acceptable outcome $(V, 0)$. Far from the "dastardly act" decried by Roosevelt later, Yamamoto's plan was sinisterly brilliant. He would communicate his strategy first, then carry out his strategy so effectively that the other player would realize that the Dove strategy pay-off (0) would be preferable to either Unsuccessful Hawk – Unsuccessful Hawk $((V - 2C) / 2)$, or even Successful Hawk – Successful Hawk $((0-2C))$.[3] To this end Yamamoto insisted that, given that Japan would go to war with the US, two things *must* happen:

1. A declaration of war had to precede any attack. And, once that communication had occurred (and only after it had occurred); then
2. A surprise attack eliminating the US Pacific Fleet had to be successfully carried out.

Had both of these two aspects of Japan's initiation of the war been carried out as intended, Roosevelt would have had a very different set of options available to him on December 8, 1941. Indeed, the situation could have been spun so that it could be argued Cordell Hull's economic bullying of a tiny nation led them to officially declare war and that, once war had been publicly declared, the very first battle deprived Roosevelt of his Pacific Fleet, and removing the option to elect a Hawk strategy even if he wanted to. And, if the US was unable to enact a Hawk strategy, then the very real threat of Japan continuing to act

---

3   Please don't misunderstand – I'm not saying Yamamoto went through these computations. I'm simply pointing out that his strategy reveals its logic once a little Game Theory is incorporated.

as Hawks, while the US was forced to act as Doves, the payoff (*V-C*, 0 − *C*) would continue unless and until America made peace with Japan, and the two nations could return to the Dove–Dove payoff (*V* / 2, *V* / 2).

Unfortunately for Yamamoto, neither of the two aspects of his plan that *had* to happen actually came off. The Japanese Embassy in Washington, DC had trouble decoding and transcribing their instructions to deliver the Declaration of War, and the Declaration itself wasn't delivered until after the entire first wave of bombers had struck Pearl Harbor. And, as if the pre-Chicken communication that Japan wasn't going to swerve wasn't bad enough, none of America's aircraft carriers were damaged in the attack. During and immediately after World War I, the battleship was considered the preeminent naval weapon. But during the late 1930s the aircraft carrier was beginning to usurp the battleship's place in the naval weaponry pecking order (to stay consistent with the Chicken analogy) because of its ability to inflict great damage across large distances. *Lexington*, *Saratoga*, *Yorktown*, and *Enterprise* were all away from Pearl Harbor (although *Enterprise* was returning as the surprise attack took place, she was still too far away to become involved), and *Hornet* and *Wasp* were in the Atlantic. In other words, Roosevelt had the option to engage a Hawk strategy.

I was long mystified why Yamamoto, who *insisted* on the surprise attack on Pearl Harbor, would have (allegedly) immediately afterward said "I fear we have done nothing but wake a sleeping giant, and filled him with a terrible resolve." But the Hawk–Dove game explains his thinking perfectly. With no communication (declaration of war) preceding the attack, he knew that Roosevelt would select a Hawk strategy if it was available to him. Yamamoto also knew, with the aircraft carriers absent from Pearl Harbor, that option was, in fact, available. In short, Yamamoto knew that this game had suddenly shifted from Hawk–Dove to Unsuccessful Hawk–Successful Hawk, and the payoffs were not in Japan's favor.

Roosevelt knew this too. In defending his Hawk strategy selection and rallying the American people behind it, he invoked the sneak attack and "dastardly act" aspects of Japan's strategy early and often, even the next day as he was asking Congress for a declaration of war. He deployed his aircraft carriers in the Pacific, challenging, then checking, and finally rolling back the Imperial Japanese Navy.

Another interesting example of the Hawk–Dove strategy from World War II's naval history involves German merchant ships which were armed and disguised as innocuous merchants. These merchant raiders avoided warships, since they weren't designed to fight against other warships. In essence, they were Hawks disguised as Doves, and were to engage only Doves. One of these merchant raiders, the *Kormoran*, after a highly successful pair of cruises, was confronted by the light cruiser H.M.A.S. *Sydney* in the Indian Ocean, West of Australia. The *Sydney* approached the *Kormoran* cautiously, asking for her identification. *Kormoran* had tried to evade *Sydney*, but when the cruiser asked for the secret identification letters, *Kormoran*'s captain, Theodor Detmers, knew the gig was up; but *Sydney* had closed to within approximately 8,000 meters. Crew members were casually standing around the secondary armament and deck railings. Detmers dropped *Kormoran*'s disguise, ran up the Kriegsmarine battle ensign, and opened fire.

The first salvo bracketed *Sydney*, but subsequent salvos quickly disabled her radio equipment and hit her bridge. Soon she was on fire, and could only fire back at *Kormoran* intermittently. In what should have been a fairly certain and one-sided fight, *Kormoran* and *Sydney* actually ended up sinking each other. Hawkish behavior is highly rewarded when it presents as Dovish – in the near term, anyway.

Now, Back to Game Theory

In the previous discussion, we were evaluating a single pair of birds and the ramifications of their adopting Hawk or Dove strategies. But what if the population were larger? What could be predicted to occur if the sample size was, say, 100 birds? Some very interesting outcomes would present, but we needed a crazy person to show us how and why.

John Forbes Nash was born in 1928, and was the subject of the film *A Beautiful Mind*. In a scene from that movie a young Nash and some of his friends are in a bar, where a group of young, eligible women are also present. One of the women was an extremely attractive blonde. As the group of young men began discussing strategies to woo the blonde, Nash speaks up and points out that, if all of the young men pursue the blonde, they will alienate the other women in the group. Further, he informs his colleagues, that even if one of them was successful, the maximum payoff would be that one and only one of the group of men would go home happy that night. A far better strategy would be the precise opposite of their initial urge: ignore the blonde, and pursue all of the other girls. This strategy would maximize their payoff, and, in the movie, that ended up being the case.

In the 100-bird version of the Hawk–Dove game, an equilibrium comes about when around 25% of the birds are hawks, and the remainder are doves. This is known as a *Nash Equilibrium*, or a state in a game where the participants cannot improve their utility, or payoff, by changing strategies – even mixed strategies (on average). A more formal definition from GameTheory.net is:

> *A Nash equilibrium, named after John Nash, is a set of strategies, one for each player, such that no player has incentive to unilaterally change her action. Players are in equilibrium if a change in strategies by any one of them would lead that player to earn less than if she remained with her current strategy. For games in which players randomize (mixed strategies), the* expected *or average payoff must be at least as large as that obtainable by any other strategy.*[4]

Note that a Nash Equilibrium does not necessarily mean that the population's payoff has been maximized. In the Hawk–Dove game, the entire population's utility is only maximized if all of the participants engage the Dove strategy. But, given that there will always be at least one Hawk participant, the Nash Equilibrium does establish the best predictable strategy selection behavior of the population engaged in the game.

A Nash Equilibrium in an environment where multiple players are engaging in mixed strategies can only be maintained for a given period of time if the mixed strategies manifest an average pattern. If some variable or rule of the game changes, this introduces a destabilizing factor in the participants' selection of strategies. For example, in the 100-participant version of the Hawk–Dove game, if V (the amount of available food) were to be suddenly reduced to the point that $V/100$ (the payoff if the entire population were Doves) was insufficient to keep a given bird from starving, then even those birds whose mixed strategies involved a minimum of Hawk behavior would either have to change their behavior or they would starve. Once the bird population began to act more Hawk-like as a whole, the Hawk–Dove game would then begin to morph into Successful Hawk–Unsuccessful Hawk games, with greater losses in the food supply, but also accelerated deaths from aggression and starvation.

---

4   Shor, Mikhael, "Nash Equilibrium," Dictionary of Game Theory Terms, Game Theory.net. Retrieved July 10, 2010, from http://www.jametheiory.net/dictionary/NashEquilibrium.html.

This would continue until V / n (where n is the number of birds in the population) exceeds starvation levels, but even then another Nash Equilibrium would not occur automatically. The next Nash Equilibrium would only occur after V/n exceeded individual bird starvation levels, and the birds would return to more Dovish (on average) mixed strategies, once again approaching the 25/75 Hawk–Dove average mixed strategy.

While this pattern of the impact to the bird population in the Hawk–Dove game has some parallels with what occurs among participants in a war, it is also analogous to situations where two or more participants have the option to act aggressively or passively in the pursuit of a given utility. Politicians employ mixed strategies when evaluating the number and tone of communications that criticize, denounce, or even ridicule their opponents (Hawk behavior) as opposed to discussing their fitness for the elected office sought (Dove behavior). Corporations will exhibit mixed strategies with respect to their competitors within a given market. For example, Apple had a long-running advertising campaign where their computers were represented by a hip young man interacting with a heavier-set, middle-aged man representing computers running Microsoft's Windows operating software. While the two men's exchanges were largely light-hearted and pleasant, there was no question that Apple's campaign was designed to mock Microsoft. In advertising parlance these are known as vampire ads, since they rely on the viewer knowing something about the competitor's product(s). Vampire ads can be very successful, but they must be used sparingly – like the politician's decision to run attack ads, or the birds employing more aggressive mixed strategies – if they are to attain a successful payoff.

While the utility in these instances are fairly clear and easy to ascertain (votes and computer operating system market share), the Nash Equilibrium may be impossible to compute in those instances where the utility involves the unpredictable behavior of those who are not technically players in the game. For this reason Game Theory calculations can never replace the feedback needed to gauge the efficacy of the amount of Hawk-like behavior incorporated into the mixed strategies employed by politicians and corporate advertisers. In other words, the value of timely and accurate polls (for politicians) and sales figures (for corporations) can't be replaced by the computation of the Nash Equilibrium in evaluating the proper mix of aggression or passivity in strategic mixed strategies. I will discuss the most appropriate use of Game Theory in specific managerial domains in Part 3.

More on the Communications of Strategies

Recall the discussion on the pre-Chicken communications from earlier in this chapter. Given that a young tough's reputation for possessing physical courage is not going to be established by a single game of Chicken, the participant will need to adopt a mixed strategy. It's also reasonable to assume that subsequent games will not be played against the same opponent. Likely (or even possible) future opponents can be anticipated to adjust their own mixed strategies based on:

1. The pre-game communications held with the existing opponent; and
2. The previously observed behavior of the participants.

Each of these bits of data can help inform the potential future opponent of the efficacy of their given strategy. In the case of Chicken, there are four possible combinations:

1. Opponent communicates a no-swerve strategy, and does not actually swerve.
2. Opponent communicates a no-swerve strategy, but actually swerves.
3. Opponent communicates a swerve strategy, and actually does swerve.
4. Opponent communicates a swerve strategy, but does not swerve.

Which is similar to the bid-up/bluff options involved in poker:

1. Increase the bet while holding a winning hand.
2. Increase the bet while holding a losing hand.
3. Place the minimum bet while holding a losing hand.
4. Place the minimum bet while holding a winning hand.

In both cases the historical selection of the combination of the communication and subsequent strategy will significantly influence the other (in the case of Chicken, possible future) participants in the game. For this reason the most appropriate combined mixed strategy must involve incorporating at least some of the deceptive alternatives (2 and 4) with the honest strategies (1 and 3), as evidenced by the fact that any canny poker player will almost always defeat the player who only bids up good hands and calls or folds on all poor ones.

Note how each of the #4 combinations appears to do nothing more than guarantee the minimum payoff if adopted as a strategy. While that is certainly the case on its face, incorporating this option does have the benefit of communicating to other participants the futility of attempting to draw conclusions from the communication/action patterns observed in previous iterations. What is happening is an attempt to disrupt an opponent's attempts to create a structure that explains patterns of observed behaviors, and then using that structure to predict future strategy selections. This establishment of structures that explain the past and predict the future and the problems surrounding such an establishment will be addressed more fully in Part 2.

A famous logic game where the participants are confronted with a boolean parameter involves the castaway who finds himself on an island, and needing to get to the town on the other side. He knows that this particular chain of islands is home to two tribes: one tribe always tells the truth, and the other tribe always lies. Our castaway sets off, but comes to a fork in the road. Next to each fork is a native, but the two are from different tribes, and the castaway has no idea which is from which tribe. He is allowed one question to ascertain the correct path. What question does he ask?

The answer is that he queries to either of them "If I were to ask you if this was the correct road to the town, would you say 'yes'?" There are (again) four possibilities:

1. He's asking the truth-teller on the correct road.
2. He's asking the liar on the correct road.
3. He's asking the truth-teller on the incorrect road.
4. He's asking the liar on the incorrect road.

But in each instance he will get the right answer. The answer in Scenarios 1 and 3 will be correct, since he is engaging the truth-teller. In Scenario 2, though, he's talking to the liar, but the correct answer will still be forthcoming because the liar must lie about what his answer would have been. If the liar on the correct road was simply asked "Is this the correct road," he would have answered "No," which is incorrect. But that wasn't the question. The question was "If I were to ask you if this was the correct road, would you say 'yes'?" The double-lie ends up being the truth – hence the two-staged characteristic of the question reveals the information needed for the game-player to adopt the best strategy.

Of course, removing the always-tells-the-truth and always-lies constraints changes the game dramatically, as well as the value of the information derived from the two-stage communication/actual selected strategy observation. *Diplomacy* is an unusual board game developed by Alan B. Calhamer in 1959, and its players must develop strategies based on this two-staged observation cycle.[5] In *Diplomacy*, players place markers on a map of Europe as shown immediately prior to World War I. There are no dice or other random-element generators, and players engage in private negotiations with each other about the intended movement of their markers, which represent armies. The actual movement of these armies is determined and written down on a piece of paper. The moves are revealed, and take place simultaneously, as in Chicken or Hawk–Dove. Alliances are formed and betrayed as players negotiate with each other about how they will move on the next turn (communication phase), and then the actual move occurs revealing if the players were accurate or deceptive in their pre-move negotiations.

There are several interesting aspects to the game *Diplomacy*. It was supposedly a favorite of both John F. Kennedy and Henry Kissinger. It's also widely known to invoke powerful emotions and passions among its fans, to the point that it may be the all-time most frequent fist-fight invoker of the board game world.

But the key interesting thing about *Diplomacy* (both the game and probably the real-world discipline) is that it's impossible to win without a mixed strategy that involves a significant amount of deceit. It's also next to impossible to win without the ability to evaluate the board situation, and combine that assessment with a two-stage analysis of:

1. What would be the best *combination* of moves for both individual and groups of the other players; and
2. Could that maximized utility be better obtained with truthful or deceitful pre-move communications?

Another level of complexity is introduced by the concept of mixed utility, since, as in the previous discussion of chess, players of *Diplomacy* must decide if an advantage on the board is worth destroying a relationship with an ally. Evaluating the frequency or pattern of bluffing, which is important information in poker or Chicken, is next to useless in *Diplomacy*. Due to the extra stages of analysis in developing the most appropriate mixed strategy, *Diplomacy* cannot be evaluated using a payoff matrix, and a calculation of the Nash Equilibrium is not possible.

This chapter's discussion of the basics of Game Theory is not meant to be exhaustive. It does, however, establish the GT lexicon and basic approaches used in evaluating the possible (probable?) strategies employed by the other participants in a given game. Next we'll examine the possible uses of Game Theory in steering business decisions to maximize payoffs.

---

5   Diplomacy (game) (June 23, 2010). In *Wikipedia, The Free Encyclopedia*. Retrieved 19:35, July 18, 2010, from http://en.wikipedia.org/w/index.php?title=Diplomacy_(game)&oldid=369649960

3 Game Theory and Cartage Schemes

Good design can't fix broken business models.

Jeffrey Veen, *Designing the Friendly Skies*, June 21, 2006

The efficacy of Game Theory in real-world business decisions was probably never better established than during the energy crisis in California from May 2000 through September 2001. Enron and other energy speculators made huge profits due to the modification of the rules by which electricity producers and retailers could operate in the State of California. California's legislature, displaying astonishing ignorance of the law of unintended consequences, arranged for the divestiture of the State's large electricity utilities, believing that the ensuing competition among the newly-formed companies would lead to a decrease in consumer costs. The new, smaller generator companies provided electricity to the California Power Exchange, from where the retailers purchased it. Unfortunately, the laws also covered the price that retailers could charge for their product, and from whom, how much, and when they could purchase electricity. These laws, when added to already-existing regulations that covered everything from scheduled power-plant downtime for maintenance to information on when power supply shortages must be reported, created the perfect environment for canny speculators to design cartage schemes – essentially, a set of canned strategies designed to be invoked when certain parameters presented. Among the more bizarre aspects of the electricity generation and retailing environment in California during the crisis:

- Retail prices were capped, but wholesale prices were not.
- Companies could charge more for electricity from out-of-State than for that generated in California.
- Transmission lines had to be scheduled to transfer large amounts of power from place to place. If the amount of power to be transferred exceeded the lines' capacity, a fee had to be paid by the power companies.
- Power generators could shut down plants (nominally, for "maintenance") at any time.

The newly-formed electricity generators didn't even have to collude: given the above parameters, it was obvious that any act that reduced supply, jammed transmission lines, or led to the necessity of buying out-of-State electricity would increase the uncapped wholesale price, and the accompanying profit. And, depending on the schedule of the transmission lines, current capacity, availability and price of electricity on the "spot market," and other parameters, a canned, sequential set of acts – a strategy, if you will

– could represent returns that would never have occurred in a genuinely unregulated market. This is a key point that will be revisited in Part 2: a specified set of actions combined into a named strategy can only be expected to be successful in an environment where the rules of the game are known and observed by all of the participants, and the strategies available to the other players are limited.

Enron's cartage schemes were given names, such as "Big Foot," "Ricochet," and "Red Congo." Depending on the mixed strategies being deployed – or could be reasonably expected to have been deployed – by the other players, Enron could invoke one of these named strategies, and just watch the profit meter spin at dizzying speeds.

S. David Freeman, who was appointed Chair of the California Power Authority in the midst of the crisis, made the following statements about Enron's involvement in testimony submitted before the Subcommittee on Consumer Affairs, Foreign Commerce and Tourism of the Senate Committee on Commerce, Science and Transportation on May 15, 2002:

> *Enron stood for secrecy and a lack of responsibility. In electric power, we must have openness and companies that are responsible for keeping the lights on. We need to go back to companies that own power plants with clear responsibilities for selling real power under long-term contracts.*[1]

Consider what was being admitted here by Mr Freeman. In Game Theory parlance:

- The State of California could not engage in a mixed strategy. The law was what it was, and to change it would require legislation being introduced, debated, voted on, and signed by the Governor.
- Nor could the State offer communication about the possibility of engaging in some other strategy.
- And, even if it could offer such communication, it could never be deceitful.
- Conversely, Enron was in a perfect position to enact mixed strategies, and they often involved little more than a couple of phone calls to initiate.
- Enron was also in a position to be deceitful in pre-game communications which, as we have seen in Chicken and *Diplomacy*, among other games, is absolutely critical to winning.

Mr Freeman is essentially lamenting that Enron had the latitude to enact mixed strategies AND engage in deceit in pre-turn communications, while California could not. But that was the nature of the game as it was developed by the representatives of the people of California! Much has been made about comments from upper Enron management along the lines of "No matter what laws the California legislature passes, we've got MBAs who will figure a way around them."[2] But, stripping aside the emotion and outrage, the participants on Enron's side of the electricity game in California in 2001 were simply in a far better position to win than their legislative and regulatory counterparts. The lawyers and regulators involved would love to portray themselves as trying to do their level best to provide a critical product to everyday consumers at affordable prices, arrayed against

---

1   California electricity crisis (July 18, 2010). In *Wikipedia, The Free Encyclopedia*. Retrieved 21:19, July 18, 2010, from http://en.wikipedia.org/w/index.php?title=California_electricity_crisis&oldid=374138603

2   Ibid.

evil, greedy power companies out to make excessive profits. An article about the crisis entitled "The Electricity Deregulation Con Game" appearing on the Center for Media and Democracy's website by Sharon Beder basically ignored the business, economic, or Game Theory aspects, and instead focused on ginning up outrage at Enron's behavior.[3] But the reality is that these same lawyers set up a game in which the rules put those same consumers – and their representatives – in a terrible (if not impossible) position to maximize their utility, while virtually guaranteeing that those who could maximize profit, or utility, at the expense of the consumer, would not lose.

If the good people of California did not want the electricity-provider game to be played out the way it was from 2001–2002, they should not have elected representatives who set the rules of the game in the way that they did.

Of course, Enron would end up going spectacularly bankrupt after having evoked the pre-game deceitful communications strategy a few times too often. But, en route to their widely-publicized crash-and-burn, they turned astonishing profits. I'm not saying that engaging in deceit is part and parcel of making profits; I am saying, though, that in those circumstances where a mixed strategy is called for, the player must take steps to manage the information that could lead to other game participants modifying their strategies to your disadvantage.

And, in those instances where a mixed strategy is called for, and a particular player cannot or does not avail themselves of a mixed strategy, that player will lose.

Game Theory and Internal Players

In his 1977 book, entitled (interestingly enough) *The Gamesman: The New Corporate Leaders*,[4] Michael Maccoby asserts that there are four types of workers in an organization and, depending on what type most closely matches a given worker, their behavior can be expected to continue to manifest in certain (predictable?) ways. The four types are:

1. The Craftsman, who really doesn't care much for whom he works, but cares deeply about the quality of his output.
2. The Company Man, who derives his working persona from the nature of his colleagues within the organization.
3. The Jungle Fighter, who engages in gossip or other, malicious tactics in order to further their standing within the organization at the expense of others.
4. The Gamesman, after whom the book is (obviously) named. To the Gamesman, salary and benefits do not necessarily translate to food on the table and a roof over the head; rather, they represent rewards in an elaborate game, a game he intends to master and win.

Maccoby asserts that, while no worker's behavior is consistently compliant with any one type, their behavior does tend to match one of these categories more than the others and, given this structure, an advantageous manner of recruiting and assigning personnel can be achieved.

---

3   Beder, Sharon, "The Electricity Deregulation Con Game," *PR Watch*, Third Quarter 2003, Volume 10, No. 3.

4   Maccoby, Michael, *The Gamesman: The New Corporate Leaders* (New York: Bantam Books, 1978) (1976).

Analyzing Maccoby's insights from a Game Theory point of view, each of the types could be said to have a predictable preference for the workplace strategies available to them; or, in the case of multiple strategies being available (which is almost always the case within an organization), which on average mixed strategies are likely to be employed. Outside of assembly-line workers in the manufacturing industry, where consistent actions are expected and required, knowledge of the most likely preferred strategies of the personnel within the organization is a critical piece of information for the manager attempting to gain insight into the development of their own mixed strategies.

For example, in the previous discussions on utility, the payoff was quantified in a single parameter. The participants in the Prisoner's Dilemma sought to minimize their sentence; players in the Ultimatum Game and the Pirate's Game sought the maximum number of gold coins. But taking into account the probable behavior of players internal to the macro organization, Maccoby's work leads to the conclusion that a series of mixed utilities, or payoffs, will come into play in any instance where an initiative to change the organization is undertaken.

The concept of mixed utility has a profound impact on the ability of Game Theory to predict the strategies most likely to be adopted by the various players. It's as if we suddenly stopped playing the Hawk–Dove game, and, instead, began playing a Craftsman–Company Man–Jungle Fighter–Craftsman game, but it goes further than that, because now not only do the participants tend to embrace different strategies, but their goals are different. If Maccoby is right, consider what would happen if a given organization were to launch a new product line. The behavior of the participants in the project team could be expected to turn based on their desired payoffs:

- The Craftsman would want to produce a high-quality product, regardless of the position of the organization to occupy the high-end of the targeted market.
- The Company Man would want to adopt a technical approach consistent with the way the macro organization has approached other projects (similar or not) in the past.
- The Jungle Fighter would attempt to engineer communications and manipulate circumstances to make it appear that they were the best contributors, at the expense of their colleagues, whether or not they had actually contributed at all.
- And the Gamesman would be inclined to engage a high-risk, high-reward technical approach, which may or may not be consistent with the organization's strategic stance or general ledger health.

As in chess, where a mixed utility makes it very difficult to anticipate if your opponent is seeking an advantage in space, time, force, or pawn structure, much less what his exact next move is likely to be, the utility trade-offs available to a project team with Gamesman-style categories make it virtually impossible to predict which set of strategies they are likely to employ.

What can be gleaned, however, are the strategies that ought to prove most useful in punishing or rewarding the behavior of the participants. Assuming that the project's manager has recognized and clearly articulated the most appropriate technical approach to the problem, she can reward her team most effectively in this way:

- The Craftsman will love quality awards, or communications that convey customer satisfaction, and an acknowledgement that the Craftsman's contribution is associated with the end product.
- The Company Man will feel appreciated with organizational (internal) recognition.
- The Jungle Fighter (if you are unfortunate enough to have some on your project) will feel rewarded if you convey to them that their standing is high with respect to their associates.
- The Gamesman will appreciate a narrative where the approach you took (and where he contributed) was fraught with hazard, but, somehow, the team made it through.

Conversely, the types are punished when:

- The Craftsman is made to believe that external perceptions of the product or service are sub-standard.
- The Company Man is told that he let the macro organization down.
- The Jungle Fighter realizes that it is known that their contribution is markedly below their colleagues.
- The Gamesman is led to believe that competitors are making inroads against them, personally, because of poor performance.

Now, I am well aware that much of this discussion presents as manipulative or deceitful. In my defense I would argue that the entire notion of using Game Theory ideas in the managerial world, by definition, reduces real human beings to players in a grand game, and that such a reduction is inherently de-humanizing. As players in a game, the manager must know what their behaviors – their most likely-adopted mixed strategies – are likely to be, and modify managerial mixed strategies to maximize managerial payoffs (which are, one would hope, consistent with the macro organization's desired payoffs).

I would like to engage in a discussion about the somewhat mushy concept of corporate or organizational culture at this point. An analysis on the external factors affecting the manifest culture of the macro organization will come up in Part 3; for this discussion I want to focus on the internal influences that shape the corporate culture.

I'm aware that the Communications Specialist/psychobabblers have made spectacular inroads in decomposing individual behavior within the macro organization into categories so subjective as to present as near-psychology to business people, and near-micro economics to psychologists. So let's present a Game-Theory-based definition of organizational culture:

Organizational culture is the perceived internal narrative behind the set of strategies (and averaged mixed strategies) that members of the organization employ as they execute their duties.

Assuming Professor Maccoby knew his subject matter, the most probable strategy (or average mixed strategy) of the organization's members can be identified and, to some extent, quantified, but only by deconstructing the selected mixed strategies employed and connecting them with trends or themes. Now consider how the values that upper management conveys to mid-level management, and thence to rank-and-file, can influence the overall organizational culture.

Back in the early 1980s I worked for a major defense contractor, now defunct. But in their heyday they were a major beltway bandit, and one of the top employers in my state. This company's culture was centered upon – I might even say obsessed with – Gamesmen, or employees who were adept at writing proposals and winning contracts from the United States Government. New managers were given a three-evening training program that spent virtually no time on how to handle personnel matters, how to ensure safety, or security – no, it was all about writing proposals and participating in the marketing system. The expectation was that, after a full day spent on billable work, the managers would spend massive amounts of overtime in proposal preparation work (all unpaid, of course). Having gone to work right out of college, I simply assumed that this was how the professional world worked, and set myself to adopt their desired behaviors. But even so, I was noticing some really odd things about the way this company functioned.

I began to notice a certain sense of dread and apprehension about the next work day when I was at home in the evenings. Soon after, I began to dream about work, almost every night. Then I started noticing the dread feeling starting to happen earlier and earlier on Sundays, until I woke up Sunday mornings dreading going to work the next day. Then the feeling started happening on Saturday evenings, then Saturday afternoons. Before I knew it the fear of underperforming at work and being let go had become pervasive.

And it wasn't just me. I started noticing small yellow post-its, with no writing on them, showing up on the double-doors that separated the major trafficked hallways and exits between the buildings in the office complex, but only on Friday afternoons. After a few weeks I asked some of my friends in the Contracts department what the story on the post-its was, and their response was "You don't know? Meet us behind the (street name) building at 5:30."

This building was an outlier office building that was used off-and-on as contracts came and went, and the company's employee population ebbed and flowed. There, in the parking lot, right at 5:30 p.m. was a tailgate party. A couple of cups full of change and $1 bills were on a pickup truck's tailgate, and cans of beer were 50 cents. Almost all of my colleagues (and a goodly share of my managers) were in attendance, loosening ties, letting hair down, and blowing off steam. And, boy, was there a lot of steam to let off. It didn't take much listening to realize that these people were so stressed, that they were in pain. Not acute pain, to be sure, but this kind of zeitgeist, low-level, always-in-the-background pain. I wasn't alone in the dread and the dreams.

Another unusual executive strategy would manifest, about once per quarter. An executive vice president would fly out from the company's headquarters on a Friday afternoon, and arrange to have a memo sent out about an hour prior to close of business, to all hands. This memo would mandate that each and every employee write out, by hand on a blank sheet of paper, name, employee number, degree(s), projects they were working on, and *any proposal where the employee was considered "key personnel."* The veep would collect these sheets of paper, and then casually go through them throughout the weekend. On Monday morning those employees who had been singled out for firing or layoff would receive the news, turn in their badges, and be escorted out of the building. Naturally, any employee who possibly could would work the entire weekend, hoping to stave off the fickle finger of furlough fate.

Although I had read *The Gamesman* by this point, I failed to recognize what was happening right before my eyes. The company was so committed to being an organization of Gamesmen that they were attempting to systematically eliminate any and all Craftsmen, Company Men, and Jungle Fighters. And, to the extent that the non-Gamesmen in the organization were trying to participate in the game, they were suffering elevated levels of stress in trying to fit into an organizational culture that was structured precisely to prevent them from fitting in. From an organizational behavior and performance perspective, it was both fascinating and sinister, much like watching great white sharks in a feeding frenzy. Interestingly, the blood that filled the water didn't belong to the Jungle Fighters, but not because they were immune. They weren't ever really in the game. In a game where the preferred strategies of the Jungle Fighter – deception, gossip, etc. – have no chance of succeeding, they would either adopt other strategies, or simply go to an organization where such strategies could work. The Company Men would quickly realize that the company culture was one of become-a-Gamesman-or-die, and would make the transition, or be furloughed. That left only the Craftsmen, and this was where the company would meet its Waterloo.

There was simply no way that the company was going to pay its Craftsmen what it paid its Gamesmen. And yet, there were strategic rivals in the work the company performed, and it's a virtual certainty that all of these competitors had a more balanced organizational structure (more on the relationship between asset, project, and strategic management in Part 3). Now, imagine yourself a Craftsman in this situation: if you could walk away from the Marianas Trench-level pressure, for the same (or, in many cases, more) money, wouldn't you jump at the chance? And jump many did. As the preferred corporate culture continued to manifest, an unstoppable brain drain was happening right under the exec's layoff-selecting finger.

The company would be bought out by a competitor in 1997, only a shell of its previous might. Other posthumous analysis might reach different conclusions on the causal factors that led to its demise; but I was on the inside, and, adding the Game Theory context, this is what I saw.

Besides providing me with some early-career trauma catharsis, this discussion does raise the question: could a Nash Equilibrium be calculated based on the assumptions that the players' strategies could be modeled after *The Gamesman* archetypes? The short answer is no, unless the analysis is absurdly long on assumptions, since there is no complete way to evaluate the interrelation among Gamesmen, Craftsmen, Company Men, and Jungle Fighters that is analogous to the ability to quantify, say, the relationship among Hawks and Dove in a multi-player, multi-iterative game. But Maccoby clearly believed that an optimal mix of his types could and should be achieved.

Maccoby and Nash, Together at Last

In his outstanding 2007 book *The Black Swan*, Nassim Taleb powerfully argues for the lack of efficacy of statistics and models to accurately predict future occurrences and circumstances, and has a singular lack of patience for the calculation of a state of equilibrium within a given "game." I will largely rely on his work in Part 2 of this book as I seek to set an intelligent and defensible upper limit to the effectiveness of Game Theory, Risk Management Theory, and Network Theory in improving managerial decision-making. In *The Black Swan*, Taleb has an ongoing recommendation for dealing with pro-Game, Risk, and Network Theory analysts, and that is to put a rat down their back, and (joyfully) watch their reactions. Even in the face of this threat, I am going to go ahead and perform the calculations involved in a payoff matrix for participants in an economic game, where the players behave consistently with Maccoby's *The Gamesman* archetypes. I'm doing this because, even though the resulting analysis cannot be relied on to illustrate even probable future business environments for a given organization, the analysis will yield some insights that are both consistent with what I have experienced personally, and will help support some of the conclusions I will assert in Part 3 of this book. If I ever have the honor of meeting Professor Taleb in person, I will attempt to avoid revealing that I am the author of this work. And, if he finds out anyway, I'll simply make sure he has no ready access to nearby rodentia.

To translate Maccoby into Game Theory-ese, we'll assert that his archetypical players employ a predictable set of strategies as they go about their workday activities. And, rather than say that each player has a major and minor inclination along one of the categories, we'll say that each player employs a mixed strategy, and that these mixed strategies will be both affected by the perceptions of the other players, and will tend towards a Nash Equilibrium.

Naturally, since we are dealing with both mixed strategies and mixed payoffs, this matrix is going to be more complex than payoff matrices associated with the other games we have been evaluating. We will quantify the strategies of the Maccoby players so:

- The Gamesman will devote most of her energy towards attracting more customers, gaining more work, and making progress against the organization's external competitors.
- The Craftsman will spend most of his energy performing the best he can against the work that the organization already has.
- The Jungle Fighter can be counted on to expend considerable amounts of energy trying to communicate to others that they are superior to competitors within the organization, while not really adding to either the customer base or the quality of the work for existing clients.
- And, finally, the Company Man will attempt to perceive the combinations of mixed strategies of the other internal players around him, and adopt their balance of mixed strategies selection. If this player happens to be adept at Game Theory, he may attempt to actually quantify the mixed strategy that mirrors that of the macro organization. Barring that, he will try to reach the most appropriate combination intuitively.

The Gamesman's greatest contribution to the macro organization will be in strategic management, or how the organization does with respect to potential new clients and market share. Similarly, the Craftsman's greatest contribution will be to the quality and timeliness of the work already in the door, or work that is part of the existing contract backlog.

Conversely, the Jungle Fighter really has no contribution in their primary strategy mode, unless it's to serve as some sort of internal spur to the actions of the others in order to try to prevent the notion that the non-Jungle Fighters aren't contributing as much as the (mostly) idle Jungle Fighter(s). And the Company Men will only contribute to the extent that they perceive that a majority of their available strategies involve emulating the Gamesmen and Craftsmen. In other words:

$$G > Cr > CM > JF$$

from the overall organization's point of view. Recall that in the Hawk–Dove game, payoff for the entire population was maximized if all the players used Dove strategy, but that the presence of even one Hawk threw that into disarray. And so it is here, since the Jungle Fighter will almost always best the Company Man in head-to-head interactions, or iterations. So here is where some fairly sweeping assumptions will need to be made in order to set the framework for calculating the Nash Equilibrium, the kinds of sweeping generalizations that can get an author rodentia dumped down his back. Let's model my earlier discussion of the high-pressure company as the organizational culture where these *Gamesman* interactions take place, using the following assumptions:

- The organization, by being somewhat tone deaf to deceitful interactions among the players, allows Jungle Fighters a fair amount of latitude when engaging in Jungle Fighter behavior.
- Attracting new work trumps all other organizational considerations, except in extreme circumstances.
- Doing the work right only matters in those instances where the customer will be sufficiently pleased to add on to existing contracts, or will engage new contracts.
- Company Men will attempt to emulate either Gamesmen or Jungle Fighters, and will do so with limited success.

With these assumptions in place, the internal strategy-selection preference becomes:

$$G \geq JF > Cr > CM$$

And, since I've assumed away so much already, what's one more? Let's further posit that the players will confine themselves to two strategies, one prevalent and the other minority.

Consider the following payoff matrices as the *Gamesmen* types interact with each other. If a Gamesman/Jungle Fighter interacts with a Jungle Fighter/Gamesman, the G/JF will tend to behave in such a way as to attract new business the majority of the time, but may engage in gossip or *ex parte* conversations with upper management to diminish the JF/G. The JF/G acts similarly, only they are more likely to engage in political machinations first, and customer attraction activities secondarily. The combinations are:

- If the G/JF (Player A) successfully engages in customer attraction activities when the JF/G (Player B) attempts to tear him down, the (successful) G/JF will be the clear victor (+2), and the JF/G will be the clear loser (-2), for not only failing to attract new business, but being exposed as a fraud.
- If the G/JF and the JF/G both engage in customer attraction activities, and are successful, then they both receive a +1 payout (the value of the new work divided between them).
- The JF/G engaging in customer attraction while the G/JF engaging in politics has the opposite payout from the first bullet (-2, 2).
- If both engage in politics, then nothing happens in new customer space, but they damage each other (-1, -1).

So, the payoff matrix becomes (Table 3.1):

Table 3.1   The Payoff Matrix for Gamesman/Jungle Fighter (Version 1)

		Player B	
		Attract Customers	Engage in Politics
Player A	Attract Customers	+1, +1	+2, -2
	Engage in Politics	-2, +2	-1, -1

As can be seen in this payoff matrix, it never benefits the Jungle Fighter to engage in politics against a successful Gamesman. But what if the Gamesman isn't successful? The Gamesman can expect to receive a minimal amount of credit for having tried (0.2) in a failing effort, but nothing else. The payoff matrix then becomes (Table 3.2):

Table 3.2   The Payoff Matrix for Gamesman/Jungle Fighter (Version 2)

		Player B	
		Attract Customers	Engage in Politics
Player A	Attract Customers	0.2, 0.2	0.2, +1
	Engage in Politics	+1, 0.2	-1, -1

Player A plays Gamesman with probability p, and plays Jungle Fighter with probability $1 - p$. Player B plays Gamesman with probability q and plays Jungle Fighter with probability $1 - q$. Player A's expected payoff from acting like a Gamesman (attempting to attract new customers without knowing the eventual outcome of those efforts) is $0.2q + 0.2(1-q)$. His expected payoff from acting like a Jungle Fighter and playing politics is $1q + -1(1-q)$. Similarly, Player B's expected payoff from acting like a Gamesman is $0.2p + 0.2(1 -p)$. His expected payoff from Jungle Fighting is $1 + -1(1-p)$. Player B will not want to change strategies when:

$$0.2p + 0.2(1-p) = 1 + -1(1- p)$$

$$0.2p + 0.2 - 0.2p = 1 - 1 + p$$

$$0.2 = p$$

So, in what begins to resemble a losing effort, a Gamesman will persist in engaging in Gamesman-like strategies only 20% of the time, which means the other 80% he could be expected to engage strategies that are not helpful to the macro organization.

This Nash Equilibrium calculation simply invites questions about other parameters in the environment. Is the Gamesman aware of the presence of Jungle Fighters, along the lines of the pre-Chicken communications among the players? And, if the Gamesman were to perceive the existence of Jungle Fighters in the game, would that not mean that he would be far more likely to employ the Jungle Fighter strategies early, perhaps even at a point prior to a critical juncture in the development of a new customer base?

We've Seen This Match Before

Next I would like to explore a theoretical combination of the Craftsman with the Company Man. Of course, this involves another multitude of rat-down-the-back assumptions, including:

- The Company Man is very interested in the company's assets, and how they perform.
- The Craftsman is more interested in producing a product or delivering a project on-time, on-budget, and meeting or exceeding their customers' expectations.
- We're no longer discussing my fevered impressions of the high-pressure company, but a typical organization that believes that Generally Accepted Accounting Principles (GAAP) provide the best structure for maximizing shareholder wealth.[5]

This matchup may very well be the basis of all of Tom Peters' writings, because it does represent such an extraordinarily yet unintuitive conflict. The focusing of managerial attention on maximizing a return on investment (ROI) while neglecting the quality of the product or the needs of the customer is the natural manifestation of years of GAAP being accepted as the most logical structure to use when establishing a business approach, or model. But while Professor Peters and outfits like the Project Management Institute can slug it out with the Asset Managers at the macro level, let's reduce it in Game Theory terms and observe it at the micro level.

Player A is an Asset-Management type, maybe even an Accountant. Player C is a Craftsman, interested in the best possible output of his product, project, or service. It is my personal opinion that Matrix Management, the organizational behavior and performance craze of the 1980s, was designed to more clearly delineate who performed the role of Company Man/Asset Manager, and who performed as the Craftsman/Project Manager. Our players are in a game where a customer is expecting the delivery of a complex product. The Company Man is in charge of procuring the assets needed for assembly of the product, and the Craftsman is responsible for the delivery of the actual product. The Company Man/Asset Manager seeks to maximize shareholder wealth, the alleged and oft-taught end goal of *all* management. As mentioned previously, the Craftsman/Project Manager can be expected to be more willing to sacrifice ultimate efficiency in order to maximize quality, or to fully comply with customer expectations. It's the classic efficiency versus effectiveness match, with the payoffs colored by the perceptions of the players. Let's posit the following payoff matrix for a project brought in successfully (Table 3.3):

Table 3.3   The Payoff Matrix for a Project Delivered Successfully

		Craftsman	
		Act Efficiently	Act Effectively
Player A	Act Efficiently	1,1	1,1
	Act Effectively	1,1	1,1

---

5   Taleb refers to the use of Gaussian Curves to predict future events as "the great intellectual hoax" of the twentieth century, and he's probably right. But the notion that all management efforts should be devoted to "maximize(ing) shareholder wealth" must be its management theory equivalent.

Forgive me, but I had to state the obvious. If the project comes in successfully, everyone wins. But what if the project encounters major delays and overruns, and the proximate cause is held to be a deficiency in project management? The payoff matrix becomes (Table 3.4):

Table 3.4   The Payoff Matrix for a Project that Overruns Cost or Schedule

		Company Man	
		Acted Effectively	Acted Efficiently
Player A	Acted Effectively	-2, -2	-2, 0
	Acted Efficiently	0,-2	1, -2

The Craftsman works to effectiveness with probability p and efficiency with probability $1 - p$. The Company Man works effectively with probability q and efficiency with probability $1 - q$. The Craftsman expected payoff from being effective is $-2q + -2(1 - q)$. His expected payoff from efficiency is $0q + 1 (1 - q)$. The Company Man expected payoff from effectiveness is $-2p + -2(1 - p)$; his expected payoff from efficiency is $0p + -2(1 - p)$.

The Company Man will not want to change strategies when:

$$-2p + -2(1 - p) = 0p + -2(1 - p)$$

$$-2p - 2 + 2p = -2 + p$$

$$-2 = -2 + p$$

$$0 = p$$

So p, the Company Man's probability of continuing to try to be effective in an apparently failing project, is zero.

The Craftsman will not want to change strategies if:

$$-2q + -2 (1 - q) = 0q + 1 (1 - q)$$

$$-2q -2 + 2q = 1 - q$$

$$-2 = 1 - q$$

$$q = 3$$

Essentially, the Craftsman will never abandon his effectiveness strategy, at least with the values we have assigned in this payoff matrix.

Which brings us back to the inherent struggle between the Gamesmen archetypes who are inclined to sacrifice return on assets in exchange for an advance in market share, the Craftsmen (who appear to be absolute heroes in the writings of Professor Tom Peters), and the Company Men/Asset Managers, who are seemingly oblivious to the needs of the organization to satisfy customers, as long as the numbers in the General Ledger indicate a good return on investment. Of course, as phrased here, it is impossible to definitively assert one approach as superior to another; however, in Part 3 of this book I will endeavor to provide a framework that will allow a quantitative analysis of the trade-offs involved in such strategic interactions. For now, suffice to say that Mr Nash has given us the tools to confirm that such a natural adversarial component in choosing mixed strategies among the Maccoby archetypes exists, much as they exist between Hawk–Dove mixed strategy adherents engaged in a common game.

Game Theory and Voyeurism

Harkening back to the discussion on the observations of pre-Chicken Game iteration communications, and the actual performance during the game, these observations and/ or the information that can be gleaned from them is of immense value. People tend to naturally gravitate towards mixed strategies in the various social, personal, and workplace environments and games in which they are compelled or volunteer to participate, or likely to participate. They naturally would like to know if known or potential participants in the various games are likely to act aggressively or passively, or like Craftsmen, Company Men, Jungle Fighters, or Gamesmen, in the event that they find themselves matched against them.

But it may go further than that. People may be attracted to events that disclose the selected strategies of people with whom they may never, ever be matched. I can understand why a boxer would be very interested in the approach that a scheduled adversary may adopt, but why would the nominal fan be interested in this? There is an astonishingly small chance that a fan of boxing would ever encounter a physical confrontation with a professional boxer. And, even if they did, there is an even smaller chance that familiarity with the pro's preferred attack pattern would be of any practical use. This being the case, why would anyone wish to watch two athletes hit each other?

Similarly, consider the popularity of the series of American television programs entitled "The Real Housewives of …," with a series of locales, such as New York, New Jersey, Los Angeles, and Atlanta, completing the title. The women who star in the series are nominally friends, but they often exhibit aggressive or negative behavior towards one another. Why on earth would anyone care about the value of the relationships among these women, apart from themselves?

The answer is understandable through Game Theory. We need to know the particulars of the conflicts in the Faculty Lounge, the locker room, the boardroom, the televised wives' get-togethers, because we have an innate need to collect data on the exhibited preferred strategies that other players select, whether we are likely to encounter them or not. Personal and untrue information about other people is slander, or gossip; personal and true information about other peoples' private behavior is broadcast across the world every day, and sells millions of magazines.

It can, actually, be considered entertaining worry. As mentioned earlier, worry is a uniquely human construct, where we can project imaginary future scenarios and engage our own potential responses. Of course, worry takes its toll, as our projection of future negative or unfortunate scenarios results in physical responses not too dissimilar than if the negative event projected had actually come about. But, what if it was other people trying out those potential strategies, or responses, in a variety of situations where the participants are engaging in the more aggressive mixed strategies? Well, we could simply observe the outcomes, without incurring any more negative response than whatever emotional investment we have in people who are, in reality, complete strangers.

I recall a quote – I believe it was from Ann Landers – that went along the lines of "Advanced people talk about ideas, mediocre people talk about things, and small people talk about other people." But the interactions of other people *do* represent the evaluation of ideas, or at least the monitoring of recognizable strategies that may or may not have a bearing in our worlds. Consider the manager who has only recently been introduced to the corporation. She will have to come to understand the nature of the game, and the personalities of the players with whom she interacts. But those people were themselves rookies at some point in the game, and would have similarly had to come to an understanding of how to play and who were the game's other participants. In this way corporate culture is passed along, as new players are introduced and adapt to the mixed, canned strategies of those around them. If a given corporation were to be founded or dominated early on by, say, Jungle Fighters, then later additions to the organization will either have to adopt strategies that are successful against the Jungle Fighters' predominant manifestations of *their* canned strategies, or else they will fail. In organizational theory, this would go a long way towards explaining why certain corporate practices or approaches can become highly contagious, even when they represent poor practices or approaches. In this light, the oft-heard defense in the face of a recommendation for improvement, "That's the way we've always done it," should not be taken as "I'm unwilling to change, even though you have made a good case for doing so." Rather, "That's the way we've always done it" is probably better understood as "This set of mixed strategies – including the strategies involved in process improvement – is currently in a Nash Equilibrium. From a pure process point of view, you are probably right. But in *this* game, someone's payoff is going to take a hit if we switch strategies, and I'm concerned that someone is me."

Our understanding of causality leads us to take away bits of information from both real-life interactions – our own as well as others – and fictional storylines, and weave them into narratives that we believe both explain how things happened in the past, as well as how things are likely to unfold in the future. Game Theory allows a quantification of this process, and the potential to quantify how the future is likely to unfold moves us ever closer to the elusive Code of Nature, or a Hari Seldon-like mathematical divination method. But such calculations only approach accuracy when we can correctly assess the payoffs, strategies available to players, and the precise parameters associated with the limits of the game. For example, from the Pirate's Game, having Pirate A suggest an acceptable division of the treasure, only to have him suddenly eaten by a large crocodile that had been stalking him from the beginning of the story would completely invalidate all of the analysis that went into what Pirate E knows about Pirate D's options, and so forth. Therefore some assessment of how canned strategies and Nash Equilibriums impact environs beyond the ones we think we're in will have to be undertaken, and THAT requires a look at Network Theory.

CHAPTER 4 Network Theory and Games

None of us is as smart as all of us.

Eric Schmidt, University of Pennsylvania Commencement Address, 2009

In observing the manifestations of sets of canned strategies in various games for their rates of success or failure, a significant leap towards identifying and predicting behaviors that are far more likely to be encountered in real-life management circumstances can be had by reviewing networked games, such as online role-playing games. Such games also provide a good starting point to incorporate Network Theory into the overarching structure of using Game Theory to identify the most effective and appropriate set(s) of strategies for effective managerial decision-making.

Probably the most basic thing the reader needs to know about Network Theory is Metcalfe's Law. This states that the value of a network is proportional to the square of the number of users in the system.[1] For example, two telephones can have only one connection (Figure 4.1), but six phones can have fifteen connections (Figure 4.2). In short, the larger the network, the more valuable or powerful it is.

The next most basic (but important) thing the manager needs to know about Network Theory is that network interactions do not behave in a linear fashion, nor in any way that can be quantified and predicted using Gaussian curves. Some networks may well exhibit behavior consistent with the Pareto Principle, and see 20% of the nodes receive 80% of the interactions, or hits. But in the majority of cases networks will exhibit far more extreme behavior, with a very small percentage of nodes receiving an overwhelming percentage of interactions, with the vast majority of nodes experiencing relatively few. Another expression of this is known as The Butterfly Effect, more elegantly presented in the question "If a butterfly flaps its wings in Brazil, does it set off a tornado in Texas?"[2]

Figure 4.1   The Connection Between Two Phones

---

1   Metcalfe's law (July 26, 2010). In *Wikipedia, The Free Encyclopedia*. Retrieved 22:09, July 30, 2010, from http://en.wikipedia.org/w/index.php?title=Metcalfe%27s_law&oldid=375494958

2   Merilees, Phillip, *Does the Flap of a Butterfly's Wings in Brazil Set Off a Tornado in Texas?*, American Association for the Advancement of Science presentation, 1972.

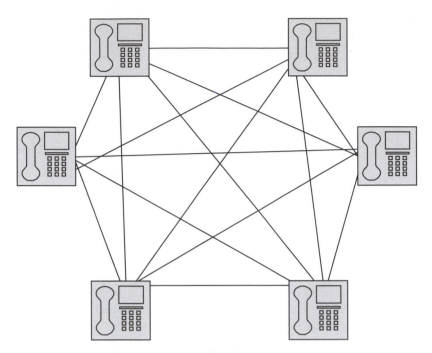

Figure 4.2   The Connections Between Six Phones

Essentially, the ability of a very small variance in a dynamic system leading to large-scale (or even cataclysmic) effects is intricately tied to Network Theory in that seemingly small changes to a small number of nodes in a given network have the capacity to cascade into massive changes to many nodes in the network, and this characteristic is practically impossible to predict. This is basically the dark side to Metcalfe's Law – an increased number of nodes in a network increases that network's influence or power at a near-exponential rate; but it also increases its variability. To the extent that people engage in the buying and selling of goods and services, they can be said to be nodes in a massive macro economic network, a network that exhibits high levels of variability, to say the least. Whenever you hear or read about economists, politicians, or other so-called experts decrying perfectly ordinary manifestations of that dynamic network, such as "income disparity," such ones are either displaying ignorance of Metcalfe's Law, or they are engaged in fraud. In Part 2 of this book I will discuss characteristics of The Butterfly Effect within networks as an upper boundary to the efficacy of structured abstracts, or models, in predicting future events and environs. For now, the manager seeking the insights of Network Theory for their decision-making need only be aware of something that is probably already ingrained in their psyche – that chaos can ensue in a dynamic environment, and the proximate cause of the chaos, when it's even identifiable, can be miniscule.

These two very basic characteristics of networks carry immense managerial implications. They are probably best evaluated in Thomas Friedman's book *The Earth Is Flat*,[3] which essentially asserts that the commercial environment has been dramatically

---

3   Friedman, Thomas, *The World Is Flat*, Farrar, Straus, and Giroux, April 2005.

altered with the introduction of communication, social, personal, and professional networks. Tom Siegfried, in *A Beautiful Math*, posits that a combination of Game Theory, Risk Management Theory, and Network Theory could potentially serve as the basis of the overarching Code of Nature discussed in the Introduction. Now, I have no intention of pulling these three theories together in order to create a crypto-Seldon Plan; however, I would like to evaluate how the selection of canned strategies by players in a networked game can mirror the selection of managerial strategies in analogous situations in the real world.

Consider that behemoth of online, multi-player games, *The World of Warcraft*. The *World of Warcraft* (WoW) is a massive multi-player online role-playing game (MMORPG) with more than 11,500,000 players as of December 2008.[4] Players create an avatar belonging to one of two opposed factions, who then explores the world ("Azeroth"), completes quests, fights monsters or other players, and interacts with other players and non-player characters. The players are rewarded for various activities by acquiring weapons, tools, property, and currency, but can also stand to lose the same. Another key aspect to *The World of Warcraft* is that the players can communicate among allies, which leads to clans forming within the alliances. Recall the discussion from Chapter 2 on the act of communicating combined with the patterns of strategy selection, and the implications to the payoff matrix. In games such as *World of Warcraft*, veteran, predatory players have been known to hang around the introduction point for new players, pretend to befriend such players, and then double-cross them at a vulnerable point in order to confiscate their gold, weapons, or other assets. Similar strategies can almost be expected from Jungle Fighters within the organization, if and when they come across the opportunities.

Another interesting manifestation of WoW players' selected strategies has to do with guild-busting attempts. Guilds are self-forming teams within an MMORPG, owing to players' ability to communicate with each other while playing, both through channels within the MMORPG itself, or through other online mechanisms, or even via telephone. These guilds, or clans, would often be centered on a universally adapted set of game-playing strategies, with observed divisions of labor and agreed-to distributions of property or achievement points. I have it on anecdotal evidence that there were instances of new players dying from exposure because they did not belong to the guild that owned all of the inns and sources of food within a geographic area, and the members of the guild had agreed to refuse to sell to any non-member. When the preponderance of guilds made it very difficult for new players to make any advancements in the game without joining one, attempts were made to automatically shuffle players' guild affiliation. When that happened, many displaced guild members continued to show loyalty to their former guild members, essentially acting as spies for their former guild and against their current. Keep in mind that these competing guilds were still within the same faction, reminiscent of the iconic scene in Monty Python's *Life of Brian*, where competing rebel factions kill each other for having lost the perspective that the occupying Romans were their real, common enemy.

I actually had a similar occurrence during my tenure as head of a Project Management Office (PMO). I inherited one Administrative Assistant, and hired another (it was a really big PMO). My predecessor, a particularly devious fellow, arranged to have the admin I inherited keep him current on my appointments and meetings. It wasn't until the admin

4   World of Warcraft (2010, July 29). In *Wikipedia, The Free Encyclopedia*. Retrieved 23:23, July 30, 2010, from http://en.wikipedia.org/w/index.php?title=World_of_Warcraft&oldid=376104479

I hired figured out what was going on and relayed it to me that I moved to put a stop to it. In the meantime my predecessor had essentially diverted some of my operating budget to take to his new organization. Since it was all within the same macro organization, no actions were taken against him. But it did serve as a lesson to me, and I would hope for the reader: in any sizable organization that you lead, at least one person will have an interest in seeing you fail, and will avail themselves of any tactic they deem safe to bring that about. I don't want to counsel as Nicolo Machiavelli did, in *The Prince*, along the lines of the new prince needing to kill off *all* of the former prince's courtiers. You just need to be aware that Jungle Fighters are in your organization; they probably have at least one network connection to you; and that they will behave as Jungle Fighters do. To ignore these two facts is to open yourself up to an entirely avoidable vulnerability.

Now, back to *World of Warcraft*. Richard Bartle developed a psychological profile test for players in massive multi-player online role-playing games, called the Bartle Test.[5] And – wouldn't you know it? – there are four such categories, which bear a striking resemblance to Maccoby's archetypes. The Bartle categories are:

- Achievers;
- Socializers;
- Explorers; and
- Killers.

Each of these categories is also associated with a suit from a deck of cards:

- Achievers are Diamonds, since they engage in strategies intended to maximize the number of points, amount of property, or achievements associated with victory in the game.
- Socializers are Hearts, and engage strategies that maximize interactions with other players.
- Explorers are Spades, since they seem to be digging around much of the time.
- Killers are Clubs – is a further explanation really necessary here?

Here's my take on how these archetypes coincide with *Gamesman* categories (Table 4.1):

Table 4.1   Comparison of Bartle and Maccoby Archetypes

Bartle Types	Gamesman Types	Comments
Achievers	Gamesman	Views interactions as a game, and does what it takes to win within that context.
Socializers	Company Men	Assumes the persona of those around him; engages in strategies based on those in the same environ.
Killers	Jungle Fighters	Get ahead by eliminating competitors.
Explorers	Craftsman	Defines success in ways that are not necessarily compatible with the original purpose of the game, or the intentions of the macro organization.

5   Bartle Test (May 6, 2010). In *Wikipedia, The Free Encyclopedia*. Retrieved 16:38, August 22, 2010, from http://en.wikipedia.org/w/index.php?title=Bartle_Test&oldid=360531356

The Gamesman was written in 1976. Richard Bartle would write the paper that served as the basis for his archetypes 20 years later. That these two men would define the exact same number of distinct archetypes, with such strong resemblance among them, decades apart and from entirely different angles is either an amazing coincidence, or else they were on to something that represents a common thread. It argues strongly against a form of confirmation bias leading to the categorizations. In massive multi-player online role-playing games, as in corporate environs, participants do tend to engage in a predictable set of canned strategies, and those sets can be characterized in one of the four archetypes.

Adversity in the Network

On September 13, 2005, *The World of Warcraft* introduced a new dungeon called "Zul'Gurub." This dungeon was controlled by Hakkar, the god of blood. Should a player overcome Hakkar, in his death throws the god would hex the player with a "corrupted blood" infection, which was highly contagious to anyone with whom the "victorious" player would later interact. Also, the fact that the player had been infected was not immediately apparent, and the infection could also be carried by non-player actors, the animals.

Although the disease was originally intended to be of short duration and confined to a specific WoW domain, players quickly discovered that, with the use of teleportation spells and infected animals, the infection could be spread over the entire WoW universe. A virtual pandemic ensued, which immediately killed lower-level players, and caused upper-level players to suddenly lose health and strength – which would also prove fatal, should the sudden onset occur while the player was engaged in combat.[6] Panic set in, as evidenced by the players' behavior and the communications both within the game and on chat boards.

World of Warcraft's creator, Blizzard Entertainment, attempted to impose a voluntary quarantine, which had virtually (no pun intended) no effect. Players told of walking through WoW towns with hundreds of dead bodies strewn about.[7] Specific buildings or even entire villages suspected of being the source of the infection were burned to the ground. Clans split apart, and individual players fled population centers. Some players who were good at healing offered their services, while others would stand on the road to villages known to be infected and warn those they encountered. While there were incidents of players teleporting known infected animals to the other faction's population centers – a type of virtual biological warfare – there were also instances of deliberate infection of players *within the same faction*.[8] Some players even rushed into population centers known to have been infected, just to see the results before rushing away and communicating what they had seen, similar to the behavior of real-life reporters. WoW play was so massively disrupted that Blizzard was forced to introduce a series of patches and hard-restarts of the game's servers, but the reason for the scale of the disruption is more easily understood in terms of Game Theory.

---

6   Corrupted Blood incident (August 18, 2010). In *Wikipedia, The Free Encyclopedia*. Retrieved 18:53, August 22, 2010, from http://en.wikipedia.org/w/index.php?title=Corrupted_Blood_incident&oldid=379546870

7   Orland, Kyle (May 20, 2008). "GFH: The Real Life Lessons Of WoW's Corrupted Blood". *Gamasutra*. United States: *Game Developer*. Retrieved August 22, 2010, from http://www.gamasutra.com/php-bin/news_index.php?story=18571

8   Ibid.

Prior to the introduction of the corrupted blood infection, the players engaged in their preferred mixed strategies, probably falling into a combination of the Bartle Types' patterns. The decisions to fight or avoid combat, explore or stay put, cooperate or defect – any of the alternatives, along with their expected (and actual) payoffs, were probably either in or close to a type of Nash Equilibrium. But suddenly, all of those payoff matrices became absolutely worthless, with the consideration of the odds of being infected trumping all other strategy-selection and payoff options.

Also consider what happened in Network Theory terms: a single node (the Zul'Gurub dungeon) initiated an occurrence that cascaded throughout the majority of other nodes (participants), utterly changing the entire network almost overnight. The Blizzard programmers who had assumed that the introduction of the tainted blood hex would be short-lived or confined to a specific area in WoW seriously underestimated the cascade effect in Network Theory. All of the early strategies intended to stem the cascading infection dealt with disengaging from the network, either by abandoning or destroying the inter-node connections (either avoiding contact with others, or destroying them). The Metcalfe's Law assertions that made the network so powerful also made its individual members extremely vulnerable. The most attractive feature of the network – its power – was instantaneously converted to its most harmful.

Back to Work

I would like to emphasize that I'm not trying to assert that there is a perfect analogy between the corporate world and *World of Warcraft*, even though many parallels exist. Rather, I would like to focus on the ways in which the macro organization exhibits network-like behavior.

While relatively few organizations maintain guilds or clans, almost all of them have cliques, or networks of friends or like-minded workers. Using Maccoby's archetypes, Company Men are obviously the most likely to be networked with a large number of others, with Jungle Fighters immediately behind. Conversely, Gamesmen and Craftsmen are least likely to be networked, with the following caveat: Maccoby discussed how individuals rarely belong to just one type, and that in most cases the types manifest as major/minor fits. The Gamesman/Jungle Fighter is more likely than the Gamesman/Craftsman to be highly networked; unless, of course, the Gamesman/Craftsman was in a game where the most "points" could be had by being highly networked.

Another common method for grouping personnel into types is the Myers-Briggs Type Indicator (MBTI).[9] Developed from the work of Carl Jung, it classifies people based on (wouldn't you just know it?) one of four indicators. But, since the results are a combination of a person's placement on each of the four indicators, the possible number of categories is 4 squared, or 16. Many organizations will pay to have key members of executive or project teams tested for their Myers-Briggs types (expressed as a four-letter acronym) in an attempt to better understand the players and advance team cohesion. In Game Theory parlance, it's indulging the voyeur impulse to gain insight into the most probable mixed strategies that members of the team will employ as the team pursues its goals. Knowing

---

9   Myers-Briggs Type Indicator (August 31, 2010). In *Wikipedia, The Free Encyclopedia*. Retrieved 18:12, September 6, 2010, from http://en.wikipedia.org/w/index.php?title=Myers-Briggs_Type_Indicator&oldid=382156719

a person's Myers-Briggs type makes it more likely that the observer can gain insight into that person's most probable payoff matrix, meaning that, given a complete knowledge of the parameters of the "game," a fairly accurate predictor of behavior can be known.

Just as members of WoW guilds cooperated to get ahead at the expense of players of the opposite faction, and even those within their own faction but not a member of their clan, members of cliques within the macro organization can be expected to further the goals of their own at the expense of non-members, even when such behavior is detrimental to the overall health of the organization. After a time this could lead to a collusion of the Jungle Fighters and Company Men within the organization – the least desirable of the Maccoby archetypes – against the Craftsmen and Gamesmen, the most valuable of the Maccoby archetypes.

This is why a pure meritocracy in any organization is a virtual impossibility (again, no pun intended). Management can't successfully tamp down networking connections – the players will simply work around any attempt, just as the WoW players would avoid using the in-game communication channels, and go to online chat rooms, or even call each other. Recall the discussion on the Hawk–Dove game, where the 100-bird population would benefit most if all of them behaved as doves; however, the introduction of even one Hawk completely disrupted the payoff matrix, leading to a Nash Equilibrium of approximately 25% Hawks (or every bird behaving as a Hawk 25% of the time in their mixed strategies). Similarly, the macro organization would best perform when comprised of Craftsmen and Gamesmen, or if the population elected to engage in Gamesman/Craftsman mixed strategies a majority of the time. But, add just one Jungle Fighter, and the payoff matrix changes dramatically. With a communication network in place, and with our inherent voyeuristic needs in play, the existence of the canned Jungle Fighter strategies within the population becomes quickly known, with all of the players adjusting their mixed strategies in an attempt to maximize their payoff in the changing environment that now, suddenly, includes elements that will detract from overall organizational performance.

Recall the calculation of the Nash Equilibrium in the game between the Gamesman and the Jungle Fighter. Of course, in a winning project environment, the payoff matrix allows for everyone to win by selecting the beneficial strategy mix. However, that changes dramatically in a losing effort. Combine this notion with the fact that:

- Communication networks exist.
- "Players," driven by their voyeurism instinct, are watching.
- The payoff matrix has suddenly changed so that the players will change their mixed strategies.
- In such a way as to increase their percentage of Jungle Fighter or Company Man strategy selections.
- At the expense of the Craftsmen and Gamesmen,and a cascading network event is almost inevitable, precipitating an organization death-spiral, should the original loss be large enough.

When the *Titanic* sank, her watertight bulkhead configuration was such that she could stay afloat should any four of her compartments be flooded. However, the iceberg with which she had collided compromised five watertight compartments. As each compartment flooded, it pulled the top of the next compartment's bulkhead below the waterline, and began flooding it. This process continued until the entire ship foundered.

Similarly, when an organization is on the receiving end of significant losses, a more broad-based and intense losing spiral becomes more likely due to the nature of the changing payoff matrices, the increased likelihood of the organization's members to employ strategies that maximize their personal payoffs while endangering the organization, and the virtual certain existence of at least one Jungle Fighter which, like the existence of a single hawk in the Hawk–Dove game, will guarantee that the entire population will not return to the set of strategies that improve their cumulative payoff.

Impact on Corporate Culture

Often, books and discussions on corporate culture take on a tone of vaguery and helplessness, as if everybody knows that:

- A corporate culture exists;
- That they can contribute to, but not significantly change; and
- That has serious implications for their prospects for getting ahead in the organization, or falling behind;
- All the while being not knowable in its entirety.

Upper-level management will usually create some sort of Mission Statement, or Strategic Vision document to serve as a way of communicating to the organization how they would like to see the corporate culture manifest, or change. There are many problems with such statements and documents, not the least of which is the fact that they are rarely considered definitive by those who read them. Recall the discussion of the board game Diplomacy, or even the analysis of the pre-game communications among participants in Chicken. The relationship of the communication to the selection of strategy (or strategies) in the actual pursuit of the organization's goals is also being evaluated. For example, almost every organization's mission statement will make some claim to placing a high priority on customer service or innovation. At the same time, every organization also has a set of mixed strategies that a majority of participants will employ to maximize their personal payoffs, and many of these mixed strategies are being originated and pursued by Jungle Fighters and Company Men. The Craftsman who sees the Jungle Fighter surging ahead in the organization can only marvel at the level of self-deception inherent in the organization making claim to valuing Craftsman-like strategies while promoting Jungle Fighters or Company Men. And, like the Diplomacy player who has been deceitfully encouraged to cooperate with another player prior to the move, and then betrayed when the actual move takes place, the organization's members will not only learn to not trust the author(s) of such grandiose mission statements, but can be expected to develop deep resentment against the same.

So for the sake of this discussion let's adjust the definition of "corporate culture" from Chapter 3 to the set of strategies that the organization's members select as they pursue both the organization's objectives and their own personal payoffs, *and the observable rate at which those strategies tend to be mixed*. The italicized part is crucial, since most organizations within a given industry are probably going to have identical or very similar strategies available to them. However, the rate at which a majority of players engage in, say, Jungle Fighter strategies at the expense of Gamesman strategies, taken as a whole, will dictate the overall character of the corporate culture.

With this definition in mind it's possible to evaluate the concept of corporate culture, and how to change it for the better, without devolving into vague, warm-and-fuzzy platitudes. For example, the next time you obtain a copy of your company's organization chart, go through the upper levels of management, and pencil in what you believe to be the Maccoby archetypes of each individual. Are the majority of these Gamesmen and Craftsmen? Then I would venture to say that your organization is in its ascendancy. They value risk-taking and innovation, and are more likely to tap into whatever technical advance is going to enhance their chances of succeeding in the marketplace.

Conversely, if your organization is headed by a sizable contingent of Jungle Fighters and Company Men, it is likely to be in decline (unless your organization is a monopoly, or government entity). Mixed strategies likely to enhance personal payoffs rather than achieve organizational goals have been rewarded with advancement, advancement at the expense of the Craftsmen and Gamesmen in the organization. The latter two types will become frustrated, and will tend to seek employment elsewhere. As this trend continues, eventually a significant setback will occur that will push the organization past its tipping point, and trigger the cascade-type tailspin described earlier. Organizations with a poor corporate culture are more vulnerable to industry setbacks, and so (mercifully) tend to remove themselves from their marketplaces.

The Impact of Information Architecture on Corporate Culture

Some years back I was asked by a friend, who had been named Line Manager over a project controls organization, to come in and re-work the information systems' architecture for the group. This organization was comprised mostly of professionals, around 50 people, most of whom had at least a Bachelor's degree. When I first encountered this group, they presented like a nest of Jungle Fighters and Company Men, and were engaged in what can only be described as organizational pathologies. Dysfunctional in the extreme, and with a poor and rapidly worsening reputation, the very need for the service these people provided was being questioned in the macro organization.

The group itself had informally self-segregated into three cliques: those who belonged to the macro organization, and those who belonged to one of the two major subcontractors providing personnel to the group. In addition, each of these cliques were using different software platforms to process their deliverable information streams. The three cliques were behaving in ways very similar to *World of Warcraft* guilds, in that they would select strategies designed to advance themselves, even at the expense of the faction (group). The Jungle Fighters engaged in slander and calumny, while the Company Men would make an elaborate show of working long hours in an effort to appear more valuable to the organization. Since each of the three teams used a different technical approach to producing their deliverables, no true advancement in one area would go unchallenged by the other two, effectively strangling innovation.

Of the problems I faced, certainly the most pervasive was the chaotic structure of the various information streams being used within the group. Their functions overlapped in some areas, and other information needs were completely unmet. In revamping the group's technical agenda, I started by mapping the nominal Management Information

System architecture to accommodate each of the clique's software platforms, identifying the data collected, processed, and delivered along each step of the way to the final products. Perhaps more importantly, I identified the points that each software platform passed along its output to the next system's input cycle, like runners passing a baton in a relay race (more on the importance of MIS theory in Part 3). With the technical agenda so set, moves were made to address the group's other pathologies.

At the next group meeting, it was announced that, should any member of the group accuse another of ineptitude or malfeasance to management, then that other employee would be called in to discuss the matter with their accuser. In essence, it was being communicated to the Jungle Fighters that their favorite strategy would no longer result in any kind of payoff. At the same group meeting, it was also announced that excessive overtime was no longer the standard by which employees' value was measured. The speech was essentially "You have families! You have lives! Why do you chain yourselves to your desks all weekend? If you're really that busy, let me know so I can hire more people." That last sentence was key: it was being communicated to the Company Men that shows of loyalty to the organization were not as important as achieving the group's goals. Craftsmen were valued over Company Men; or, in other words, the group should start using Craftsmen-oriented mixed strategies, and abandon Company Men or Jungle Fighter strategies.

The effect of these three tactics was astonishing in both their effectiveness and the speed at which the change came about. With the technical agenda set and clearly articulated, process improvements were fairly evaluated, and either implemented or discarded, instead of being ruthlessly attacked irrespective of their merits. The walls that had been erected between the cliques began to dissolve as the players came to realize the greater payoffs to be had from cooperating rather than defecting. Simply knowing that excessive amounts of free overtime was no longer expected or even appreciated had, by itself, a marked positive influence on morale. The unrepentant Jungle Fighters saw their supply of allies dwindle, as well as their ability to glom on to the contributions of the Craftsmen. After having been given opportunity after opportunity to cease engaging in Jungle Fighter strategies, and refusing to do so, they would be given the less-appealing assignments. Sometimes this would be sufficient to turn them into contributors, but the hard-core Jungle Fighters would come to realize that their preferred strategies no longer resulted in any kind of payoff, and sought environs more suited to their chicanery. Within five months the combination of resetting the technical agenda, combined with the personnel moves, had utterly transformed this group into a cooperative, high-achieving unit, with good morale and improving reputation.

So, how was this accomplished, exactly? The tactics can be simplified as follows:

- First and foremost, the rules of the game changed. The chaotic MIS architecture, where the various outputs of the contributing systems could not be evaluated on their merits, was replaced with a clearly articulated, simple plan to produce the project cost and schedule performance information required. The systems – and their advocates – were no longer overlapping their areas of responsibility, nor leaving gaps. This act alone went a long way towards relieving much of the hostility and animosity within the group.
- Even with the rules changed, I knew that Jungle Fighters and Company Men would remain in the game. The latter could be tolerated (or converted), but not so much the

former. By eliminating the tactic of approaching the group leader and complaining about other players, I removed the Jungle Fighters' favorite strategy, rendering them second-class players overnight. I modified the communication/voyeur network in such a way that the Jungle Fighters would be frustrated at every turn.

- And, finally, by adjusting the organization's culture to be more accommodating of Craftsmen and Gamesmen, those strategies became dominant, and technical excellence naturally flowed as a result.

A more extensive discussion of the role of information streams in influencing organizational behavior and performance is in Part 3; for now, suffice to say that information is the life-blood of the organization, and its flow and usage has a profound effect on the inner workings of the macro organization.

I can't finish this story without a discussion of an event that was both highly illustrative and hilarious. One member of the group, a fellow I'll call Neil, was a Jungle Fighter through and through. I mean, when Maccoby wrote that nobody manifests exclusively in just one of his archetypes, he did so only because he had never met Neil. About three months in to my tenure, one of the team members arranged for our group to take on another group within the same division in a paintball game. It was a great way for former adversaries to learn to trust each other. At the appointed time the two groups arrived in a mountainous play area, where it was discovered that there were a couple more in our team than in the other group. Neil was assigned to the other group to even out the number of players in each.

The two groups separated and, at a given signal, began playing "Capture the Flag." The first battle took around 45 minutes, after which the air horn sounded indicating that all the players should return to the main camp for drinks and re-supply of ammunition. When we arrived back at the camp, Neil had been hit in the back by a paintball that was the color of his own team.

Hey, Neil, what happened?

I got out in front of the rest of my guys, and was mistaken for one of you.

Oh.

Neil had been fragged, and the rest of us tried desperately to stifle our laughter. We had five more heats throughout the day, and, after every single one, we would come back to the main camp to discover Neil had another paintball hit on his back from his own team. Jungle Fighters are neither respected nor liked, and, given the opportunity, the other players will find a way to communicate as such.

Neil would stay involved in our team for some time, but his powers of persuasion never recovered from that Saturday afternoon paintball match. Of course, word spread quickly, and the mixed strategies that included unhealthy doses of Jungle Fighting accelerated their decline throughout the group.

5 *Win Using the Rules of the Game*

Human beings, who are almost unique in having the ability to learn from the experience of others, are also remarkable for their apparent disinclination to do so.

Douglas Adams (1952–2001), *Last Chance to See*

From analyzing the dynamics of energy distribution cartage schemes to evaluating the structure of tactics employed in turning a profoundly dysfunctional group around, it's clear that Game Theory has much to offer the world of management. But, as we have seen, Game Theory by itself, as offered up by Von Neumann and Nash, is of limited utility. When combined with Network Theory, traditional Risk Management techniques, and Maccoby's (and Bartle's) archetypes, however, it becomes the basis for identifying and eradicating commonly-held pathologies of decision-making that are rampant in many organizations. For the remainder of this book I will refer to this combination of theories as Macro Game Theory, or just MGT.

Thus far I have been moving back and forth between Macro Game Theory's main beneficial attributes, without examining the efficacy of these attributes. Macro Game Theory provides a structure – a concept, if you will – that allows a more prescient analysis of things that have occurred within the organization. However, in those instances where the payoff matrix can be accurately known and the set of strategies available to the players can also be known in its entirety, Macro Game Theory may also have the capacity for predicting a probable future. Good non-team-play athletes, like boxers, will have a pretty good idea of the strategies and tactics their next opponent is most likely to employ by watching film of the opponent's previous contests. However, the exceptional fighter can come to the same knowledge about strangers by evaluating how the surprise opponent stands, holds his hands, advances or retreats, and distributes his weight – all prior to the first strike being thrown.

Of course, any management model or theoretical structure that lays claim to predicting the future in a usable manner is fraught with hazards. To further examine these hazards, I want to further review some more interesting goings-on in *World of Warcraft* (WoW).

Back to Azeroth

As I mentioned earlier, players in *World of Warcraft* accumulate goods and in-game currency. These goods or currencies can be used or spent, or sold at in-game auctions –

or given to others, either within the player's guild, or to complete strangers. Why, you may ask, would a WoW player give away hard-won virtual gold to a complete stranger? Because the stranger paid them in real-world currency to do so.

These virtual economies mirror real economies in many ways, much as the Tainted Blood incident mirrored real responses to epidemics in real life. A Yahoo! search for "WoW Gold" yielded 134,000,000 hits.[1] Players known as "Gold Farmers" have been known to accumulate WoW gold and sell it for real currency as a way of making a living. Some experts speculated that the virtual currency market would exceed subscriptions by 2009.[2] Of course, engaging in currency transactions or speculation is a highly regulated industry, and the extent that virtual currency was bumping up against real currency regulations has become a source of concern for economists and lawmakers alike. The movement of virtual currency into real currency markets raises issues associated with gambling and taxation, and even virtual crime. In South Korea, with its relatively high number of per-capita personal computers and online game players, virtual WoW gangs have sprung up, forcing new players to pay "protection" money to keep from being killed, or even robbing vulnerable players outright.[3]

One of the more fascinating aspects of players' behavior within the WoW universe resembling real people's behavior in the business world has to do with the relationship between the WoW players and Blizzard Entertainment programmers and administrators. As players began to manifest unwanted behaviors or implement undesirable strategies, Blizzard would change the parameters of the game to circumvent them. A certain low-level antagonism between some of the players implementing the undesirable strategies (and wishing to continue to do so), and Blizzard sprang up, with characteristics resembling the relationship between government and the governed. Like the California State Legislature attempting to prevent Enron from making huge profits at the expense of the State's energy consumers, each new attempt from Blizzard to curtail undesirable behavior was met with work-arounds or evasions from parts of the players' population. As in real legislatures, the Law of Unintended Consequences often leads to behaviors or strategies being implemented that are worse than the strategies originally targeted for correction.

Nor are massive multi-player online role-playing games immune from macroeconomics problems. Often new players are introduced with a nominal sum of money, but without an automatic increase in the number or amount of goods or real estate in the game. As more virtual currency is introduced into the virtual economy, it chases fewer true resources, meaning that inflation can (and does) set in. If such an unintended consequence has sufficiently far-reaching effect, it can drive away players and lead to dramatic imbalances among the remaining subscribers. In Game Theory parlance, the payoff matrices can change dramatically and suddenly, and from causes that have nothing to do with deliberately-introduced epidemics, like the Tainted Blood incident. In short, observing the behavior of players in MMORPGs can provide key insights to the behavior of participants in the real-world free marketplace.

---

1   Retrieved from Yahoo! August 29, 2010.

2   Virtual economy (August 25, 2010). In *Wikipedia, The Free Encyclopedia*. Retrieved 18:47, August 29, 2010, from http://en.wikipedia.org/w/index.php?title=Virtual_economy&oldid=380901352

3   Ibid.

The Role of Incomplete Information

The innovation of the adversarial players in *World of Warcraft* far outpaces Blizzard Entertainment's ability to quickly and effectively return the world of Azeroth to Blizzard's ideal, intended state. This innovation, generated by and communicated through multiple nodes in a grand connected network, creates a vast library of information, only some of which is knowable by Blizzard employees at the time it is developed, or at the time it leads to the widespread adoption of strategies considered undesirable. I'd like to restate that last sentence, specifically for the manager or executive seeking to realize the advantages to be gleaned from an understanding of Game Theory in the organization: incomplete information about the likely strategies of the players in a game is the biggest obstacle to generating and implementing decisions designed to create the preferred business environment or circumstances. Blizzard Entertainment wants their virtual environment to present in such a way as to be attractive to new customers (players), while remaining interesting enough as to limit the number of experienced players who may be otherwise inclined to leave. However, groups of existing players have learned, communicated, and adopted strategies that maximize their own payoffs, often at the expense of the new players. Blizzard moves to thwart these undesirable strategies, but the network is so powerful, innovative, and complex, that the mountain of incomplete information can be counted on to ensure that Blizzard can be expected to remain frustrated in their management decisions' effectiveness in bringing Azeroth completely to where they want it to be.

Information, as Complete as Possible

All valid management information systems (MISs) have the following basic structure:

Figure 5.1   Valid MIS Structure

Of course, managers must make decisions based on incomplete information all of the time, but it is blindingly obvious (or, at least, it should be) that the more accurate, timely, and relevant management information available, the better the odds that the decision-makers will make the right call. Indeed, the impact of the incompleteness of information on the realization of organizational success cannot be understated. The very best managers with 20% of the information needed to obviate a given decision will be beaten every time by the very poorest managers who have access to 80% of the information so needed (my very own slant on the Pareto Principle).

But what information is relevant? I once worked with a Vice President at the now-defunct Advanced Sciences Incorporated (ASI), who had a Ph.D. in Statistics. He simply loved to read reports that listed project expenditures, and compared those to the project's original basis of estimate (BOE). When he came across a discrepancy, he would automatically assume something had gone wrong, and raise the inconsistency as a management issue. As head of the Project Controls Office for ASI, I attempted to get him to reconsider his perspective using the following story.

"David," I would tell him, "imagine a project that had estimated a total cost of $100,000. In the basis of estimate, there was $75K for labor, and $25K for heavy equipment. At the project's 90% complete point, they had spent $68K for heavy equipment, and $18K for labor. By your analysis, this project would be in major trouble. But, by simple Earned Value analysis, they are in great shape, due to come in under budget. Do you not see that simply comparing budgets to actual costs leads to the exact wrong conclusions about cost performance?"

The short answer was no, he didn't. He had latched on to an invalid management information stream, and the decisions and stances it led him to adopt were, well, wrong. He didn't last long among the company's executive team.

Similarly, there was a rash of books and articles early in the millennium that attempted to quantify the value of Project Management (PM), and many of these were predicated on the idea that PM's Return on Investment (ROI) could be calculated. If this were so, and the calculation produced a positive number, project management practitioners could, at long last, justify their callings and enjoy the organizational support of executives and asset managers that had been so cruelly withheld. Alas, it was not to be, and anyone with even a passing knowledge of Game Theory could tell far in advance that it wouldn't work out the way the ROI-pushers envisioned. The players in organizations that work on projects are either in, or close to, a Nash Equilibrium with respect to adopting strategies or behaviors consistent with accepting the Project Management or Asset Management approach (recall the Craftsman versus Company Man discussion in Chapter 3). Calculating the Return on Investment (calculated revenue generated/cost of the asset) is an Asset Manager's tool, and he's already clear on his preferred strategies and expected payoffs. In short, these oft-touted assertions weren't game-changers, nor did they alter anybody's payoff matrix; so, it should come as no surprise when they fail.

Now, there is a distinct possibility that they did not fail in all cases. It's conceivable that some frustrated Project Management practitioner plopped a copy of *Researching the Value of Project Management*[4] on their company executive's desk, saying "See? *See*? I told you it was worth doing!" And the executive immediately slapped herself on the forehead, and replied "Wow! You were right all along! Let's set up a large Project Management Office, with you as its head!" But I kind of doubt it.

The only way management information streams can become game-changers is if they deliver accurate, timely, and relevant information. In the last two examples I have used, the information was accurate, and it was timely. But it wasn't relevant, and that was what mattered most. "All things fail by irrelevant comparisons." I don't know who said that (and neither does Wikiquotes), but it most certainly holds true in the realm of management information.

Keeping with the Titanic example, she received a transmission from the steamer *Amerika* that there were icebergs in her vicinity on the night of April 14, 1912. The information was accurate, timely, and relevant, and Captain Edward J. Smith changed course towards the South in response. Of course, the exact position of the very iceberg

---

4   Janice Thomas and Mark Mullaly, *Researching the Value of Project Management*, PMI Publishing, 2008.

that would get hit by the ship would have been useful, but that kind of positioning technology was still decades off.

The next time accurate and relevant information was available concerning that particular iceberg, it was coming from the forward crow's nest, when Frederick Fleet rang the bell three times, and then called through the telephone line to the bridge, "Iceberg, right ahead!"[5] However, given the speed and rate of turn of *Olympic* class passenger liners, the information wasn't timely enough. Perhaps they should not have been staring at Leonardo DiCaprio and Kate Winslet kissing on the foredeck.

Information takes time and money to generate. As shown in Figure 5.1, data must be collected based on a certain structure or technical approach. It must be processed into information, using specific methodologies. And finally it must be communicated to those in a position to decide (or act decisively) in a manner that they will understand the significance of the information. Naturally, the information must be timely and accurate. And, just as no valid conclusion can be drawn from a flawed premise, the only usable information that can be gleaned from inaccurate or irrelevant data, or a flawed MIS structure, is by pure accident.

I once worked with a manager who wanted to change the organization's management information systems so that they could relay a comparison of the number of hours in a project's original staffing projection with the actual hours of people on the project team (to recognize and discourage latitude in switching people between projects, I suppose). This upgrade would bear significant costs and effort to deliver. When I challenged the relevance of the information, he replied "Why *wouldn't* you want to know that information?" The (blindingly obvious, at least in my opinion) answer was that the kernel of information he sought flunked the accurate, timely, and relevant test; but, not only that, it would cost money and effort, while other information streams, costing less and passing the ATR test, would not be pursued. But, since I couldn't convince him that his desired information was irrelevant, it was pointless to try to educate the fellow. So I didn't.

Now we can see that, in addition to a Management Information System's valid function (accurate, timely, relevant), successful MISs have a strategic goal: that of providing a narrative for why the things that have gone wrong did go wrong, why the things that went right went right, and try to predict future conditions and events in a way that's accurate enough to capitalize on them. We have already seen how Game Theory, and especially Macro Game Theory, provides utility in explaining why things unfolded the way they did, and its limited ability to predict probable manifestations of players' mixed strategies in a given environment. And, since the resources used to create these information streams aren't limitless, any stream that doesn't satisfy the function and strategic standards is a waste of time and money, and will lead to the introduction of more pathology in managerial decision-making.

Predicting the Future

In Project Management space (and *only* in Project Management space) the future cost and schedule performance of a given project is performed by Earned Value and Critical

5   RMS Titanic (September 5, 2010). In *Wikipedia, The Free Encyclopedia*. Retrieved 02:46, September 5, 2010, from http://en.wikipedia.org/w/index.php?title=RMS_Titanic&oldid=382981789

Path methodology, respectively and exclusively. Earned Value is a method for placing a monetary value on work that has actually been performed. For example, on a project to create 2,000 widgets, with a budget of $2,000 (USD), and a schedule of two months, the project manager budgets $1,000 for Month 1, and $1,000 for Month 2. At the end of Month 1, the project's accountant tells the project manager that the project has spent $1,100. How is this project doing?

If you answered "It depends on how many widgets have been made," go to the top of the class. My ASI veep would have concluded, sans the data on the widget number, that this project was in trouble, based on a comparison of the cumulative budget ($1,000) and actual costs ($1,100), yielding an apparent overrun of $100, or 10%. However, this particular widget manager has actually produced 1,300 widgets. And, if the reader has already reached the conclusion that the amount of the project's budget actually earned is, therefore, $1,300, then ... well, I'm dashed, because I already sent you to the head of the class. Okay, well, umm, good job.

Not to dwell on my unfortunate ASI veep, but this story problem vividly demonstrates the invalidity of the commonly-used technique of comparing budgets to actual costs in attempting to evaluate project cost performance. In the widget project example, this comparison was not only irrelevant, it produced misleading information, and, had a manager acted on it, would have resulted in management decisions that were the exact opposite of what should have been done.

In this example, the project team was able to earn $1,300 in project value against an actual cost of $1,100. At this rate of performance, they will be able to complete all 2,000 widgets for a cost of $1,692. Also, at this rate of performance, the project team won't need all of the two months. They can be expected to complete the project on the 17th day of Month 2. These two projections are possible by calculating something called the Cost Performance Index (CPI) and Schedule Performance Index (SPI), both of which are predicated on the value of the work already accomplished. For example, the widget project's CPI is the amount earned divided by the cost it took to accomplish it, or:

$$CPI = \text{Amount Earned/Amount Spent}$$
$$CPI = \$1,300/\$1,100$$
$$CPI = 1.18$$

Dividing the CPI into the overall budget ($2,000) produces the $1,692 figure. How accurate is this prediction of the future? Professor Dave Christiansen performed an analysis of the stability of the CPI figure,[6] and showed that, once a project has passed its 15% complete point, the CPI almost never changes more than ten points in either direction. The implication is that any estimate of at-completion costs based on the CPI (after 15% of the project is done) will almost never be more than 10% off.

The same is true of Critical Path Methodology (CPM), since it shares many of Earned Value Methodology's processing techniques. Say a given task is originally estimated to last 100 days. On day 50, the scheduler asks the task's manager his percentage complete. If that manager answers that he is only 40% complete, and the scheduler enters this information into a CPM-capable software package, the software will calculate that the task will not be completed in 100 days, but 125 days, at that rate of performance. And,

6   Christensen, David S. and Kirk I. Payne (1992, April). "CPI Stability-Fact or Fiction?" *Journal of Parametrics*, 10: 27–40.

if there is a task manager who is counting on Manager A to be done on day 101, he had better be notified of the delay – otherwise, he will make uninformed (read: bad) decisions about how (or when) to execute his task.

These information streams – unique to Project Management – have truly remarkable predictive capabilities. I have to laugh at Asset Managers' techniques for predicting cost performance on a given project, which usually center on two techniques, both of which are utterly invalid. One is to perform some sort of regression analysis on cumulative actual costs. I think the widget project example shows the utter futility of this approach – regression would have predicted a total project cost of $2,200, as opposed to the $1,692 CPI-derived amount. The other is the practice of re-estimating remaining project work, and then adding this amount on to the cumulative actual costs. As I discussed in a paper presented to a Project Management Institute® conference,[7] the American Association of Cost Engineers[8] asserted that a detailed estimate, performed by a professional estimator using off-the-shelf software, could produce an estimate accurate to within 15% of the total realized costs. Hmmm. 10% accuracy, with a relatively easy calculation using objective data, versus 15% accuracy, with the costs associated with a professional estimator, using some subjective data (cost of remaining work), some objective (actual costs so far). The preferred method seems pretty obvious to me, but the practice of continually generating so-called bottoms-up estimates not only continues, but is often encouraged, or even mandated. Returning to the widget project example, we know that the project had spent $1,100 through Month 1. We also know that there were 700 widgets left to make (ironically, we could only know this through an assessment of how much work has already taken place). Assuming we have the same set of estimators who came up with the original estimate still on the team, they'll probably conclude that it's going to take $700 more to finish the project (though there is much truth in the old saw about how no two estimators will come up with the same numbers based on the same work, nor will the same estimator come up with the same number for the same work on two different occasions). We now have an at-completion estimate of $1,800, which is closer than the regression version, but still high. Essentially, this technique is a quasi-Earned Value derivative, only substituting massive amounts of subjective data (each line item of the new, improved estimate of remaining work) for EV's calculations. Clearly, it fails the accuracy test when compared to the CPI-based calculation; and, since it takes longer, it fails in the timeliness arena, as well.

I've written often about the calculated versus estimated Estimate at Completion issue, both in my regular columns in *PM® Network* magazine ("The Variance Threshold"), and in my blogs on the Project Management Institute's website. The riposte I hear most often has to do with how the incorporation of more current knowledge about project conditions overcomes the subjective nature of the re-estimating remaining work technique (although not in those terms. It's usually articulated as something like "Things change! Calculated EACs can't know that!," or some such). The problem with this counter-argument is that it doesn't take into account the way in which the information about how what has gone wrong so far has impacted the project's performance. The PM's knowledge of what went wrong, and the size of the mishaps' impact, gets integrated into a narrative that

7   Hatfield, Michael, *The Bottoms-Up Myth*, a paper presentation to PMI – Boston, 1996.

8   Now known as the Association for the Advancement of Cost Engineering, International (AACEI).

exonerates the project manager, if not large parts (or all) of the project team. And, of course, nothing like those mishaps will occur again, don't you know.

The Earned Value/calculated version of the Estimate at Completion has none of those problems. It doesn't need a narrative, nor subjective (read: optimistic) projections of how everything will go as planned from that point forward. It only knows the current level of the project team's cumulative performance, and unblinkingly forecasts the future – and can be counted on to do so accurately. These attributes, as desirable as they are in the Management Information game, often stand in stark contradiction to the project team's narrative of how they have been performing, and, as such, must be denigrated if everything hasn't gone according to plan, which is often the case. Unable to assail the Earned Value technique on accuracy, ease-of-use, or objective vs. subjective nature of the information, opponents instead try to thread the needle in epistemological space, on the utility of information as it presents in time (again, articulated as "Things change!").

Pulling the Threads Together

Let's evaluate the different types of management information systems as compared to their utility in the explaining the past and predicting the future functions (Table 5.1).

Table 5.1   MIS Streams and Management Types

Management Type	Explaining Setbacks	Explaining Successes	Predicting the Future
Asset	- GAAP (Profit & Loss statement) - Estimating	- GAAP (Profit & Loss statement)	- Return on Investment, Opportunity Costs, et.al.
Project	- Earned Value - Critical Path - Quality Management (including 6 Sigma) - Estimating	- Earned Value (w/ GAAP data) - Critical Path	- Earned Value (calculated cost & schedule performance) - Critical Path - Risk Management
Strategic	- Game Theory - Maccoby Archetypes	- Game Theory	- Game Theory - Maccoby Archetypes - Capability Maturity Model®

I will engage in a more thorough discussion of the types of management in Part 3. For now, the following definitions will suffice for continuing the analysis:

• Asset Management covers the organization's assets, including personnel. Its main MIS stream comes from the organization's General Ledger, created consistent with Generally Accepted Accounting Practices, or GAAP, and the main products of this stream are the balance sheet and profit and loss statements.
• Project Management pertains to attaining the scope of a specific project within the customer's parameters of cost, schedule, and quality.

- Strategic Management is the standing of the organization with respect to its competitors, and its main performance measure is market share.

These three types of management are different utterly; they have different goals, techniques, and tools. Because of this difference, attempting to use a management information stream that is germane to one type in an attempt to gain information in another type is a futile gesture, wasteful of resources and misguided in result. Similarly, attempting to use a tool within the same management type but for a different function will also lead to failure. For example, calculating a Return on Investment for the purpose of deciding to purchase a printer produces a highly relevant piece of information, which turns to utter irrelevance if the decision at hand is to discover which projects perform better than others, or to attempt to squeeze out a competitor in a certain market. Similarly, attempting to use the Risk Management techniques discussed in Chapter 1 to help fill in the narrative on why a project ran into difficulties is an invalid use of those techniques, even though we're staying within the project management type (more on this later; for now suffice to say that it's irrelevant if a certain problem that was predicted to have happened did happen, but the project team's response was the same). While that is something of a dramatic example, the principle holds true even when the desired information stream appears to belong to more than one management type. They don't, except as noted in Table 5.1, and attempts to force them into cross-functional utility are, again, a waste of time and resources.

However, used within their appropriate function and type this overarching MIS architecture can be powerful in the extreme. Eliminating confirmation bias when putting together the narratives of what has gone wrong, and why, and what has been successful, and why, is of monumental importance to the odds of the future success of the organization. Returning to the example of the *Titanic*, the story would seem to be as simple as a boat hit an iceberg and sank – except for the fact that 1,517 people died because of it.[9] So, we have the loss of an asset, and a huge one at that. In putting together the narrative of how and why, confining the information streams to just one type will not provide a satisfactory basis. For example, we know that the lookouts saw the iceberg, and warned the bridge prior to the collision. Why did the collision still take place? Because the ship couldn't turn fast enough. Why not? Because it was going too fast. Why was it going as fast as it was? Was that the ship's most economical speed? No, it wasn't. It was going that fast because the White Star Line could gain a competitive advantage over its rivals by demonstrating that its ships could make the Atlantic crossing more quickly than others.

Okay, given that the ship didn't avoid the iceberg, why did so many people die? Because the water was freezing, and there weren't enough lifeboats. Why weren't there enough lifeboats? Because the *Titanic* was considered so robust by its builders that the possibility of her sinking was considered remote. That being the case, the cost of including enough lifeboats for every passenger and crew member, in both money and deck space, was considered inefficient use of resources, or assets. An asset management consideration in favor of efficiency had a huge impact in the project management sphere (assuming that the project we're talking about here was to successfully deliver all on board to their destination, safe and sound).

9   RMS Titanic (September 6, 2010). In *Wikipedia, The Free Encyclopedia*. Retrieved 17:52, September 6, 2010, from http://en.wikipedia.org/w/index.php?title=RMS_Titanic&oldid=383240161

But given that each of these factors – and hundreds others – were either known or knowable, why the level of controversy on the particulars of the narrative of how and why the *Titanic* sank? Because if the generally accepted narrative could be manipulated to show that the proximate cause of the tragedy was simply the blind, damnable bad luck of having an iceberg drift into your path, and nothing could have really been done to avoid it, the implications for the White Star Line would be very different than if the narrative was that the ship was poorly designed, or used inferior materials, or was improperly operated by the White Star Line, and the whole tragedy could have been easily avoided if certain people had performed their jobs and responsibilities with due diligence. And, if the latter narrative was found to be the most accurate, the ability of the organization to accept that narrative, and act upon its lessons learned, would tell a very different story than if the organization refused to accept that narrative, even in the face of direct evidence supporting it, and clung to its own version in the hope of limiting strategic damage. Such a fate awaited the White Star Line, which merged with its chief rival of the time, Cunard, in 1934.[10]

Information-Powered Winning

Arthur Conan Doyle's Sherlock Holmes was famous for not wanting to know about things that had no bearing on his ability to solve mysteries, much to Dr Watson's surprise. Similarly, the successful organization will seek to develop valid Management Information Systems that produce accurate, timely, and relevant information in the phase and management type that are appropriate for the circumstance. MISs can be mapped like the taped-off areas in an assembly plant, where various products enter into a certain zone at a certain level of completion, and the person working that zone is expected to add to it before it proceeds to the next person's taped-off area. Without a clear distinction of exactly who is doing exactly what at which point in the process, chaos ensues, like a relay race where the runners do not have an exact zone where the baton can be passed, and don't come to a consensus amongst themselves about where the hand-off should occur, either.

But using the classifications and process guides shown in Table 5.1 and discussed in this chapter, optimization of the organization's information stream's efficiency, effectiveness, and, most importantly, relevance can be attained. And, as discussed earlier, the very best manager with 20% of the information needed to reach the best (or even sufficient) decision will be bettered by the poorest of managers who have access to 80% of the information so needed. It follows, then, that the better (or best) managers who have 80% (or more) of the information they need will be virtually (no pun intended) unbeatable.

Indeed, it can be argued that the combination of Game Theory (including Nash Equilibrium and cartage schemes), Risk Management Theory, Network Theory, MIS architecture techniques, Maccoby, Bartles, and Myers-Briggs archetypes, can yield a crypto-Code of (Management) Nature, well-nigh guaranteeing organizational success

---

10   White Star Line (September 3, 2010). In *Wikipedia, The Free Encyclopedia*. Retrieved 18:26, September 6, 2010, from http://en.wikipedia.org/w/index.php?title=White_Star_Line&oldid=382672428

as predicted future environs and events come about regularly, and are acted on more quickly and appropriately than the competition.

Or can it?

2 *The Upper Limit*

Art, like morality, consists of drawing the line somewhere.

G.K. Chesterton

This part of the book will show how some of the assertions in Part 1 are wrong; well, maybe not *wrong*, but have a limit as to their efficacy, and that this limit can be reasonably assessed and quantified.

In Chapter 5, I discussed the appropriate function and use of management information streams within the confines of types of management, and how, when those information tools are used outside of their appropriate domains, inefficiencies and irrelevancies manifest. But with many of these information structures and constructs, similar inefficiencies and irrelevancies can (and do) develop, *even when they are used as intended*.

One of the problems with taking on epistemological issues within Management Information System (MIS) theory is that these MIS streams often have their own groups of supporters, supporters who have oftentimes benefited impressively by overselling their MIS stream's capabilities. I've already discussed the difficulties I've encountered when asserting the estimators' tools' incompetence when attempting to predict the future, even though such an assertion is demonstrably true. But that's only the beginning of the fracas. As I discussed earlier, while I was earning my MBA, the common thread among virtually all of my professors was what they held to be the ultimate point of all management actions: to maximize shareholder wealth. It was positively axiomatic among the lot of them; however, we have seen that, while this may be the ultimate point of all *asset* managers, it's hardly the ultimate goal (or even consideration, really) of the project manager, or the strategic manager. But the business world has been so imbued with the asset managers' approach to organizational success that even their terminology dominates the decision-maker's lexicon. People who would not have a clue on how to read a profit-and-loss statement will refer to the perceived end-state of a process as "the bottom line." The insanity has reached the point where project management practitioners will repeatedly attempt to justify their type of management using the asset managers' tools (a Yahoo! search on "ROI" and "Project Management" yielded over 1.6 million hits on September 6, 2010). Referring to the widget project example in Chapter 5, recall the calculation for determining a Cost Performance Index:

Cost Performance Index (CPI) = $ Value of Work Performed/Amount ($) Spent

Now, compute the CPI of, say, a company vehicle. See? It's impossible, because the asset does not actually accomplish any work itself, but can only be used in pursuing the project's objectives. And, if the PM tool is irrelevant in the assessment of assets, why should the reverse be considered any more relevant? But so entrenched is the asset manager's vernacular and approach in the management world as a whole, such misapplications are common, even rampant.

So, in tackling the study of the limits of knowledge – epistemology – as it pertains to the world of business in general, and Management Information Systems in particular, I am certain to directly and severely challenge many of the groups of people who have combined into massive multi-player online role-playing game-like guilds, supporters of and adherents to the payoffs of their selected information stream and technical approach. All of these structures and approaches have limits, past which they return less and less relevant information, until they pass foursquare into the realm of misleading information.

In short, the purpose of Part 2 is to overturn much of the conventional wisdom with respect to the true utility of various common technical approaches to management, and the information streams that make them possible. So, with no further ado, let's let the deconstructing begin.

6 *Deconstructing Game Theory*

Prediction is very difficult, especially about the future.

Niels Bohr (1885–1962)

Among the quotes in the "Praise for *A Beautiful Math*" part of the dust jacket on my copy of *A Beautiful Math*, Steven Strongatz, Professor of Applied Mathematics, Cornell University, and author of *SYNC* wrote:

> *Fast-paced and wide-ranging, A Beautiful Math chronicles the quest for the laws of human collective behavior. Along the way, Tom Siegfried takes us to the frontiers of modern science, from neuroeconomics to network theory. By the end you'll see why game theory – the beautiful math pioneered by John Nash – just might be at the very center of it all.[1]*

Wow. The quest for the laws of collective human behavior. While I won't pretend that anyone who earns a living as a Professor of Applied Mathematics at Cornell couldn't significantly out-score me on those tests MENSA gives out to see if you can join them, I still can't help but marvel at the sense of proportion or perspective that would lead someone to believe that the "quest for the laws of human collective behavior" is anything other than completely futile.

Right out of college I lived with a couple of roommates, one of who was a car mechanic specializing in Porsches. He was a lover of fast cars himself, and participated in many Sports Car Club of America events. He also subscribed to *Car and Driver*, as well as *Road and Track*. One day after work Steve began to discuss with me his passionate rejection of Corporate Average Fuel Economy (CAFE) standards, based on an article he had read in one of his magazines. These are laws issued by the federal government of the United States that mandates the minimum number of miles per gallon that automobiles must attain, on average, for car manufacturers. While I agreed that these laws were simultaneously silly and destructive, the arguments Steve employed were interesting. He began by asserting that the government should have no authority over the car manufacturers (other than taxation or worker safety) in the first place. I asked him if he had ever read Upton Sinclair's *The Jungle*, with its depictions of filthy and dangerous conditions in Chicago's feed lots and slaughterhouses, conditions made possible due to a lack of government authority over how those businesses should be run. Steve immediately shifted his argument to one of the government ought not to have such authority over the automobile industry specifically.

---

1   Strogatz, Steven, as quoted on the dust jacket of *A Beautiful Math*, Joseph Henry Press, 2006.

I then asked what made the automobile manufacturing industry so different from other industries that the government should not have authority over them, specifically. Steve's argument then shifted back to the government ought not to have that authority over industry in general. After a couple more shifts back and forth, I realized no progress was being made in influencing either of our points of view, and so I dropped it.

A similar rhetorical slight-of-hand occurs in *A Beautiful Math* and other books on the topic of Game Theory. Recall the discussion of the utility of valid management information from Chapter 5, where I asserted that all such information needed to make informed decisions had to be able to help describe what has happened in the past that resulted in a setback, what has happened in the past that led to success, and what is likely to happen in the future. The information emanating from these systems had to be accurate, timely, and relevant if it was to help clarify and define the most appropriate, most truthful narratives. It's in the creation of these narratives that the rhetoric shifts, from explaining the past via an accurate narrative based on the rules of causality, over to creating a probable timeline of future choices, decisions, strategies, and behaviors. There's something about the temporal shift from past to future that renders the Game Theory-derived narratives weaker, even bordering on irrelevance. But before I go there, let's review cases where even the simplest, most straightforward attempts at using Game Theory to predict the future failed.

Recall the Ultimatum Game from Chapter 2. In this game, an amount of money (usually $100) is to be split between two players, A and B. Player A proposes how much each player should receive, and if Player B approves, the money is so distributed. However, if Player B rejects the distribution, then neither player receives anything. By evaluating possible payoff matrices, the Game Theoretician would recommend Player A propose a split of A receiving $99, and Player B receiving $1, under the assumptions that:

1.   Player B is "rational," and
2.   Player B would rather receive $1 than nothing at all.

These assumptions being the case, Player A would maximize his payoff by proposing the 99–1 split, at least in theory. This strategy is identified as the most appropriate by using a process known as *Backward Induction*, which was initially proposed by none other than John Von Neumann, in the previously-discussed *Theory of Games and Economic Behavior* (1953). The maximum/minimum (non-zero) payoff strategy also represents a *subgame perfect Nash Equilibrium*,[2] meaning that, mathematically speaking, the 99–1 payoff strategy is strongly consistent with Game Theory predictive models.

But some funny things happened on the way to depositing Player A's $99 in the bank. In experiments using real currency, the maximum/minimum (non-zero) payoff proposal was almost universally rejected.[3] In fact, the vast majority of offers that failed to give at least 20% to Player B were rejected. In Mongolian culture, proposals of a 50–50 split were often made, even though Player A was well aware that their Player B would accept a lower amount. There were even instances of Player A proposing Player B receive *more* than 50%

2   Subgame perfect equilibrium (April 14, 2010). In *Wikipedia, The Free Encyclopedia*. Retrieved 20:17, September 10, 2010, from http://en.wikipedia.org/w/index.php?title=Subgame_perfect_equilibrium&oldid=355958323

3   Nowak, Martin A., Page, Karen M., Sigmund, Karl, *Fairness versus Reason in the Ultimatum Game*, Science, September 8, 2000.

of the currency, with Player B actually rejecting the proposed split – presumably, due to cultural concerns with Player B being perceived as (or perceiving) being in debt to Player A.

There has been a lot written about the phenomena of the dramatic, consistent delta between the Game Theory-expected strategies' utility and the outcome of real-life strategies employed in the Ultimatum Game.[4] Much of this material addresses so-called cultural issues overriding Player B's "rational" choice of strategy, while others examined possible psychological elements being manifest, such as Player B's desire to punish Player A for the act of proposing a perceived inequitable distribution scheme. But even as these writers examine the reasons why Player B does not appear to act "rational," they tend to treat the additional data points as if they were clues that could be used to perfect the original Game Theory formula used to predict Player B's strategies. To me, this scholarship is completely invalid. Recall the earlier discussion of the concept of a mixed payoff from Part 1. The existence of a mixed payoff in any "game" prevents the computation of a Nash Equilibrium, since the Nash Equilibrium needs a single variable to represent the value of a payoff (or loss of a payoff). As simple as the Ultimatum Game is, it simply cannot preclude a mixed payoff that goes well beyond the boundaries of evaluating an amount of money in assessing Player B's potential gain. Indeed, instead of attempting to analyze why real-life players in the Ultimatum Game appear to behave irrationally, these writers would do much better to evaluate why the people laying out payoff matrices and calculating Nash Equilibriums are irrationally assuming that the payoff can be reduced to a single variable.

The discussion of how a "rational" participant in a free market economy can be expected to, or "should," act as a consequence of the elected strategies of other participants, governments, or natural events has been around since at least the writings of Adam Smith. However, they all butt up against the central problem of the impossibility of quantifying mixed payoffs. For example, consider the concept of Inequality Aversion. Inequality Aversion is the preference for fairness and resistance to incidental inequalities.[5] The formula for quantifying it is:

$$U_j(\{x_j\}) = x_j + \frac{\alpha}{n-1} \times \sum max(x_j - x_i, 0) + \frac{\beta}{n-1} \times \sum max(x_i - x_j, 0),$$

Where α parametrizes the distaste for disadvantageous inequality in the first nonstandard term, and β parametrizes the distaste for advantageous inequality in the final term.[6] Now, without actually adding values to the parameters and executing the formula, consider the concept of quantifying a person's "distaste for disadvantageous inequality" as an integer. It simply can't be done, at least not accurately. Recall from Chapter 5 that the information being used to create or refine the narratives we build must be timely, relevant, and *accurate*. As impressive and sophisticated as this formula is, it simply can't be considered reliable in the production of an accurate data point with respect to when or under which exact circumstances a given player will select a strategy that is detrimental to themselves in order to prevent a perceived injustice.

Of course, after the facts concerning the difference between the expected strategies Player A in an Ultimatum Game would employ and what was actually observed in real

---

4   Ibid, among others. A Yahoo! search on "Ultimatum Game" and "experiments" yielded 62,500 hits on September 10, 2010.

5   Fehr, E. and Schmidt, K.M. (1999). "A theory of fairness, competition, and cooperation". *The Quarterly Journal of Economics*, 114: 817–68. doi:10.1162/003355399556151.

6   Ibid.

Ultimatum Game experiments came out, it was possible to go back and explore aspects of Player B's strategy selection that went beyond the basic payoff matrix and Nash Equilibrium, like the concept of Inequality Aversion's influence. But this train of thought merely continues down the path of assuming that all of the parameters in a mixed payoff matrix can not only be known, but quantified. As we have seen, in reality, neither is the case, even in that simplest of games, the Ultimatum Game.

A similar deviation occurred in experimental occurrences of players involved in the Prisoner's Dilemma. Recall from Chapter 2 that this game involves two players who are held in jail. The jailer approaches Player A and makes him an offer: if Player A would inform on his cellmate (Player B), then Player A's sentence would be reduced. The problem is that Player A knows that the same offer will be made to Player B. The potential outcomes are as follows:

Player A informs, but Player B does not. Player A walks free, and Player B gets 10 years.

Player A informs, and so does Player B. Both get 5 years.

Player A does not inform, and neither does Player B. Both get 11 months.

Player A does not inform, but Player B does. Player A gets 10 years, and Player B walks free (this is known as the "Sucker's Payoff").

In Chapter 2 we reviewed the payoff matrix, where it was apparent that the preferred strategy for Player A (actually, either player) would be to always defect. However, in a tournament where competing computer programs played 200 iterations of the Prisoner's Dilemma in 1980, the always-defect strategy did not win. The winning mixed strategy was employed by a program called "Tit for Tat." Tit for Tat did not inform on the first iteration; thereafter it did whatever its opponent did in the previous move.[7]

After Tit for Tat won the overall competition, analysts set out to discover why that particular strategy was successful. Variants of Tit for Tat were developed, ones that did inform on the first iteration, and then engage the Tit for Tat strategy, another refused to inform for the first five iterations, and then would revert to the Tit for Tat strategy, and so on. The original defeated all of the variants, leading the experts to determine the three major factors in Tit for Tat's success:

It was initially nice, or cooperative.

It retaliated immediately for defection.

It forgave completely and immediately for cooperation.

What I found interesting about these success factors is that there was no facility within Game Theory's payoff matrices or Nash Equilibrium that could identify, much less quantify, these key factors, even though we're talking about a relatively simple game. In

---

7   Tit for Tat (August 21, 2010). In *Wikipedia, The Free Encyclopedia*. Retrieved 19:47, September 11, 2010, from http://en.wikipedia.org/w/index.php?title=Tit_for_tat&oldid=380130721

this case, not only did traditional Game Theory analysis techniques fail to identify these factors beforehand, it couldn't even predict that a mixed strategy was superior to a single strategy in maximizing the payoff.

And, if Game Theory's techniques are not able to identify the best strategy in games as simple as the Ultimatum Game and the Prisoner's Dilemma, how could these analyses be considered valid for their far, far more complex cousin games?

The Integration of Other Realms

The very title of Von Neumann's book, *Theory of Games and Economic Behavior*, implies an attempt to set boundaries on the available payoffs in Game Theory by specifying that the subject matter is restricted to "economic behavior." And, in fairness to the genius Von Neumann, he did specify that the analysis in that book pertained to zero-sum games, with perfect information (i.e., players are aware of all of the other players, the total number and nature of strategies available to them, and the exact payoffs available). So please don't misunderstand: I'm not taking on Von Neumann. I'm taking on all of those writers and thinkers who believe that Von Neumann's theories and calculations pertain to areas outside of zero-sum games, where perfect information is quite impossible to attain.

Also consider the impossibility of confining potential payoffs within the realm of economics. Webster's New Collegiate Dictionary defines economics as "a social science concerned chiefly with description and analysis of the production, distribution, and consumption of goods and services." This definition, while (probably) accurate, is so broad as to exclude very little involving human behavior.[8] Even a person dying and receiving the appropriate sacraments is receiving the services of a priest. By this definition, very little of anthropology (again, from Webster: "the science of man; *esp*: the study of man in relation to distribution, origin, classification, and relationship of races, physical character, environmental and social relations, and culture") falls outside of economics, at least those aspects of anthropology that can be quantified. Ah, but if only the payoff could be confined to a single parameter, and that parameter could be accurately quantified! Then the selection of strategies, or mixed strategies, could be predicted accurately, leading to the establishment of a Code of Nature. And, with a valid Code of Nature, a paradise on Earth couldn't be far behind. The smartest possible move on the chessboard of life could always be known, with those doing the knowing moving into positions of authority and guiding mankind to the greatest possible total-population payoff!

But even within the narrow realm of the hawk–dove game, we see this is impossible. The total population payoff is greatest when the entire population of birds select the dove strategy; but, with the introduction of even one hawk, the payoff matrix is changed utterly. Unless some power were to be in a position to exclude all hawks from the population, the maximum utility payoff for the population could never be achieved. And, for such a power to be in a position to eliminate hawks, they would have to be in a position to eliminate the latitude of the players to select the hawk strategy. In other words, such a power would have to be either a tyrannical man with complete control over the population, or else, well, God.

---

8   I asked my son, Troy Hatfield, if he could name any activity that fell outside of Webster's definition of economics. His reply was "watching the stars."

Since I've skated so sharply into politics and religion, I may as well finish making my points before retreating off of this thin ice. When evaluating the analogous hawk–dove game strategies and using the lessons from that game, if we are talking about hawk behavior manifesting as criminal behavior, with dove strategy being analogous to obeying the law, then the use of government authority to police the population becomes an obvious good. However, if we are attempting to use this analogy in economics, with its previously-noted broad definition, where hawk behavior equals entrepreneurial risk-taking (which is, by definition, aggressive), then governmental authority curbing hawk behavior detracts from the overall population's payoff.

Further, an oft-heard criticism of believers from agnostics or atheists is "If there is a God, why does He allow evil in the world?" Re-stated in Game Theory parlance, "Since only God has the power to enforce the set of strategies that would lead to the maximum payoff for the entire population, and we are not in a Nash Equilibrium where the population's maximum payoff has been realized, doesn't that argue against the idea of a 'just' God?" The believers' response is (usually) "In order for God to remove all evil from the world, He would have to remove our free will, and He is unwilling to do that." This response changes very little in the Game Theory vernacular: "In order to eliminate strategies that are inconsistent with the population's maximized payoff, certain players – if not all of them – would have to have the option of engaging in hawk strategies removed from their repertoire."

We see something similar in the way system administrators attempt to eliminate strategies they see as undesirable from the massive multi-player online role-playing games for which they are responsible, with varying levels of success. But these administrators' effectiveness can be relatively narrow in scope and ineffective, or broad in scope and astonishingly effective. On YouTube® there is a video entitled "Greatest Freak-Out Ever." In the setup you see (fuzzily) a young man who informs the viewer that he just cancelled his little brother's *World of Warcraft* subscription, after which he apparently hides a camera in the unfortunate brother's bedroom. You then see the younger brother enter the room, order the camera-hider to leave, close the door, and then engage in behavior that I would consider consistent with a nervous breakdown, though I'm no psychologist. What's apparent, though, is that the younger brother is in a great deal of emotional pain, with no satisfactory way of expressing his anguish and distress. He strikes himself, tears at his clothing, throws himself into walls. I vaguely recall an insipid little article about how shopping mall managers have an inordinate amount of power over ordinary people, since they decided things like the temperature of the mall, the mix of fast food to shoe stores, the number of large department stores, the level of security or cleanliness of the facility, etc. But the people who are in charge of the virtual worlds of MMORPGs have a god-like power in comparison to mall managers, and the emotional health of thousands is affected by their decisions.

I'm not trying to relay political or theology insights here. Far from it. I'm simply pointing out that attempts to attain "perfect information," in even the simplest of games, is ultimately futile. There are simply too many factors in play, and these factors cannot be defined out of existence or relevance. Further, even when all of the factors can be known – which is almost never – many (if not most) of those factors are far too abstract to capture as an integer. In *A Beautiful Math*,[9] Tom Siegfried asserts that the efficacy of Game Theory is enhanced in larger populations, and uses the analogy of gas (and, no, I'm not kidding).

---

9   Siegfried, Tom, *A Beautiful Math*, John Henry Press, 2006.

Just as the behavior of one gas molecule is virtually impossible to predict, but a container filled with billions of molecules of the same gas does contain predictable properties, so, too do populations exhibit predictable behavior patterns that are not applicable to the individual. But even here, Siegfried allows "(i)magine how much trickier chemistry would become if molecules could think."[10] Well, in the game of management the players *can* think, making the Game Theory alchemy very tricky indeed.

Incoming Black Swans

I immensely enjoyed Nassim Nicholas Taleb's book *The Black Swan, The Impact of the Highly Improbable* (apparently, so did a lot of other people, it was a *New York Times* best seller), and I'm not just saying that in an attempt to avoid having him or one of his students put a rat down my back. *The Black Swan* was the fifth book I read when researching this book (after *Theory of Games in Economics*, *The Gamesman*, *A Beautiful Math*, and a review of *A Guide to the Project Management Body of Knowledge*), and Taleb caught me just in time. I was well nigh convinced that *some* combination of Game Theory with Network Theory, Risk Management Theory, the Maccoby and Bartles archetypes, and examples of successful cartage schemes, could, at the very least, produce a powerfully insightful structure for predicting players' (and organizations') most probable selected mixed strategies, yielding all sorts of advantageous insights. It might even bring the next generation of Von Neumanns and Nashs to the very brink of an Asimov-like Code of Nature (as it turns out, it did help lead me to a usable version of the former, as we will see in Part 3, but convinced me of the impossibility of the latter).

A review of Taleb's insights is forthcoming, I promise. But to understand Taleb, you really have to know about Karl Popper. Popper was born on July 28, 1902, and would become a professor at the London School of Economics. He is widely regarded as one of the most profound philosophers of science in history. Popper sought to overturn the idea of scientific advancement via inductive reasoning by asserting that falsifiability ought to be the manner by which science was advanced. Using an example that Taleb also uses, if one were to seek to come to a scientific rule concerning the color of swans, they would (presumably) go out and begin observing swans, and documenting their color. While asserting that all swans are white after only one observation could hardly be considered scientific, such an assertion would have more weight if our swan scientist had observed thousands of swans, and had never encountered one that was not white.

The problem with declaring the "all swans are white" assertion scientific is that it is not falsifiable, since there is always the possibility that a previously unknown population of swans exists somewhere that are not white, which is exactly what happened when black swans were discovered in Australia in 1697. The vast majority of scientific advancement is based on the idea of the sequence of:

1. Developing a hypothesis;
2. Testing the hypothesis empirically, via experiments that could be repeated and would provide the data needed; to

---

10   Ibid, p. 61.

3. Assemble the data into a valid logical construct, or argument, that would validate the hypothesis, elevating it to theory status.

The third step, of using inductive logic to establish the link between available data and theory validity, is the point that Popper sought to overturn.

In classical logic, *modus ponens*, also known as affirming the antecedent, is the argument most often used in the scientific method discussed in the previous paragraph. It is a valid argument, and takes the form:

If P, *then* Q

P;

Therefore, Q

Popper maintained that modus ponens was a far weaker argument than its near relative, modus tollens. Modus tollens, also known as denying the consequent, takes the form:

If P, *then* Q

Not Q;

Therefore, not P.

For a scientific theory to be falsifiable does not mean it is false; it simply means that, if the theory were false, it would be possible to demonstrate its falsehood. For example, the theory that all matter is made up of atoms is not falsifiable, since it is impossible to observe all of the matter in the universe. It will always be possible that, in some far corner of a particularly far-flung galaxy, there exists a material consistent with the definition of matter that is not comprised of atoms. Nevertheless, much scientific advancement has come about because of the non-falsifiable atomic theory, and many of those resulting theories are themselves falsifiable. Note that the atomic theory uses modus ponens to make the leap between data and validity, and not modus tollens. It's easy to see why Popper's ideas were met with the level of opposition they encountered.

Enter Taleb

The invaluable service that Nassim Taleb performed was to bring Popper's theories out of the scientific realm and into the arena of economics. In *The Black Swan*, Taleb often evokes the situation of a turkey being raised on a farm. Every day for three years the farmer comes out and gives food to the turkey. Based on that data set, the turkey will wake on the day of his execution fully expecting to be fed. If our turkey were logical, he would employ modus ponens thus:

If it's a new day, the farmer will come out here and give me food.

It's a new day.

Therefore, the farmer will come out and give me food.

The argument is valid, but it's not true. Interestingly, the similar argument expressed as modus tollens is both valid and true:

If it's a new day, the farmer will feed the turkey.

The farmer did not feed the turkey.

Therefore, it was not a new day (for the turkey, anyway, having been executed the day before).

Taleb then goes on to evaluate how the use of inductive reasoning in economic decisions has led to a multiplication of "pathologies in our decision-making." He's particularly hard on Game Theorists, as indicated by the following quote:

Legions of empirical psychologists of the heuristics and biases school have shown that the model of rational behavior under uncertainty is not just grossly inaccurate but plain wrong as a description of reality.[11]

Enter Kuhn

Thomas Kuhn was born in 1922, and wrote extensively on the history of science. In 1962 he wrote the book *The Structure of Scientific Revolutions*, where he asserted that changes in the preferred scientific theories tended to follow a predictable cycle.[12] At any time, and for any scientific realm, a certain theory – let's call it Theory T – will be widely accepted by scientists in that field because it explains the observed phenomena and available data. Once observations and data come in that seem to overturn the theory, additions or modifications to the theory will accumulate in order to continue to explain the anomalies. This continues until the additions and revisions become overly complex, or even contradictory. An alternative theory is then introduced, which will appear to explain the anomalous data as well as the data set explained by the previous theory; however, only a minority of the scientists in the field can be expected to embrace the new theory. This division of scientific opinion continues until the previous theory's inability to explain the ever-expanding data set becomes so prevalent that most or all of its previous supporters abandon the previous theory and become supporters of the replacement theory, and the cycle starts again. Kuhn also asserted that this cycle was not linear; advancements in science did not come about steadily, as more and more data was accumulated. Rather, it tended to advance in leaps or bounds, interspersed with periods of stagnation. This philosophy of advancement coming in "leaps" is also shared by Taleb, and is mentioned often in *The Black Swan*. *The Structure of Scientific Revolutions* introduced

---

11   Taleb, Nassim, *The Black Swan, The Impact of the Highly Improbable*, Random House Trade Paperbacks, 2010.

12   The Structure of Scientific Revolutions (August 26, 2010). In *Wikipedia, The Free Encyclopedia*. Retrieved 01:52, September 19, 2010, from http://en.wikipedia.org/w/index.php?title=The_Structure_of_Scientific_Revolutions&oldid=381201596

the terms "paradigm" and "paradigm shift" into the lexicon. Of course, any manager or participant in the business world has heard these terms, often to excess, making it obvious that Kuhn's work has made its way into the realm of economics.

Kuhn's assertions can be summarized (somewhat bluntly) as science and technology advancing via a survival-of-the-fittest competition among modus ponens-based theories. This is clearly at odds with Popper, who advocated falsifiability, or modus tollens, as being the logical structure that advanced science. Before I demonstrate the significance of these competing ideas to the limits of Game Theory in business, I need to invite one more thinker into the room.

Enter Alexander Tytler

Alexander Tytler was a Scottish-born lawyer, writer, and historian, who lived from 1747 to 1813. Although it appears in none of his works, he is commonly attributed to having created the Tytler cycle:

> *The average age of the world's greatest civilizations from the beginning of history has been about 200 years. During those 200 years, these nations always progressed through the following sequence:*

- *From bondage to spiritual faith;*
- *From spiritual faith to great courage;*
- *From courage to liberty;*
- *From liberty to abundance;*
- *From abundance to complacency;*
- *From complacency to apathy;*
- *From apathy to dependence;*
- *From dependence back into bondage.*[13]

Note that the Tytler cycle is truly cyclical, in that it implies a return to a nominal state prior to re-initiation. In contrast, the Kuhn cycle implies a repeating set of steps as scientific knowledge continually advances. In other words, Kuhn's cycle does not suggest that, once Copernicus' version of astronomy was adopted, we would ever return to Ptolemy's theory.

So, what do Tytler, Kuhn, and Von Neumann all have in common? They all attempted to present a structured narrative that accommodated known facts and observations into a causation cycle that could explain why historic things happened the way they did, and, perhaps, predict the way the future would unfold. A graphic way of presenting this would be (Figure 6.1):

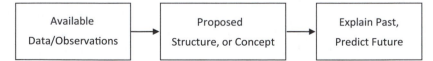

Figure 6.1   A Graphic Way of Presenting a Structured Narrative

13   Alexander Fraser Tytler (August 17, 2010). In *Wikipedia, The Free Encyclopedia*. Retrieved 02:37, September 19, 2010, from http://en.wikipedia.org/w/index.php?title=Alexander_Fraser_Tytler&oldid=379331491

Recall the structure of a valid Management Information System from Chapter 5 (Figure 6.2):

Figure 6.2   Valid MIS Structure

The two are very similar for a reason. Consider the rivalry between modus ponens and modus tollens discussed earlier in this chapter. What they have in common is the first premise:

If P, *then* Q

But in classical logic, the relationship between P and Q may be valid or invalid, true or false, genuinely causal or simply incidental. Taleb's turkey had every reason to believe that it would be fed on its execution day, just as the sixteenth century zoo keeper had every reason to expect that all swans were white. While both modus ponens and modus tollens have such a premise, only modus ponens returns true if the link between P and Q is merely incidental. In short, Popper was right.

The implications for Game Theory in economics are numerous – myriad, even. For example, while the Tytler cycle seems true on an intuitive level, and obviously carries grave implications for nations such as the United States (which would seem to be somewhere in the Abundance-to-Apathy or Apathy-to-Dependence stage), it is also falsifiable. In other words, if just one of the "world's greatest civilizations" did not go through the cycle in around 200 years, then the predictive capability of the cycle would have to be considered highly questionable. Well, it just so happened that, ever since William the Bastard became William the Conqueror on October 14, 1066, England has had a system of government that has kept them out of bondage to anyone, unless you want to try to make the argument that they were in bondage to their own kings. But even then, the English dynasties were switched out from time to time, essentially rendering the Tytler cycle's ability to predict the future highly suspect. And, if it can't adequately predict the future, could there be something wrong with its narrative that arranges the facts of history in that particular manner? In short, Taleb is right, too.

The Implications for Game Theory

I believe it is safe to say that this chapter's discussions yield two strong implications for the role of Game Theory in management:

1. Game Theory's capability in the realm of predicting likely strategies – mixed or pure – to be adopted by participants in an economic environ should be considered severely restricted (a detailed analysis of these limits will be taken up in Part 3).

2. Its ability to support specific narratives on why things went well or poorly for the organization, in an economic sense, deserves stricter scrutiny than is often afforded, especially when the logical connection between facts and narrative is based solely on modus ponens.

But what of Siegfried's assertions of the predictive capability of Game Theory when it is combined with other techniques, such as Risk Management? I will attempt to overturn this notion in the following chapters, as I take on the Maccoby and Bartles archetypes, and Risk Management theory, in that order.

But here's an assertion I will repeat until I am blue in the face: the payoff grids of economically or managerially analogous games *can't* be quantified, at least not accurately. That being the case, Game Theory ought not to have any greater sway in general management than Eric Berne's Transactional Analysis has in current psychological practices. It most definitely has its limits, especially and particularly if we are trying to use it to predict the future.

No, dear reader, I was not gaslighting you throughout Part 1 of this book. Game Theory has a powerful and valuable structure to bring to management – just not *general* management. As discussed in Chapter 5, its relevance is maximized when its practice is targeted to a specific type of management. The appropriate structure, and target of use, will be discussed in Part 3 of this book. For now, suffice to say that Game Theory can't predict the future, is suspect when providing a framework for linking the causalities that go into our organization's narratives of what went right, and why, and what went wrong, and why.

And a Harry Seldon-esque Code of Nature is right out.

CHAPTER 7

The Pieces Move Like This ...

A preoccupation with the future not only prevents us from seeing the present as it is but often prompts us to rearrange the past.

Eric Hoffer (1902–1983), *The Passionate State of Mind*, 1954

Do you remember learning to play chess? The 64-square board was pretty much self-explanatory, but the ways in which the different pieces moved took some memorizing. Once you had some command over those different movements, you played a few games, and were probably beaten each time as you began to get a sense of how the pieces' specific characteristics worked together to attain some desired strategic objective, however ill-defined that may have been at the time.

Do you remember your first managerial or leadership role? The technical agenda was pretty much self-explanatory, but the ways the different personnel in your team would respond to your instructions and outside influences took some time to inculcate. Once you had assumed your leadership position, you probably had to address some difficulties along the lines of the clichéd teaming cycle of Forming–Storming–Norming–Performing, and may have encountered some setbacks along the way.

Ah, but if only the players had a specific, limited set of strategies that they could employ, and there were obvious visual clues as to what those strategies were! The entire discussion of mixed payoffs and macro Game Theory's ability to predict probable outcomes could become usable reality! Alas, it was not to be, which didn't mean some considerable scholarship didn't go into trying.

In 1964, psychiatrist Eric Berne published *Games People Play: The Psychology of Human Relationships*.[1][2] Berne introduced Transactional Analysis, in which he posited that human interactions took the form of "transactions," and that these transactions would often take the form of a predictable series of strategies designed to accomplish specific emotional payoffs. These transactions took place within a structure similar to Freud's classical definitions of the self, of Super Ego, Ego, and Id. In Berne's version, the personal internal structure was Parent, Adult, and Child, and transactions were mapped as in Figure 7.1.

So, with a "healthy" interaction between two individuals' "adults" being shown in the figure, along the lines of one person asking information of another, and receiving it. Berne's Games would often be characterized by a switch in roles, or ego states, towards

---

1   Berne, Eric, *Games People Play*, New York: Grove Press.

2   Honestly, could a book entitled *Game Theory in Management* sufficiently cover the topic *without* taking into account *Games People Play*?

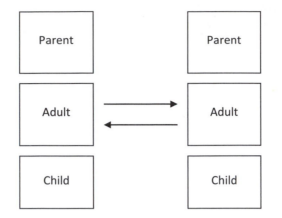

Figure 7.1   Nominal Berne model

the end of the game, resulting in the acquiring of the desired emotional payoff. Conflicts would arise when the communication paths crossed. For example, consider the following figure (Figure 7.2):

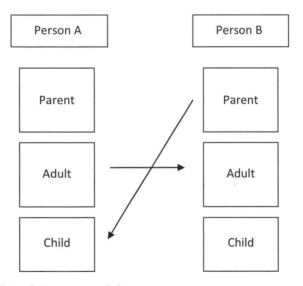

Figure 7.2   Conflicted Berne model

Suppose Person A engages Person B as an adult, perhaps asking for important data. Then suppose Person B responds in a manner that includes an overly critical response, along with a request for why Person A wants the data in the first place. Person A's adult attempted to connect with Person B's adult, but Person B's parent tried to communicate with Person A's child. Since the communication channels crossed, a conflict can be expected to come about in this transaction.

Not all instances of mixed communications result in conflict. For example, if Person A were to ask Person B for important data and Person B were to respond along the lines of "Let's just blow this off, and go have some drinks," the modeled transaction would look like this (Figure 7.3):

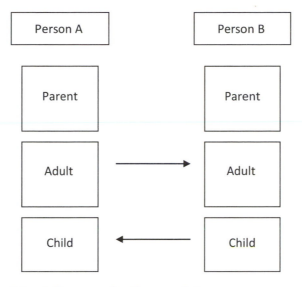

Figure 7.3   Inconsistent Communication model

While no conflict would necessarily take place, Person A would probably come away with a sense that Person B had engaged in an irrelevancy. In addition to mapping communications among individuals, Transactional Analysis also posited that the individual's communications patterns could be quantified and analyzed, with the goal of quantifying and analyzing the emotional payoffs inherent in such transactions. In other words, the transaction game could be identified, with the payoff matrix not far behind.

Okay, so where did the basis for the emotional payoff come from? A key part of Transactional Analysis is that people tend to create and maintain a narrative, or script, about who they are and why the things that have happened to them happened. These scripts, or narratives, become the structure we use to project how future events will unfold. By now, even the most casual reader is coming to the realization that the parallels between Berne and Von Neumann are striking. I do not know if either was aware of the other's work. But consider: psychiatrist Berne and physicist Von Neumann both assert a model for explaining observed behavior, or the adoption of a set of mixed strategies based on the behaviors or mixed strategies of others. Both posit a payoff being sought, and an evaluation, quantification, and comparison of the decisions that players select to maximize the odds of realizing those payoffs. Both refer to canned strategies and expected payoffs. In fact, the parallels are so strong that not only is the vernacular similar, but the only difference appears to be that, where Von Neumann was evaluating payoffs that could be captured numerically (dollars, or avoidance of time in jail, etc.), Berne was analyzing emotional payoffs, which reinforced or modified the "scripts," or internal narratives of the players. And, just as the behavior of the players in experimental instances of the Ultimatum Game who rejected the 99–1 split were held to be "irrational," so, too, do players whose behavior is at odds with what the Transactional Analysis model maintains is the best selected strategy find themselves labeled as engaging in a psychologically detrimental "game."

By happy accident of birth, I happen to have two highly accomplished older sisters. The eldest, Marcia, is married to an executive professor in a prestigious State university system. The other is a professional psychologist, practicing in California.[3] I posed the question to them both: why is Transactional Analysis currently out of favor with counselors? My middle older sister was in a position to answer directly, while my eldest sister could pose the question to professors of psychology at the university where she was engaged. As it turned out, they both delivered their answers within an hour of each other, one week later. The interesting thing was, the answers were identical.

"It's too simplistic." The reason Transactional Analysis (TA) had fallen out of favor with practicing counselors was that it was too simplistic in its ability to explain and correct many of the psychoses encountered by professionals. Indeed, Wikipedia itself has classified TA away from a school of psychological thought, and placed it as a "belief system."[4] I found the parallels striking and ironic. Game Theory's proponents, with their formulae and quantified analysis, were widely considered geniuses (Von Neumann and Nash, among others). Conversely, Berne's ideas, which closely paralleled the Game Theorists, were considered "too simplistic," and the only obvious difference being that of the ability to quantify the payoff grid. As we have seen, the ability to accurately quantify the payoff grid in even the simplest of games is illusory, which ought to land Game Theory advocates in the same "too simplistic" category as Transactional Analysts' supporters.

Bias in our Narratives

Simplistic as it may be, I believe Transactional Analysis does provide valuable insights into assessing the pursuit of the emotional payoffs people seek, and in revealing how the selection of certain strategies can serve as an indicator of the nature of some of the characteristics of the internal narrative, or script, that people maintain. Maccoby asserted as much, in positing a structure of the four *Gamesman* archetypes. Maccoby didn't get into *why*, say, the Jungle Fighter engages in duplicitous behavior in pursuing his desired payoff; only that he did tend to select those types of strategies, and could be counted on to do so in the future.

So if we are to accept Berne's idea that people maintain an internal narrative, or script, about who they are, and why the things that happened to them in the past came about, how are these narratives created? By their observations of things that have happened in the past, and linking them via their notion of causality into storylines, these storylines then come together to create the overall narrative. But these narratives can veer sharply away from reality through four powerful influences:

• Cognitive Bias, where the facts are distorted as they become part of the narrative.
• Confirmation Bias, where nascent, invalid storylines are not detected as faulty, and continue to serve as part of the overall narrative.

---

3   This sister asked me to avoid referencing her by name.
4   Ibid.

- Emotional or unintellectual influences on a person's concept of causality.
- Lack of knowledge of the rules of evidence and logic.

The structure of creating our narratives, then, resembles the valid Management Information System structure discussed in Chapter 5. If you will recall, I posited that the structure had three sequential steps:

1. Data is collected, using a certain structure or discipline.
2. It is converted into information, using a certain process.
3. The information is delivered to the decision-makers, for use in guiding their decisions.

The information as integrated by the decision-makers is only useful if it is timely, accurate, and relevant. Similarly, the narratives we maintain are authentic if and only if the storylines that comprise them are comprised of accurate memories and assessments of events in our lives, recognizing where a causal link exists and the nature of that link, and a correct projection of the significance of that storyline in more clearly defining who we are and what the implications for future actions might be. Obviously the path to arriving at a narrative that is accurate and genuine is fraught with hazards, just as any MIS stream can be. Let's take a look at those hazards in the context of the aforementioned valid Management Information System.

The Data Could Be Wrong

Cognitive Bias is the tendency to make systematic errors in certain circumstances based on thought processes rather than the objective evidence on hand. It is why eyewitness accounts of the same event can often vary significantly. Theoretically, people engage in *framing*, or imposing a structure onto perceptions and events that help fit them into a narrative. These frames serve as filters, allowing in the evidence that seems to fit the narrative, and discounting or eliminating the evidence that overturns the script. (The late Douglas Adams had a hilarious take on this phenomenon in his *Hitchhiker's Guide to the Universe* trilogy. A floating sofa that could take Ford Prefect and Arthur Dent off of a planet where they had been marooned flies near the two, but only Ford can see it because the idea of a floating inter-dimensional sofa was so fantastic to Arthur that his brain would not allow him to process its existence.)

Those who maintain a certain narrative in the face of objective evidence that contradicts it are said to be delusional. The problem with the term "delusional," though, is that it has come to be used to mean that a debate opponent does not share one's assessment of the available facts. As such, another perfectly useful psychological term has been rendered useless by misuse among those who would insist on the primacy of their narrative over those of others. The competition of narratives, being as personal as it is, is probably the prime reason behind the advice to avoid discussions of religion or politics – once narratives that touch on these subjects are set, their holders can almost assuredly be assumed to have collected the data set that supports such narratives, and contradicts others. Others' unwillingness to accept the particular data set that supports the tightly-held narratives can only present as delusional, with the accompanying frustration with a debate partner's lack of respect for the rules of evidence. But, as we have seen, such "evidence" can be (and almost always is) highly subjective. So, right off the bat, the pursuit of the genuine narrative has a major strike against it: the data we collect is almost certainly biased, at least to a small degree.

One of the most profound services provided by lawyers is that they are familiar with the rules of evidence (or, at least, they should be), and can be relied on to prevent narratives devoid of objective facts from being brought against their clients. The successful elimination of such narratives is often derisively dismissed as "technicalities," but they serve a key function in the pursuit of justice. Even if we are trained in the legal or scientific professions, the likelihood of our internal narratives being fed exclusively by facts that pass muster with the rules of evidence is extremely remote. It then follows that any process we use to create our narratives, no matter how logical, is almost certain to yield a flawed final product. The computer experts' name for this is "garbage in, garbage out," meaning that no matter how valid the process, the data feed for any MIS stream can be ruined by the inaccuracies in the initial data feed.

The Process is Almost Certainly Wrong

Even if the facts as perceived and absorbed are completely accurate, the process we use to assemble them into information, or the narrative, is often flawed. There was a widely-distributed e-mail years ago from an English Professor that constituted a history of the world, based on sentences pulled from essays submitted by his students. As I recall, one part of this "history" contained the following:

John Milton wrote Paradise Lost. *Then his wife died, and he wrote* Paradise Regained.

While those facts were accurate, the conclusion, or narrative, seems to have a causal connection between Milton's wife's death, and the writing of *Paradise Regained*, as if being free of the marital state was the equivalent of paradise to the famed writer. In fact, *Paradise Lost* is a more detailed re-telling of some parts of the Apocrypha and Genesis, chapters 1–3. *Paradise Regained* is a re-telling of Matthew, chapter 4, verses 1–11. Neither work has anything to do with marriage.

Which touches on a key ingredient in the narrative-creating process: things that happen within a sequential timeframe will often be interpreted as if the previous event caused the latter. Consider this entry from the Forgotten English calendar's definition for "zuckblood" from Thursday, June 17, 2010:

Leeches for Weather Forecasting?

In What Do the Leeches Say? *(c. 1859), Elisabeth Woolams presented a variety of weather predictions based on the activities of jarred leeches, which were used at that time – and still are – by doctors to suck blood from patients:*

"Leeches remain at the bottom during absolutely calm, wet weather. When a change in the former is approaching, they move steadily upwards in advance. If a storm is rapidly approaching, the leeches become very restless, rising quickly, while previous to

a thunderstorm they are invariably much disturbed and remain out of the water. When the change occurs and is passing over, they are quiet and descend again.

If they rise during a continuance of east wind, strong winds rather than rain are to be looked for. When a storm comes direct from a distance, observe the rapid rising alluded to above. When heavy rains or strong winds are approaching, the leeches are restless but their movements are less rapid and they often remain half out of water and quiet."[5]

Indeed, it could be argued that the entire basis for all superstition rests on a foundation of incorrectly attributing a causal relationship to unconnected events that just happened to occur in sequential order to an observer who connected them into a narrative that appeared accurate. (How else could something as strange as the American tradition of Ground Hog Day have come about?) And yet, the entire voyeurism aspect to Game Theory rests on just that – the ability to observe events or behaviors, assemble them into a structure, or narrative that describes why what has happened, happened, and use that narrative to try and predict what is likely to happen in the next iteration of the game.

Individually, and in Groups

Corporations are not only legal entities – they can (and do) take on the characteristics of a thinking, or psychological, entity (otherwise, exactly what or whom is being emulated by Maccoby's Company Man?). Entire macro organizations are perfectly capable of arranging observable facts into a narrative that supposedly reflects a deeper or more widespread message about who they are, and what the future is likely to hold for them based on their narrative-supported view of selves.

For example, there is a famous story about Federal Express founder Fred Smith and the financial difficulties FedEx was having in its early days. Smith was waiting for a flight home to Memphis from Chicago when he impulsively flew to Las Vegas, and won $27,000 playing black jack, helping him to make payroll that week.[6] When I first heard that story, it was being touted as evidence of the corporate culture at Federal Express being one of a can-do spirit, of taking risks for the sake of the others in the corporation. Now, Smith couldn't have been the only company owner in history to raise capital from winnings at gambling. But his company was the first I had ever heard of that translated a successful weekend in Vegas into a narrative that both reflected well on the organization and its owner. I mean, let's think this through: does the predilection of an owner of a delivery company to resort to gambling to make payroll have anything at all to do with that company's ability to deliver packages to the right address, on time, and for a good price? Clearly the event and the organization's capability have no causal or logical link; and yet, in hearing a description of FedEx's corporate culture, this story almost always gets told. And if the facts that are combined into a narrative that describes the characteristics of an organization have no causal or logical link to them, what will happen when parts of that self-identification narrative are used to predict the organization's future?

---

5   Kacirk, Jeffrey, *Forgotten English*, entry for June 17, 2010, used with permission.

6   FedEx Express (September 26, 2010). In *Wikipedia, The Free Encyclopedia*. Retrieved 19:50, September 27, 2010, from http://en.wikipedia.org/w/index.php?title=FedEx_Express&oldid=387206149

While not identical, Berne's *Games People Play* archetypes are similar to Sigmund Freud's structural model of the psyche. Indeed, Freud posited that infant children are completely dominated by their Ids, and that their ego develops as a result of the need to satisfy the Id's demands in a world that requires interaction with others. The following table provides a high-level comparison of the Freudian and Berne archetypes (Table 7.1):

Table 7.1   Comparison of Freud's and Berne's Classifications

Freudian Psychic Apparatus	What They Have In Common	Berne Archetypes
Id	Completely self-centered; illogical and irrational; decisions and actions serve only the internal self.	Child
Ego	Aware of others and the rational world; interacts with the outside world in such a way as to bring benefits to the self.	Adult
Super Ego	Seeks perfection; is critical and seeks improvement of the self; works in contradiction to the Id/child.	Parent

Now recall the discussion of the similarities between the Maccoby and Bartle archetypes from Chapter 4.

Table 7.2   Comparison of Bartle and Maccoby Archetypes

Bartle Types	Gamesman Types	Comments
Achievers	Gamesman	Views interactions as a game, and does what it takes to win within that context.
Socializers	Company Men	Assumes the persona of those around him; engages in strategies based on those in the same environ.
Killers	Jungle Fighters	Gets ahead by eliminating competitors.
Explorers	Craftsman	Allegiance to others or respect of authority is not key to these types – they participate largely on their own terms.

Maccoby provided an analysis of people engaged in economic activities, or business. Bartle's types represent people engaged in massive multi-player online role-playing games. Both Freud and Berne were providing a structure that could help to explain the decisions and behavior of all people, including those engaged in economics and playing in MMORPGs. These disparate analyses and structures do have some interesting parallels, though. Consider the alignment shown in Table 7.3:

Table 7.3   Alignment Between Freud, Berne, Bartle and Maccoby

Freud	Berne	Bartle	Maccoby
Super Ego	Parent	Achiever	Gamesman
Ego	Adult	Socializers, Explorers	Craftsmen, Company Men
Id	Child	Killers	Jungle Fighters

Bartle's Achiever, like Maccoby's Gamesman, must engage in an ongoing evaluation of the tactics he is using in order to maximize the odds of future successes, and minimize the odds of failure. In this sense he engages in Super Ego/Parent evaluation and criticism of the self. These four types also have in common their placement atop their respective structures.

Bartle's Socializers have an obvious parallel to Maccoby's Company Men. Maccoby's Craftsmen, like Bartle's Explorers, are fully engaged in the other players in the game/corporate world where they find themselves, and yet play by their own set of rules. A Bartle-style Killer exhibits rather primal behaviors as they go around attacking other players in order to get ahead. But the conflation of these four structures also seems to imply a sequential or progressive process by which we become better massive multi-player online role-playing gamers, managers, and, well, people. Neither Bartle nor Maccoby asserted that any of their archetypes was superior to others per se, i.e., Socializers are not superior gamers to Explorers. Maccoby does discuss a parallel between personal development and professional development, but I do not want to take up that part of the discussion.[7] What I do want to examine is whether or not the proffered analysis structures of Maccoby, Bartle, Berne, and even Freud can be used to reveal:

- What facts went into any given player's or organization's narrative;
- If those facts were processed into something representing a narrative that reveals the archetype of the person possessing the narrative; and
- Even if the previous two points are shown to be true and valid, could the belonging in the particular archetype lead to an ability to accurately predict the selection of available strategies for a given event, or circumstance?

The Pieces Don't Always Move That Way

Participants in experimental playings of the Ultimatum Game who, as Player B, fail to accept a $1 payoff, with Player A receiving $99, and the only alternative being to receive nothing at all, are held to act "irrationally." People who engage in interactions with others, and cross channels of communication among the Child–Adult–Parent ego states are probably engaged in an unhealthy psychological "game." Someone who presented as so passionate about an issue that he appeared to lack sufficient perspective might be diagnosed by Freud as having an undeveloped ego, or in a state of arrested development, and might be given a prescription for morphine.

Don't misunderstand – I'm not knocking the contributions of Von Neumann and Nash, Berne, Maccoby, or Freud. Quite the contrary, I sincerely applaud their contributions.

But the basic fact of the matter is that scientific theories exist to explain why observed phenomenon occurred, or why the observed data is what it is, *and to provide a structure for the prediction of how future phenomenon and observed data will present*. When we talk about these ideas in the realm of economics, they begin to lose efficacy due to the unknown and unknowable parameters that will have an impact on the experiment where the theories are being tested. This aspect of scientific discovery has a huge impact when we attempt to use these theories in a broad application in the realm of management. In other

---

7   Maccoby, Michael, *The Gamesman: The New Corporate Leaders*, Simon and Schuster, 1976, p. 210.

words, there are managers, or management practitioners, who are using these ideas and structures in areas where they simply do not belong.

Why can't the Maccoby archetypes be used for predicting the behavior of the members of a macro-organization – even when credible evidence exists for the accurate assignment of the employee's type? For the same reason that Transactional Analysis has fallen out of favor with professional counselors. It's too simplistic. We can't possibly know all of the facts or fictions that went into the creation of the individual's, or organization's, narratives. Nor can we know if those facts were scrutinized as to accuracy, or reasonable weight, and assembled using the rules of logic, or genuine causation. Nor can we know if they were illogically grouped together in order to flatter the narrative's owner, or buttress some poorly conceived but deeply-held aspect of the organization's narrative. The Id exists in our subconscious, and is knowable through dreams. The narratives that originate there – and there has to be a lot of them – are thoroughly untestable, and therefore largely unknowable to others. In short, virtually any attempt to reverse engineer another person's narrative based on their observed behaviors, or even intimate conversations, will almost certainly yield inaccuracies.

The attempts to reduce the payoff of players in any given game to a single, quantifiable variable, such as money, are a tacit acknowledgement of the impossibility of accurately assessing the narratives of the players around us. Both Bartle and Maccoby assign people their categorizations through answers provided to questionnaires – essentially, trying to glean some of the characteristics of people's internal narrative. But those internal narratives change, and can do so dramatically, from causes both sublime and catastrophic. Today's Jungle Fighter could be tomorrow's Gamesman, tomorrow's Explorer the following day's Killer. And, if there is anything to the idea that a natural progression could or should occur within the Id–Ego–Super Ego, or Child–Adult–Parent classifications, then it is reasonable to assume that progression through the Bartle and Maccoby archetypes is not only plausible, but desirable.

The Bartle and Maccoby archetypes strike hard against the rocks that mark the border between explaining why the things that have happened happened the way they did, and the ability of that narrative to predict behaviors into the future. So, for the moment, let's discard the entire future-predicting capability business. We have seen the cognitive biases and information processing flaws that are inherent in creating the scripts we hold to. Do such structures lend credence when evaluating the validity of the processes that lead to the creation of such narratives?

When Things Go Good …

As we saw in the computation of the Nash Equilibrium between the Gamesman and Jungle Fighter in Chapter 3, when things are going well for the organization, then there is no reason for anybody to adopt any set of strategies that will either endanger the organization's success, or reveal a predilection for strategies that could endanger success. But the tendency to select detrimental strategies, while eliminated in the universe where a Nash Equilibrium could be calculated based on quantified payoff matrix parameters, still exist in the universe where internal narratives, and not payoff matrices, rule the behavior of participants. We have already seen how such narratives are, by their very nature, unknowable and unquantifiable. So, when an event has come about that is seen as favorable to the organization, do the Maccoby archetypes aid in constructing an accurate narrative about why the favorable event came about?

My guess is probably not. Each Maccoby type will assume that the success was due to their approach to winning the work, or successfully completing it, or however the event manifested. It's the whole "Success has many fathers, but failure is an orphan" effect.

When Things Go Badly ...

Here is where the Maccoby archetypes become invaluable but, sadly, are not used often enough. A management analyst with knowledge of the Maccoby types is in a position to create a lessons-learned narrative far superior to analysts with no such knowledge. In Project Management space, the creation of Variance Analysis Reports is common. Similarly, when evaluating the performance of an asset, objective data is usually readily obtainable. But, in the arena of Strategic Management, the only objective data is the size of the organization's market share. If that amount of market share represents a setback, Maccoby's archetypes provide one of the few structures that can provide an accurate and logical approach for constructing the causal analysis of what went wrong.

For example, let's posit a project goes terribly wrong, and costs the owning organization market share. In creating the narrative that describes the root cause of the disaster, each and every analyst who contributes to the final report brings with them their own narratives, their own structures for assigning facts into a sequential this-led-to-that script. The Craftsman can be counted on to generate an analysis revealing a lack of expertise within the project team, and the Jungle Fighter will find specific scapegoats (probably including many seen to be rivals, whether or not a logical causality loop can be established). Company Men will look to so-called risk factors beyond the ken of managers as the exonerating causal element, and Gamesmen will take in evidence to modify their how-the-game-is-played narratives to increase the odds of adopting a strategy with better results should they find themselves in a similar game. Maccoby holds the Gamesman type to be the most successful. Could that be because the Gamesman's response to project disaster is the most robust, the most accurate, the most appropriate inclusion in the internal narratives that explain what has happened and, more importantly, what is likely to happen in the future?

It All Comes Down to the Narratives

In *The Black Swan*, Taleb presents us with two analysts: one is highly educated, formally, while the other is more street-smart. Each has been informed of a fair coin having been tossed 30 times, with heads being the result each time. What will be the result of the next coin toss? The educated fellow selects tails, knowing the odds of a fair coin being tossed 31 times with the same result being astronomical. The street-smart fellow, however, selects heads, since the premise of a "fair" coin is clearly flawed. In Transactional Analysis parlance, the educated analyst has been taught to adopt a narrative that leads him to predict a future event – the coin toss – one way, while the street-smart analyst has obviously built a narrative that leads him to challenge the premise that the coin is, in fact, fair.

In short, it's all about the narratives we adopt, and use in making managerial decisions. However, as we have seen, this narrative can be highly subjective, if not out and out illogical, therefore leading to the conclusion that the decisions we make based on these narratives can be profoundly misguided. It goes without saying – though I'll say it here – that misguided managerial decisions lead to career limiting events, if not out-and-out catastrophes (see the "Big Dig"). Does Game Theory offer a remedy? It does, but I'll need to place guard rails around another commonly-used management discipline: Risk.

8 *Deconstructing Risk Management*

Great deeds are usually wrought at great risks.

Herodotus (484 BC–430 BC), *The Histories of Herodotus*

The Preliminary Edition of PMI®'s *Project and Program RISK MANAGEMENT: A Guide to Managing Project Risks and Opportunities* defines "project risk" as "… the cumulative effect of the chances of uncertain occurrences adversely affecting project objectives."[1] As broad as that sounds, an even broader definition was offered up by Risk Management guru Dave Hillson, as he quoted the *PMBOK® Guide*'s definition in a comment to one of my columns in *PM® Network* magazine:

> *Michael Hatfield's* PM® Network *columns are often stimulating. Unfortunately, his January 2007 column on* A Guide to the Project Management Body of Knowledge (PMBOK® Guide) *included a significant mistake. While discussing the value of knowledge areas, Mr Hatfield talks about quantifying risks in terms of "potential costs, delays, or changes in scope."*
>
> *He should know the* PMBOK® Guide *risk management chapter defines risk as "an uncertain event or condition that, if it occurs, has a positive or negative effect on at least one project objective." In other words, risk includes both threat and opportunity. Upside risks can therefore be quantified in terms of potential savings in time or cost, as well as potential enhancements in performance or quality (though not scope enhancements, of course). In this view, we should be using the risk management process to find ways of working "smarter, faster, cheaper," as well as exposing potential traps.*
>
> *As a risk specialist, I was delighted with Mr Hatfield's conclusion that "risk is cool!"[2] But I think it's important to know what we mean by the term and to be sure that people get the full benefit available from proactively managing both good and bad risks.*
>
> *David Hillson, Ph.D., PMP*

As it turned out, this fairly mild exchange would turn into a rather nasty rhetorical brawl with other members of the Risk Management community when I replied to Dr Hillson's

---

1   Project Management Institute, *Project and Program RISK MANAGEMENT: A Guide to Managing Project Risks and Opportunities*, no publication date given.

2   I didn't use the exclamation point, nor was the fact that it was only part of the sentence mentioned.

comment by quoting Wikipedia and Webster's definition of the word "risk," and pointed out that neither definition made any reference whatsoever to opportunities, or "upside risks." Members of PMI's Risk Special Interest Group sent belligerent missives to my editors, insisting that my column had no place in a PMI publication.

The tempest would blow over, and even lead to a friendly and professional point-counterpoint-style exchange between Dr Hillson and I in *PM® Network* a little later, on the topic of whether or not Risk Management legitimately included opportunity management. That article came about from the transcription of a three-way discussion between me, Dr Hillson, and editors from PMI. Through the course of that discussion, I pressed Dr Hillson for a working definition of a "risk event." Dr Hillson responded – and I'm paraphrasing here – in a similar manner as in his letter, that a risk event was any occurrence, positive or negative, that impacted the realization of project objectives.

"Dave," I objected, "by that definition, anything that happens in the pursuit of project objectives qualifies as a 'risk event.' Using your definition, you simply cannot articulate the distinction between risk management, and, say, scope management, or quality management – or any other kind of management, for that matter."

Dr Hillson would not offer up either a modified definition of a risk event, nor an acid test for determining where Risk Management began, or ended, and other management types began. I suspected that the assertions of Risk Management practitioners had far outstripped their legitimate boundaries, if, for no other reason that those boundaries could not (or would not) be defined by Risk Management's own experts.

Another incident had started my suspicions about the efficacy of Risk Management techniques, and the information streams they created. I was working as a project controls analyst on an environmental program, and had actually coded a program that interacted with Primavera Project Planner® software to create a contingency budget, based on a single-tier decision-tree analysis of the scope of the activities at the project's reporting level. This program delivered a written analysis of the potential difficulties that the tasks could encounter, with an estimate of the odds of the difficulty happening, and an estimate of the costs in resources and time. These analyses were printed out and assembled in (large) notebooks for each of the remediation projects in the program.

One of these projects began to experience large cost overruns and schedule delays. The cause was the encountering of a layer of shale in the drilling of a test well in an area mostly comprised of tuff, a far softer type of rock. I guess those guys were going through drill bits at an exponential rate, but the only alternatives were to place the well elsewhere, or stop the work altogether. Placing the well elsewhere would have been futile, since the data sought had to do with a specific aquifer beneath the existing drill site. A representative of the customer came out to perform an audit of the project, and this person was a Risk Management specialist. He spoke with the project controller who was working that particular project, a woman named Donna. One of the auditor's first questions was: Did you perform a risk analysis, and was this event evaluated as a potential threat?

"Oh, I don't know. Let me look." Donna took down the hard copies from the risk analysis software reports, and looked up that particular set of tasks. And, wouldn't you know it, there it was, number one on the list of possible threats to successful task completion, with a comment that the potential cost overruns should a layer of shale be struck by the drilling team could be in the millions.

What happened next was, in a strange sort of way, simultaneously amazing and predictable. He simply folded up his notebooks, requested a copy of that specific risk analysis report, and left. I do not know the extent of his further investigation, but a check for the amount of the overrun was received within the month.

Note that the existence of the report citing the striking of shale as a risk event had nothing to do with the fact that the shale would be hit. And, once the shale was hit, the risk analysis had absolutely no impact on the response of the project team. None whatsoever. They would have responded in an identical manner, with or without the analysis. And yet, hearing Donna tell me what had happened led me to believe that the outcome with the customer representative would have been very different indeed had she not produced the report showing that the analysis had been done, as well as the risk event that ended up happening been quantified, as haphazard as that quantification would be.

Do I have to say it? That makes no sense, none at all. The risk assessment didn't lead to an avoidance of the so-called risk event, nor did it change the response to the event one iota. And yet it does point to the elusive, but logical, limits to the relevancy of Risk Management: Risk Management is relevant if and only if its information products can lead decision-makers to either avoid a future negative event, or changes the response to such an event should it happen. Let's evaluate the two separately.

Can Risk Management techniques lead to the avoidance of events that have a negative impact on a project in the future? The plain answer is no, they can't, with the sole exception being those cases where an identified risk leads to changes in the way a given project's goals are planned or pursued. As we saw in the previous chapter, we all create narratives that provide both structures for explaining why things that have happened in the past happened the way they did, and serve as a basis for extrapolating how things will unfold in the future. But Risk Management can't even provide the former. Consider a supposedly fair coin, tossed 30 straight times and coming up heads each time. Ask a Risk Management guru what are the odds that it will come up heads the next time, and you can bet (get it?) that he will respond "50–50." However, in real life, the odds of a fair coin coming up heads 31 straight times are, well, astronomical. Any reasonable person would immediately come to the conclusion that the coin is (obviously!) not fair, and predict that the next iteration will yield heads.

For the sake of argument, though, let's say the 31st flip did come up tails. What has that added to the narrative? Not a thing. Neither probability nor statistics can provide a structure that adds causality to a narrative of why the things that happened, have happened. The coin was flipped. It came up tails. Why? Probability can't tell you – it only knows that prior to the flipping the odds of a fair coin coming up tails were one-half. So, it came up tails. What does that say of the odds of the coin coming up tails in the next iteration? Nothing – the analysis stays the same, at 50–50.

Management ... Science?

I want to explore this notion a bit further. In order for an idea to be considered scientific, it must meet two standards:

- It must be observable; and
- It must be repeatable, preferably in a laboratory setting.

Insisting that individual electrons spin on an axis parallel to its atom's nucleus, therefore, isn't scientific, since it can't be observed (at least not with 2011 technology). Nor are ideas concerning the source of the 1908 Tunguska fireball considered truly scientific, no matter how well they fit the available data, since that event can't be recreated – especially not in a laboratory. Unless and until a significant amount of new fireball data becomes available, any explanation is little better than rank speculation.

Put another way:

- The hypothesis ready to become scientific theory must provide a structure, or a narrative, that explains why the data collected was the way it was; and
- It must provide the structure (or narrative) that accurately predicts the outcome of the experiment the next time it's tried.

By now the alert reader has realized the similarity between what constitutes genuine science, and how people tend to create their internal narratives. Keep in mind that these internal narratives do two things:

- They provide a structure for explaining why the things that have happened, happened, based on our understanding of causality; and
- They provide a structure for predicting how events will, or should unfold in the future, should similar occurrences or causal factors present themselves.

Now, let's return to coin flipping. If we assume a perfectly fair coin, the odds of it coming up heads on the first flip are ½, or 50%. The odds of this coin facing heads-up two straight times is ½ times ½, or ¼ (25%). Continuing in this vein, the odds of heads coming up 30 straight times is one in one billion, seventy-three million, seven hundred and forty-one thousand, eight-hundred and twenty-four (1 in 1,073,741,824). If you were to take ten seconds to flip a coin, observe its face-up side, and write that result down, it would take you 10,214 years of non-stop coin-flipping before you should expect to see a 30-straight heads-up event. As a point of reference, you would have had to begin flipping 4,214 years before the beginning of known history to expect to see such an event in the present day.

So, let's say our very long-lived and determined coin-flipper has put in his 10,214 years, and has realized the 30-heads event. Now, he is ready to flip the coin for the 31st time.

Wait a moment. The odds of tossing a coin and having it come up heads 31 straight times is actually 1 in 2,147,483,647. Adjusting for the additional ten seconds involved in multiple 31-toss sets, this would take 21,110 years – prior to any direct evidence of Homo Sapiens Sapiens attaining behavioral modernity, incidentally.

The difference between the odds of tossing the coin 30 times straight, with heads as the result, and 31 times straight, is 1 in 1,1073,741,824, or ½ times the odds of 31 straight. And yet, still assuming the fair coin, the odds of any one of those flips coming up a specific way is ½, or 50%. So, for that 31st toss after 30 straight heads, which is it: 50%, or 0.0000000931%?

As any Risk Manager could tell you, it's 50%.

What our little foray into numerous repetitions of coin-flipping should have inescapably demonstrated to all but the most experienced Risk Managers is that Risk Management techniques cannot add any insight – none whatsoever – to the creation or modification of a narrative that describes why the things that have happened, happened the way they did. Therefore, it fails the first standard for a scientific theory: it can't help explain observed data, or phenomena. The question then becomes: if Risk Management can't explain observed phenomena, can it be used to predict the future?

To be fair, though, one of the very first things that students of probability and statistics learn is that correlation is not causation. And yet, without some notion of causation, creating a hypothesis about why a certain data set or observed phenomena occurred the way it did is completely futile.

If any insight on causation is automatically off the table when probability and statistics is discussed, and our concept of causation is key to both the narratives we maintain to explain the things that have happened, as well as the things that can be expected to happen, then doesn't that mean that any such analysis can't possibly lend any insight to the unfolding of future events? And isn't that exactly what Risk Management pretends to do?

In short, the Risk Management experts can't have it both ways. The correlation-is-not-causation meme gets pulled out whenever a statistical assertion is found to be wrong, as a sort of intellectual get-out-of-jail-free card. When a probability analysis returns a result that is consistent with how events actually unfolded, these guys never remind us that correlation is not causation – the clear (if unspoken) implication is that there is a causal relationship. This analytical sleight-of-hand sets up a monstrous confirmation bias cycle, one so pervasive and influential that it could lead to members of Risk Management special interest groups maintaining a strict vigilance for and intense opposition to any writer of management topics who dares to fail to include invalid notions of "upside risk" when addressing the topic.

If risk analysis can neither support a particular narrative for why things happened the way they did, nor serve as a structure for forecasting likely future events, on something as simple as tossing coins, no less, how could it possibly be of use in evaluating situations and circumstances far, far more complex?

Do You Know Who You're Taking On Here?

And yet Risk Management is big business. A Yahoo! search conducted on October 2, 2010, on "Risk Management" yielded over 136,000,000 hits. But it must be asked: does Risk Management, as it is currently practiced (and as defined in Chapter 1), represent what Taleb called "flawed tools of inference"?

On January 17, 2003, the late Michael Crichton delivered a Caltech Michelin Lecture entitled "Aliens Cause Global Warming." Similar to Taleb's condemnation of "flawed tools of inference" in the business world, Crichton essentially dismantled some of the commonly-held "truths" that rest upon junk science, and how the pattern of unproven or poorly established theories drive the creation of ultimately wasteful or even destructive public policy. Early in the lecture, Crichton discusses the Drake equation, developed by an astrophysicist named Frank Drake to try to assess the number of planets that might have intelligent life. The formula is:

$$N = N * fp\ ne\ fl\ fi\ fc\ fL$$

Where N is the number of stars in the Milky Way galaxy; fp is the fraction with planets; ne is the number of planets per star capable of supporting life; fl is the fraction of planets where life evolves; fi is the fraction where intelligent life evolves; fc is the fraction that communicates; and fL is the fraction of the plant's life during which the communicating civilizations live. As serious as this formula appears, Crichton points out that there is absolutely no way of knowing any of the variables. The result could be anything from "billions and billions" to zero, making it essentially a structure for mere speculation. Or, as Crichton put it, "An expression that can mean anything means nothing."[3] The way the Drake equation was presented to me was in the vein of "even if each of the multipliers is extremely small, that still leaves thousands upon thousands of planets that might sustain intelligent life." But, as with all equations, if only one of those parameters happens to be zero, then the end result is zero. And, if the answer really is zero, then any decisions – particularly public policy decisions – made in anticipation of a non-zero result would be flawed.

Let's revisit one of the risk analysis techniques from Chapter 1, the Decision Tree analysis. A version of its formula is:

$$Cn = BAC - [(E1\$ * E1\%) + (E2\$ * E2\%) + (En\$ * En\%)]$$

Where Cn is the contingency budget, BAC is the budget at completion, E1\$ is the cost of possible event one occurring, E1% is the odds of event one occurring, all the way through event n, which is the last possible event included in the analysis.

I was struck by the similarity of the Decision Tree analysis formula to the Drake equation. Consider: what's the basis for identifying these events? It's the internal narrative of those engaged in the analysis, projected into the future. This basis introduces massive amounts of subjectivity into a supposedly objective process. For example, how do we know that some amount of cognitive bias hasn't invalidated the narrative? What if the narrative is comprised of false causality loops? For that matter, how do we know if event n was a sufficiently high number to be reasonably said to encompass the number of different events that could impact the project? As in the Drake equation, there is simply no way of knowing these things, meaning that one of the primary models for performing risk analysis (and, by extension, Risk Management) does not provide the level or type of management insight that it purports to deliver.

I must point out that Risk Management, as it is currently practiced, is rendered weaker than advertised, not by its probability and statistics mathematics, but by its underlying logic. It follows, then, that the Monte Carlo analysis technique, which is essentially a version of the Decision Tree with its probability-and-statistics components accentuated, is also of more marginal utility than advertised, and for the same reasons.

To be clear, I'm only addressing Risk Management techniques within the realm of project management. These techniques are apparently valid within the disciplines of engineering and architecture, among others. My assertions of the weakness of Risk Management specifically target the approaches from, well, the *PMBOK® Guide*, and *Project and Program RISK MANAGEMENT, A Guide to Managing Project Risks and Opportunities*,[4] also from PMI®.

---

3   Crichton, Michael, *Aliens Cause Global Warming*, Caltech Michelin Lecture, January 17, 2003.

4   Project Management Institute, *Project and Program RISK MANAGEMENT: A Guide to Managing Project Risks and Opportunities*, no publication date given.

A Convenient Escape Hatch

Risk Management experts invariably respond to the above criticisms by pointing out that their risk analysis techniques are only designed to quantify the so-called "known–unknowns." Recall from Chapter 1 the classification of risk events into those that can be "reasonably" expected to occur – and, therefore, be identified and quantified – and those that cannot be "reasonably" expected to occur, such as natural disasters, or acts of God. This latter category are labeled "unknown–unknowns."

The distinction between risk events as known–unknowns and unknown–unknowns has to be one of the most sophomoric frauds perpetrated upon the managerial community. Prior to a negative-impact event happening to a project, what's the difference between a known–unknown, and an unknown–unknown? The unknown–unknowns aren't in the risk analysis. After the event happened, if it was not foreseen, how is it determined to have been a legitimate unknown–unknown? If the event could have been "reasonably" foreseen. "Reasonable" based on whose standards? If the event was consistent with the narrative of the person responsible for the project, then the event will be held to have been "reasonably" foreseeable, and if not, then it's (voila!) an unknown–unknown. This reclassification of the risk events legerdemain is eerily similar to the response of Game Theory practitioners, when the actual playing of the Ultimatum Game yielded results that strongly contradicted their expected results – the players weren't acting "rationally." We find ourselves returning to the previous questions: how do we know that cognitive biases haven't rendered the "reasonableness" of the assessors' narrative invalid? Does she have a strong sense for determining causality?

When I was preparing for my Certified Cost Consultant® test, I was working on problems associated with the Risk Management part of the exam. One of these practice questions involved calculating the expected amount of time that a person would take to get to work, and the parameters offered included the distance from his apartment to workplace, number of traffic lights, length of time that the unsynchronized traffic lights stayed on their colors, average speed of the car, among others. I had memorized the equation, and just went through the motions of plugging in the data, and produced the answer expected.

Driving home from the study session, my Volkswagen Dasher broke down, and I arrived home late. I realized that the premise of the problem I had "solved" was all wrong, and began to think of perfectly predictable events that would render the risk analysis invalid. Some of these included:

• The aforementioned car malfunction.
• Sick spouse, or child.
• Snow packed streets.
• The onset of a sudden craving for a triple latte from a nearby Starbucks.
• Auto accident happening to the commuter.
• Auto accident happening to the car in front of the commuter, and commuter stops to help.
• Auto accident happening anywhere on the intended path, forcing a detour.
• Observing spouse disembarking at a hotel with your best friend.

And the list went on and on. Were any of these events unforeseeable by a "reasonable" person? Certainly not (except for maybe that last one). But if they were knowable, could they be quantified with respect to the odds of their occurrence, and duration added to the commute? Not really – they all depended on other initiatives, other people's decisions – and that didn't even take into account the odds of more than one of these events occurring during a single commute. When one takes into account that this risk analysis technique, and its accompanying formula, are intended for use in larger, more complex situations, the fact that it can't even adequately capture the schedule contingency in its simplistic driving-to-work setting becomes all the more stark.

The central difficulty with all risk analysis techniques is their exclusive dependence on modus ponens. Recall from Chapter 7 that modus ponens takes the form:

If P, then Q

P

Therefore, Q.

But modus ponens, while representing a valid argument, does not guarantee that conclusions so reached are true. For modus ponens to produce truth, the premises must be true for any true instances of the conclusion. Let's say that the commuter's shortest calculated time to drive to work is 20 minutes, and that is based on hitting every single green light. Our commuter could take 25 minutes after having hit all green lights, and slipping through the drive-through at Starbucks. If we stipulate that the driver hits only green lights, this particular risk analysis technique failed by modus tollens as follows:

If P, then Q

Not Q

Therefore, not P

If *the complete set of risk factors is confined to the driver hitting only green lights*, then *he will arrive at work in 20 minutes*.

The commuter did not arrive in 20 minutes.

Therefore, *the complete set of risk factors was not so confined.*

Modus tollens is a valid logical argument, and, as we have seen, can return a conclusion that highlights possible weaknesses in the major premis(es) of modus ponens. The "theory," in this case, of the major premise was falsifiable, since the occurrence of a single instance of the commuter arriving at work past 20 minutes while encountering nothing but green lights would invalidate it. The potential for a flawed major premise is a major threat to conventional Risk Management techniques – which is, perhaps, one of the reasons Karl Popper pushed for the rejection of modus ponens as the main driver behind advancing scientific research. But, again, if modus ponens is even remotely unsuitable for advancing scientific theories, where the experimental parameters can be identified and controlled, how could modus ponens be considered a suitable argument for advancing risk analysis theory, where virtually none of the essential parameters can be known to any degree of precision, as in Drake's equation?

The time-to-destination exercise didn't end with calculations of the maximum and minimum times. No, we were expected to be able to calculate the most likely amount of time needed to complete the commute, as well as the odds of arriving at the earliest or latest possible times. The conflation of the techniques involved in assessing the unfolding of a (perfectly predictable) series of events in a pre-determined narrative, with the probabilities derived from the application of Gaussian curves, created an inferentially flawed monster, which quickly dominated far, far more areas of legitimate management and information system theory than it ever had the rights to do so.

Valid or Not, It's Everywhere

There's even an ISO standard (ISO 31000)[5] for this intellectually vacuous mess. Hundreds of organizations offer Risk Management services, and thousands upon thousands of managers are convinced of its efficacy. Many professional organizations attempt to further the use of Risk Management's tools, and there are dozens, if not hundreds, of software packages that perform some version of risk analysis (including the previously-mentioned one that I wrote!).

To borrow an oft-used phrase from Barrack Obama, I want to be very clear about this: Risk Management does have a valid and valuable function in engineering and architecture, and in a very specific segment of management; however, that function is far more restricted than its practitioners believe, or even dream. I will discuss the valid use of Risk Management in Part 3. For now, though, I want to review those areas of managerial theory that have been invaded by Risk Management, but where Risk Management has no legitimate intellectual stake.

One common use of risk analysis on a project is the creation of a contingency budget. This is actually not a bad use of the afore-slammed techniques, especially if a blanket 25% of the estimated budget for contingency reserve isn't backed up by enough mind-numbing statistics to inspire confidence in the project's customer. But the creation of the contingency reserve piece of the project's baseline is the absolute boundary for Risk Management's efficacy in generating useful project management information. Unfortunately, that's not how the common management science intelligentsia sees it.

A Guide to the Project Management Body of Knowledge® has this to say about "Risk Response Control: ... respond(s) to changes in risk over the course of the project."[6] This sort of assertion is rather frequent in Risk Management literature. It simply won't do for

---

5   ISO 31000 (September 3, 2010). In *Wikipedia, The Free Encyclopedia*. Retrieved 23:55, October 3, 2010, from http://en.wikipedia.org/w/index.php?title=ISO_31000&oldid=382645713

6   Project Management Institute Standards Committee, *A Guide to the Project Management Body of Knowledge*, PMI Publishing, 1996.

these professional worry warts to guess at the amount of reserve budget projects ought to have in case something goes wrong; no, they want to stick around for the life of the project, re-assessing and trying to quantify things that might go wrong along the way. According to the *PMBOK® Guide*:

> *Risk identification consists of determining which risks are likely to affect the project and documenting the characteristics of each. Risk identification is not a one-time event; it should be performed on a regular basis throughout the project.*[7]

Unless this contingency planning leads to a substantial difference in the manner that the project team responds to the risk event(s), this is a monumental waste of time and money. Worrying about – or, to put it more kindly, projecting – things that might go wrong on a project, and knowing an appropriate response when things do go wrong, is what project managers *do*. In fact, it's next to impossible to keep them from doing just that. Is their ability to engage in these two behaviors enhanced by endless probability-and-statistics pseudo-quantification? The aforementioned environmental project manager – was his decision to continue to drill through the shale improved (or, indeed, altered in any way) by the knowledge that someone had estimated his odds of hitting the shale in that particular geological formation? Or even what those odds were?

An Honest Application of Risk Management

Keep in mind that the analysis techniques being advocated here:

1. Have no validity in establishing a structure for explaining phenomena or observed data; and
2. Therefore have no standing when trying to predict the unfolding of future events.

That being the case, what are the legitimate functions of Risk Management within the management world?

First, let's define the "management world." As we saw in Chapter 6, the common definition of economics is so broad as to include almost all human interaction, and Dr Hillson's previously mentioned definition of a risk event is similarly so expansive as to eliminate next to nothing from being considered such an event. The reason these definitions are so absurdly all-inclusive is that they are attempting to serve the function of establishing the major premise for modus ponens or modus tollens:

If *P*, then *Q*

If *something impacts the production, distribution, and consumption of goods* then *it must be economics.*

If *a future event impacts the attainment of managerial objectives,* then *it must fall under the purview of Risk Management.*

---

7   Ibid, p.111.

But, as we have seen, this definition and approach in Risk Management is utterly invalid. The narrower and more appropriate use of Risk Management techniques is confined to its utility in the creation of management information streams, information streams used to test the robustness of the narratives or structures that we use to both understand why our personal or organization's history unfolded the way it did, and how our futures are likely to unfold, given the successful implementation of our plans. If our personal narratives are accurate, then we have achieved Socrates' first rule of wisdom, "know thyself." People whose personal narratives are notably at odds with reality are said to be delusional, while those with personal narratives starkly and provably at odds with reality are said to be insane. For that person who is planning on winning the lottery, and therefore believes that they do not need to save for retirement, the citation of the odds against that plan coming off is a perfectly appropriate use of risk analysis techniques.

The honest and appropriate use of Risk Management, then, becomes one of testing for robustness in the existing situation or condition of the organization, and a test of the strength of the narratives or structures being used in projecting the outcomes proposed courses of action. It's something of a narrow distinction, and I don't want to be accused of resorting to semantics to finish my arguments against Risk Management as practiced, so I'll put it another way. Risk Management can't tell you why things happened the way they did, nor can it predict the likelihood of things that will happen in the future. What it *can* do is inform you if the narratives you are using to understand why things happened the way they did are invalid; it can tell you if the narratives that serve as the underpinnings of your understanding of yourself (or your organization), and serve as the springboard from which to ascertain if your plans for the future, are inaccurate. And, to make an even finer distinction, it should be noted that Risk Management cannot inform you if your narratives are accurate, only if and where they are inaccurate. If we're younger than 10,214 years, and we just flipped the 29th head, then stop assuming a fair coin!

We will further explore this, the proper use of risk analysis in the management world in Part 3. For now, though, I think it's safe to say that Risk Management's upper limit is that it *cannot*:

1. Add context to the narratives we use to understand why history has unfolded the way it did; and
2. Provide insight as to the likelihood of events yet to happen.

And when I say "safe to say," I mean purely from an intellectual or rhetorical point of view. Much of Risk Management, as it is currently practiced, is predicated on its analysis techniques being able to generate a narrative of likely future events, and any writer who directly confronts this as I have should expect significant blow-back. No, I'm not going to try to compute the odds of such a negative future event happening, nor attempt to estimate its impact if it does. This prediction is just from my experience – my fact and perception-based narrative – that informs me that identical (if less complete) forays into this area have resulted in opposition that appears completely divorced from any sense of proportion, so I expect to see similar occurrences in the future, given the execution of my plans to finish this book.

Since we are teetering on the edge of managerial epistemology, let's go ahead and plunge into the nature and utility of management information, in Chapter 9.

9 *On the Limits of Knowledge and Management Information*

Knowledge must come through action; you can have no test which is not fanciful, save by trial.

Sophocles (496 BC–406 BC), *Trachiniae*

What we've seen time and again in the realm of management theory is the introduction of a concept, or a narrative, that seems to explain why historical economic events have unfolded the way they have. This concept is then projected or expanded, either from the exact circumstances and environs from whence it was originally hatched and into other types of management, or else from explaining the past into predicting the future. This expansion will continue apace until the concept has so dramatically outstripped its ability to structure reality and bring anything of value to the decision-making process that it begins to fade away, discredited.

Take Quality Management as an example. According to the *PMBOK® Guide*, Project Quality Management "includes the processes required to ensure that the project will satisfy the needs for which it was undertaken."[1] If that definition is insufficiently broad, consider this gem from Draft International Standard 8402, Quality – Vocabulary. It asserts that Quality Management includes:

> *… all activities of the overall management function that determine the quality policy, objectives, and responsibilities and implements them by means such as quality planning, quality control, quality assurance, and quality improvement, within the quality system.*[2]

Once the same word gets used five times in a single defining sentence, I start to lose track of what that word really means, much less what the writer's intended meaning for the entire sentence might have been. Webster's New Collegiate Dictionary has a boatload of definitions for quality, but the following appear to be the ones pertaining to management:

---

1   Project Management Institute Standards Committee, *A Guide To The Project Management Body of Knowledge*, Project Management Institute, April 1996.

2   International Organization for Standardization, *Quality – Vocabulary, Draft International Standard 8402*, ISO Press, 1993.

1a: peculiar and essential character; 1b: an inherent feature; 2a: degree of excellence; 2b: superiority in kind.[3]

And Webster is a bit more precise with the definition of Quality Control:

... an aggregate of activities (as design analysis and statistical sampling with inspection for defects) designed to ensure adequate quality in manufactured products.[4]

Note the difference in the definitions: when did quality management cease being confined to eliminating flaws in manufactured goods, and transform into encompassing "the processes required to ensure that the project will satisfy the needs for which it was undertaken?"

Once Quality Management broke free of its intended confines, it went viral. Consider this definition of Six Sigma, the business strategy vanguard of the quality management movement:

Six Sigma seeks to improve the quality of process outputs by identifying and removing the causes of defects (errors) and minimizing variability in manufacturing and business processes. It uses a set of quality management methods, including statistical methods, and creates a special infrastructure of people within the organization[5] (emphasis mine).

Quite a leap, from minimizing flaws in manufactured products to minimizing variability in the business process. Motorola University admits as such:

Six Sigma originated as a set of practices designed to improve manufacturing processes and eliminate defects, but its application was subsequently extended to other types of business processes as well. In Six Sigma, a defect is defined as any process output that does not meet customer specifications, or that could lead to creating an output that does not meet customer specifications.[6]

And what does that mean, exactly, "minimizing variability in ... (the) business process?" Variability between what and what? Well, between what was expected as the outcome of the organization's efforts, and the actual outcome. Where did these expectations originate? In the organization's plans for the characteristics of the manufactured product – er, no, I mean, the organization's efforts.

See how easily those bounds are slipped? As long as we're just talking about reducing flaws in manufactured products, sure, bring in all the statistical analysis you want. But the moment we expand these ideas past that specific venue, and start talking about variability in the business process, then we step firmly into the domain of creating a narrative about why the past unfolded as it did, and projecting that narrative into the

3   Woolf, Henry Bosley, *Webster's New Collegiate Dictionary*, G. & C. Merriam Co., 1977.

4   Ibid.

5   Six Sigma. (October 8, 2010). In *Wikipedia, The Free Encyclopedia*. Retrieved 21:02, October 8, 2010, from http://en.wikipedia.org/w/index.php?title=Six_Sigma&oldid=389550751

6   "Motorola University – What is Six Sigma?". Retrieved September 14, 2009, from http://www.motorola.com/content/0,,3088,00.html. "[...] Six Sigma started as a defect reduction effort in manufacturing and was then applied to other business processes for the same purpose."

future as a plan, and then crying foul when things don't go according to plan, i.e. a "variance" in the "business process," with ample amounts of statistical information to back it up, don't you know.

Quality management's heavy reliance on statistical data should, all by itself, be considered an indicator that QM has suspect bearing on assessing "business processes." It's simply too one-dimensional, a view of the business world while wearing Gaussian-colored glasses. But to oppose the quality zealots' take-over-the-business-world agenda is to be against quality, and who can stand to have that stigma attached to them? It's tailor-made for the Jungle Fighters in the organization – simply master college-level statistics, sprinkle in some quality management jargon, and become the final arbiter of which business processes are legitimate, and which are not. It makes me wonder if a Six Sigma analysis has ever been performed on the efficacy of the Six Sigma process, or the organizations they form.[7]

The Great Estimate-at-Completion Debate

One of my favorite examples of a legitimate management process that suddenly turns invalid once it leaves its originally-conceived confines has to do with the creation of an Estimate-at-Completion, or EAC, within the realm of project management. Once a project is underway, knowing what the final costs are likely to be prior to the actual completion of the project within a few percentage points is obviously extremely valuable. The availability of an accurate EAC could have conceivably been used to avoid some of the biggest project disasters of our time, like the "Big Dig" in Boston, or the National Ignition Facility at Lawrence Livermore National Laboratory, in California.

There are several approaches to generating this highly coveted number. The asset management advocates (read: accountants) will try to bring their Generally Accepted Accounting Principles to the table, and perform some sort of regression analysis on the actual costs expended thus far in the project. The unacceptability of this approach is demonstrated by the story problem example from Chapter 5.

In case you have slept since reading Chapter 5, the story goes like this. Imagine that you are a project manager, and your project is to manufacture 2,000 widgets. You have two months to do so, and your budget is $2,000. You budget $1,000 in Month 1, and $1,000 in Month 2, and get to work. At the end of Month 1, your accountant comes to you and announces that you have spent $1,100.

Two questions present themselves: how is your project performing, and what will be the total costs at project completion? The accountant will probably inform you that you are doing poorly, having spent $100 more than budgeted for Month 1, and, at this rate, your project will overrun by $200, since you can be expected to have at-completion costs of $2,200, assuming you spend another $1,100 in Month 2.

As luck would have it, you have access to an Earned Value specialist, who wants to know just one more bit of data: How many widgets did you make in Month 1? The answer: your project team cranked out 1,300 widgets in Month 1. The EV specialist immediately knows two things:

---

7   In the interest of full disclosure, I happen to be a Black Belt in Kenpo Karate. The whole Six Sigma deal with calling their experts "Black Belts" or "Green Belts," I find highly irksome. A Kenpo Black Belt takes a lot longer to achieve than the Six Sigma version, with a lot more effort, blood, fatigue – and expertise.

- On the question of how you are doing, your accountant was wrong. You're doing great. You've made 300 widgets more than planned, and it cost you $200 less than anticipated (each widget is worth $1; your team has made 1,300 of them, but it only cost $1,100).
- At this rate of performance, your accountant was also wrong in projecting an overrun. You can be expected, in fact, to finish with an underrun of $308 (the Cost Performance Index is 1.18. At this rate of performance, you will accomplish all $2,000 worth of work for $1,692).

In short, attempting to predict a project's at-completion costs using a "burn rate," or observed behavior in the amount of project money spent, is an invalid approach.

Another common method for generating the Estimate at Completion is to have an estimator estimate the amount of money it will take to complete the remaining work on the project, add this number to the cumulative actual costs, and, voila! An EAC is here. This approach, known as the "bottoms-up EAC," is so prevalent that it is actually expected of many American contractors as a sort of sanity check on project performance. As it turns out, this approach is flawed, as well.

To reiterate some of the discussion from Chapter 5, according to the American Association of Cost Engineers (predecessor organization to the Association for the Advancement of Cost Engineering, International, or AACEI®), there are three types of estimates. The most accurate is known as the Detailed Estimate, and it is so detailed that once it is completed it can be used to procure the materials and labor for the project. It is produced by a professional (hopefully, certified) estimator, using off-the-shelf software. At its most accurate, it can be expected to be within 15% of the real end-costs of the project, assuming no major changes to the baseline are incurred.

In a paper entitled *Cost Performance Index Stability*, David Christensen and Scott Heise demonstrated that a project's Cost Performance Index, or CPI, only rarely changes more than 10 percentage points in either direction once the project has passed the 20% complete point.[8] The formula used by Earned Value practitioners to calculate the Estimate at Completion is to divide the project's budget (Budget at Completion, or BAC) by the Cost Performance Index. It therefore follows that this method of calculating the EAC can be expected to be accurate to within 10% of the actual final costs, once the project has passed the 20% complete point. This calculation does not require specialized software or advanced expertise in cost engineering, and, in fact, is routinely performed on projects with a functional Earned Value Management System.

So, to recap (Table 9.1):

Table 9.1 Types of Project Progress Estimation

Type of EAC:	Regression	Re-Estimated	EV-Calculated
Performed by:	Accountant	Pro Estimator	Just falls out of the system
Effort/Time Required:	Not much	A lot	Virtually none
Accuracy Rate:	Comically In-	15%, at best	10%, at worst

8   Christensen, David S., and Heise, Scott R., *Cost Performance Index Stability*. Retrieved October 8, 2010, from http://www.suu.edu/faculty/christensend/evms/CPIstabilityNCMJ.pdf

And yet the other methods are prevalent, even in organizations that consider themselves advanced in management in general, and project management in particular, and even in the face of direct evidence that these other approaches are inferior.

More on Management and Kuhn

I introduced Thomas Kuhn in Chapter 6. In 1962, he published *The Structure of Scientific Revolutions*.[9] While Kuhn's insights were written about advances in the physical sciences, the parallels to advances in management science are inescapable.

Kuhn asserted that one of the aims of science is to find models that will account for as many observations as possible within a coherent framework.[10] One of his best examples involved cosmology. Ptolemy believed that the movement of the stars and planets were based on cycles and epicycles, with a stationary Earth at its center. However, with the invention of the telescope at the beginning of the seventeeth century, data was collected and phenomena observed that appeared to represent exceptions or anomalies to Ptolemy's models, so more and more epicycles had to be proposed in order for the Ptolemy model to remain viable. Johannes Kepler was among the first to abandon the Ptolemy view of the cosmos, and posited that the Sun was at the center of a solar system, where the planets orbited. At first, however, there was insufficient data or observations to establish the Kepler model as superior to Ptolemy's cosmos, and it was therefore not readily accepted. But, as more and more data and observations became available, it became clear that the Kepler model not only explained the known data better, but explained the new data in a way that Ptolemy's model could not, as well.

Another interesting aspect of Kuhn's writing involves the introduction of the term "paradigm shift." Though the term's precise denotation has often been overcome by its connotation, it originally referred to the phenomena of new scientific theories displacing previously-held beliefs, as the cycle of new information and observations coming in that challenge the currently-held theories and those theories being added to in order to explain the anomalies begins again.

I believe that something very similar occurs in the realm of management theory, but with a key difference: theories deemed to be scientific can be used to explain observed data, and can be empirically tested in an experimental setting. Not so for management, which will be forever locked into an infinitely complex system. In the realm of management – or even in that subset of microeconomics – the players are so numerous, conditions and environs so vast, that it is a virtual impossibility to isolate single parameters, or even sets of parameters, in such a way that a theory of their consistent future behavior can be empirically tested, and thence trusted as viable. At best, certain narratives can become widely adopted, after they appear to successfully explain observed economic or managerial events and their consequences, or if these narratives can make that step across the timeline and accurately describe the future in such a way that success follows.

Again, that's the best-case scenario.

---

9   Kuhn, Thomas S., *The Structure of Scientific Revolutions*, University of Chicago Press, 1962.

10   The Structure of Scientific Revolutions (September 20, 2010). In *Wikipedia, The Free Encyclopedia*. Retrieved 02:27, October 10, 2010, from http://en.wikipedia.org/w/index.php?title=The_Structure_of_Scientific_Revolutions &oldid=385851715

In the less-than-best-case-scenarios, the vulnerability of commonly-held management narratives to inaccuracies, biases, and flat-out falsehoods is enormous. There are far too few opportunities to test management theories empirically, leading to a susceptibility to trendiness. Nassim Taleb writes in *The Black Swan* "I will repeat the following until I am hoarse: it is contagion that determines the fate of a theory, not its validity."[11]

To be fair, the validity of a given managerial or economic theory is far more difficult to establish, if, for no other reason, than due to the aforementioned complexity of the environment where such theories are introduced, and then either accepted or rejected. In an extraordinary piece on the American Thinker blog site for August 31, 2010, Monty Pelegrin (a pseudonym) posted an article on the topic of how Keynesian economics did not gain popularity in the 1930s because it seemed to explain observed data and economic phenomena better than Adam Smith's economic theories: it was adopted by the United States Government because Franklin Roosevelt needed some sort of defensible theoretical cover for his attempts at introducing massive amounts of statist power over a country that had been previously defined by the very absence of statist power.

Could Keynesian economics be tested empirically? A great historical debate rages over whether or not FDR's policies alleviated the Great Depression, or if they prolonged it. (As a side note: whenever you see the expression "historical debate," in expanded Game Theory parlance this represents historians' – peoples' – competing narratives about how perceived historical facts unfolded, and the causality loops being overlaid on these occurrences.) Amity Schlaes' book *The Forgotten Man* makes this case very effectively.[12]

After the Great Depression, probably the next best clear opportunity to test Keynesian economics occurred during the presidency of Jimmy Carter. Keynes hypothesized that a nation's gross domestic product (GDP) was comprised of two elements: what the private sector created, and what the government contributed. Since the government was in a position to print currency, and spend that currency in the private sector, Keynes argued that it was a participant in generating output that should be considered part of the GDP. Since inflation is, by definition, too many dollars chasing too few goods or services, a central government should be encouraged to print money until the inflation rate drove prices up. At that point, the marketplace would signal that there was too much currency in play with low interest rates from lenders, since currency would be so readily available. Therefore, another part of Keynesian economics was the idea that high inflation and high interest rates could not happen concurrently. Consistent with Keynesian theory, under Carter, the top marginal federal income tax rate was 70%. However, the inflation rate in 1979 was 13.3%, with interest at 15.5% (November, 1979).[13] Like the attempts to keep Ptolemy cosmology as the commonly-held model, additional tenets of Keynesian economics were posited to explain the observations which had previously been asserted to be impossible, should the Keynesian model be valid. But unlike the Ptolemy-Kepler transition, the arguments for the maintenance of the Keynesian model tapped into data points that had been previously neglected, or ignored. In other words, when the Keynesian narrative became untenable, its proponents appealed to the very complexity leading to the uncertainty of the macroeconomic realm where they had previously claimed mastery and validity. Whether or not these arguments are true, they do

---

11   Taleb, Nassim, *The Black Swan: The Impact of the Highly Improbable*, Random House, 2007, p. 277.

12   Schlaes, Amity, *The Forgotten Man: A New History of the Great Depression*, Harper-Collins, 2007.

13   Retrieved October 8, 2010, from http://www.wsjprimerate.us/wall_street_journal_prime_rate_history.htm

represent a profound departure from logic. Paul Krugman may approve, but Aristotle is rolling his eyes.

In 1980, Ronald Reagan was elected president of the United States (in a landslide: 489 electoral votes for Reagan, 49 for Carter).[14] In a speech given by economist Arthur Laffer entitled *The Four Pillars of Reaganomics*, Laffer asserted that two of the four key components to the economic policies of Reagan were lower taxes and a far stricter monetary policy – both concepts singularly at odds with Keynesian theory.[15] The United States economy responded with the longest peacetime expansion in history.

Were Ronald Reagan's economic policies the proximate cause of this expansion? I believe that it is intellectually safe to conclude so, but it's not scientific – any environ as mind-numbingly complex as the economy of the United States prevents the isolating of parameters and causal loops definitively. We can only generate narratives that seem to explain why historical events resulting from human decisions unfolded the way they did, and test such narratives when projecting them into future settings. On this basis, then, the free-market-centric narrative of Von Hayek and Adam Smith present as being far more robust and successful than the narratives of Keynes or Marx, who advocated systems contrary to free markets.

And yet not only is the debate far from over, the passions aroused from advocates of the various hypotheses bring an intensity to the analysis that displaces the last vestiges of the scientific approach. The same is true in micro-economics, and in management theories. The story I relayed earlier, about incurring the wrath of the Risk Management crowd, is in no way an oddity restricted to the realm of risk. Try telling a Six Sigma black belt he has no business telling a person who is not engaged in manufacturing how her business process can be improved and you will very likely receive an impassioned – if unscientific – rebuttal.

So when Eric Berne posited that people adopt narratives that structure their perceptions into a model of who they are and what types of strategies they could be expected to employ in future circumstances, he could have just as easily been referring to how workers adopt narratives that structure how their economic decisions impact their organizations as well as their specific careers. These narratives become personal – they're part of how we perceive ourselves, and expect others to perceive us. Informing a Risk Management specialist that his techniques have no relevancy past a project's baselining or planning phase does not typically lead to a dispassionate discourse on how MIS relevancy can be empirically tested in an experimental setting; rather, it's a direct challenge to their professional relevancy, the validity of their narratives – their very intellect. The same is true of Six Sigma quality specialists, Keynesian economists – like I said, it's everywhere.

I believe this is part of the reason that high-level changes in organizations are always met with a great deal of trepidation. This new Vice President – what's his narrative? Is it similar to mine? Does he have the intellectual heft to recognize what parts of his narrative have been rendered invalid by cognitive bias? Does he have a good grasp of causality? Is he quick to respond when his narrative is shown to be invalid as a decision

14   United States presidential election, 1980 (October 7, 2010). In *Wikipedia, The Free Encyclopedia*. Retrieved 04:59, October 10, 2010, from http://en.wikipedia.org/w/index.php?title=United_States_presidential_election,_1980 &oldid=389387901

15   Laffer, Arthur, *The Four Pillars of Reaganomics*, WebMemo #1311, January 16, 2007, retrieved from http://www. heritage.org/Research/Reports/2007/01/The-four-pillars-of-Reganomics on October 11, 2010.

structure when events do not unfold as he is anticipating? Does he even know what "cognitive bias" and "causality" are?

Key Narrowing Distinctions

Continuing to attempt to analyze the nature of our personal and professional narratives in relation to our experiences and events to come is becoming hopelessly broad, so I would like to narrow the confines of the discussion along the lines of how we can construct truer, more valid, and more successful professional narratives. While becoming fluent in types of cognitive biases in order to recognize them in our current narratives and root them out, as well as reading more Aristotle so as to allow the power of logic to shore up our causal analysis capabilities would be a great start, I think a more effective approach begins with the answer to the following question: Do you, as a manager, seek to force a change, or to inform a change?

To show why this is relevant, let's return to our friends, the Risk Managers. What are they trying to accomplish? Based on the *PMBOK® Guide*, "Risk identification is not a one-time event; it should be performed on a regular basis throughout the project."[16] So, as we discussed in Chapter 8, they want to stick around the project throughout its life, doing … what? Well, identifying risks, of course. And what happens when these risks are identified? And how, exactly, are they identified? Well, a description of the risk event, along with some kind of quantification of its impact and odds of occurrence are documented in some format, and transmitted to the project team's decision-makers. What happens next? Ah, this is the question that turns this discussion. If the project team's decision-makers eagerly await the risk identification analysis, consume its contents greedily, and immediately make significant changes to their previous decisions and technical approaches, then the Risk Managers (and fans of Risk Management everywhere) are ecstatic. These guys get it! Our narratives are confirmed! But, should the risk identification analysis be not so coveted, and simply take up space in a dusty binder in the decision-maker's bookshelf until such a time that an auditor wants to see if the risk analysis had taken place, then the risk aficionados are less giddy.

But why should that be so? The Risk Management-types are (presumably) paid the same amount of money for performing identical assignments. The reason is because the Risk Management crowd is, generally speaking, not content to generate an information stream that may or may not provide valuable managerial insights. They want to change the way managers *behave*. And the only way to do that is to find a way to change these managers' internal narratives, the way they perceive the structure that accounts for what has happened on the project, and what can be expected to occur.

This is the point at which management theory leaves the intellectual space where the scientific method can be brought to bear, and enters into psychological influence and manipulation (which is, incidentally, the planet where the Jungle Fighters thrive). For if the information stream provided by "risk identification" analysis can be shown to be both accurate and relevant for specific phases in specific managerial arenas, then risk identification analysis would no more need advocates among managers than Bunsen

---

16   Project Management Institute Standards Committee, *A Guide to the Project Management Body of Knowledge*, PMI Publishing, 1996.

burners would need advocates among chemists. The same is true for Six Sigma quality advocates. And Keynesian economists.

But the fact that these theories, and many, many others, do need and have advocates demonstrates that their utility is not entirely predicated on the scientific method, and have left the environs of competing information streams in the evaluation of their relevancy. I'll continue to pick on Risk Management, because its precepts are particularly vulnerable in this respect. A particular risk identification and analysis technique can be evaluated with respect to its accuracy in estimating the appropriate amount of reserves for a given project during its planning phase. But post-planning phase, the output from a risk identification system simply can't be accurately quantified. If a programmatic event occurs that was neither planned nor contained in the risk assessment analysis, then Risk Management fails open. And if an unplanned event occurs that *was* addressed in the risk identification analysis, then the only way Risk Management could be shown to have any efficacy at all would be if the project's decision-makers had responded to the event differently than they would have otherwise which, of course, is impossible to establish, much less quantify. Assessing Risk Management techniques exclusively within the realm of information stream validity, accuracy, and relevance allows usage of the scientific method; in all other cases, we're back to competing internal narratives and manipulating behavior.

Accurate, Timely, Relevant Information

The daily entry from the *Forgotten English* calendar for Saturday and Sunday, June 19 and 20, 2010, reads:

Buying Low and Selling High

On June 19, 1815, financier Nathan Rothschild started a rumor that the Battle of Waterloo had gone badly for Napoleon's enemies the day before and England's future looked bleak. Rothschild sold some of his British-backed government securities to reinforce the appearance that the news for Britain was bad. His banking competitors followed suit, dumping these same investments and causing their value to plummet. Rothschild then bought up the securities at bargain-basement prices, later reselling them at an enormous profit. Rothschild was among the first to hear – via a message carried by scandaroon (carrier pigeon) across the English Channel – that, in fact, Napoleon had been defeated at Waterloo.[17]

We see this time and again whenever some story of an extraordinary bit of success is realized, that of a decision-maker having access to accurate, timely, and relevant information before the competitors, and this information leading to decisions that bring about success. Nassim Taleb discusses the concept of the knowledge we possess versus the knowledge we need at length in *The Black Swan*, beginning on the very first page by discussing Umberto Eco's library.[18] Professor Eco's library is vast, and those who encounter it usually wish to know how much of it Eco has read. But that's not the question: the question is, how much of it remains un-read?

---

17   Kacirk, Jeffrey, *Forgotten English*, entry for June 19 and 20, 2010. Used with permission.
18   Nassim, *The Black Swan: The Impact of the Highly Improbable*, Random House, 2007, p. 1.

When presented with accurate, timely, and relevant information, even the most experienced accountant can be counted on to make the right managerial decisions. Note that I did not list "complete" information. I excluded "complete" for two reasons: we can never really have complete information, or all of the data involved in a given decision. Managers advance their competency by coming to appropriate conclusions and making the right decisions with less and less "complete" information. The other reason that the desire for complete information is a fool's errand has to do with the definition of "complete information," and the innate desire for certainty in our lives. Information that is sufficiently complete for one manager will not be so for the next, and our desire for certainty in our lives prevents any logical test for completeness from being derived, much less employed. Taleb discussed this concept at length; for my purposes, suffice to say that the pursuit of complete information is counter-productive, and a waste of time.

Some Examples of the Importance of TAR Information

Perhaps one of the most historically significant instances of the impact of timely, accurate, and relevant information occurred during World War II, at the Battle of Midway. Midway is a two-island atoll in the North Pacific, roughly mid-way between Hawaii and Japan. In April 1942, Colonel James Doolittle led 16 Army B-25 bombers off the deck of the USS *Hornet*, and bombed several cities in Japan. The Japanese military did not know where the bombers had come from (President Roosevelt's comment that they had come from "Shangri-La" was not very helpful), and suspicion fell on Midway Island. To prevent the Empire from having to endure the ignominy of another such attack, the Japanese planned to attack and occupy Midway.

The Japanese had the ships to mount a massive attack. The Imperial Japanese Navy forces included 4 heavy Aircraft Carriers, 1 light Aircraft Carrier, 3 seaplane tenders, 11 Battleships, 13 Heavy Cruisers, and multiples Destroyers, Submarines, and other craft. Against this, American Admiral Chester Nimitz could only muster 3 Aircraft Carriers (one of which, the *Yorktown*, had been severely damaged at the Battle of the Coral Sea, and had to put to sea in a partially-repaired state), 6 Heavy Cruisers, 1 Light Cruiser, and far fewer Destroyers, Submarines, and other craft. Against this apparent mismatch, Nimitz would have the winning advantage: he had more timely, accurate, and relevant information.

Nimitz's first information advantage came about when the Allies broke the JN-25 Naval Code, and discovered not only that the IJN was targeting Midway, but knew the approximate Japanese order of battle. Nimitz used this information to stage his carriers to the North and East of Midway, a position named "Point Luck," from where they could be in a position to mount counterattacks on the Japanese forces.

Nimitz's opponent, Chuichi Nagumo, had no equivalent information about the American forces. A picket line of scouting submarines was late in arriving at their stations, allowing Nimitz's carriers to reach Point Luck undetected.[19] A second attempt at reconnaissance, using four-engined flying boats to determine the presence or absence of Aircraft Carriers at Pearl Harbor, was thwarted when the submarines sent to refuel them

---

19   Battle of Midway (October 14, 2010). In *Wikipedia, The Free Encyclopedia*. Retrieved 18:22, October 16, 2010, from http://en.wikipedia.org/w/index.php?title=Battle_of_Midway&oldid=390645610

found the island to be used as their rendezvous point was occupied by American forces.[20] Finally, Japanese intelligence did detect an increase in radio traffic immediately prior to the battle, which would normally indicate that enemy fleet units were underway. The information was relayed to the overall IJN commander, Admiral Isoroku Yamamoto, who accompanied the invasion forces well to the rear of Nagumo's carriers. Yamamoto did not want to break radio silence to notify Nagumo of this information, and assumed Nagumo had also received the signal from Japan concerning the increased radio traffic. However, Nagumo's flagship, the *Akagi*, had a damaged long-distance antenna, and was unaware of this information.

So, prior to the Battle of Midway, the American commander Nimitz was in possession of information that included:

- The enemy's objective;
- Approximate positions;
- Planned timetable; and
- Strength of forces.

By contrast, Nagumo had none of these. In fact, the Japanese were unaware that *any* American naval forces were in the area until well after the onset of fighting. By the standards set out by Sun Tzu in *The Art of War*, the outcome of this battle had already been determined.

One more story about this battle illustrates the essential quality of timely, accurate, and relevant (if incomplete) information in our decisions leading to success or failure. Most of the aircraft on carriers during the Second World War were used to either attack other ships, or defend against aerial attacks. In large formations, such as the Japanese Attack Force, the job of scouting was largely performed by the seaplanes assigned to the non-carrier capital ships, such as Battleships and Heavy Cruisers. At the beginning of the Battle of Midway, on the morning of June 4, 1942, these seaplanes were assigned to various sections to search for what Nagumo thought would be the unlikely arrival of American naval forces.

The ordnance used to attack land facilities is different from the weapons used to attack naval vessels. Not suspecting the presence of naval opposition, Nagumo's first Midway attack wave was equipped with bombs for land targets. While the first wave of Japanese planes were attacking Midway, the float plane from the cruiser *Tone* was delayed in launching, due to problems with the *Tone's* catapult. The sector that this float plane was to cover included Point Luck.

In keeping with Japanese carrier tactics of the day, Nagumo had kept half of his planes in reserve, should any American naval forces arrive. As the first strike aircraft were returning to the Japanese carriers, a group of American aircraft based on Midway Island itself arrived over the Japanese task force, and bombed them from high altitude. This attack resulted in no hits or damage to the Japanese fleet, but it did underscore in Nagumo's mind the need to neutralize the Midway facilities. He ordered his reserve aircraft be loaded with land-based weapons.

As this arming was getting underway, the delayed float plane from *Tone* finally arrived at its search sector, and sent back a message that they had observed warships in the area.

---

20   Ibid.

Nagumo signaled the float plane, demanding more detailed information on the sighted vessels. Forty minutes passed before the float plane signaled that the ships appeared to be accompanied by an Aircraft Carrier.

Nagumo was now in a quandary. His first strike was re-arriving, and would be short on fuel and needing to land. His reserve aircraft were being armed with land-based bombs, but needed to be armed with anti-ship weapons in order to deal with the more immediate threat. At least in part because he believed he was facing a lone American carrier, Nagumo elected to stow the reserve aircraft, have them re-loaded with anti-ship ordnance, and recover his first strike aircraft. He could then launch a massive strike against the American naval forces, eliminate that threat, and continue with the Midway invasion.

The results of this decision would change history. Throughout the arming, disarming, recovering and refueling process, bombs, torpedoes, and gasoline lines were stored or stashed somewhat haphazardly on the decks of the Japanese carriers. Just as all of the refueling and rearming was being completed, and the first plane of the second strike was launching against the American forces, an officer on the bridge of *Akagi* announced "Enemy dive-bombers overhead!" The American dive bombers would inflict fatal damage on three of Nagumo's four carriers within the next ten minutes of battle. The remaining carrier, the *Hiryu*, would be sunk later that afternoon. The Americans would lose the damaged *Yorktown*, and one destroyer.

Much has been written about the Battle of Midway, with multiple explanations and narratives presented to help explain why the events of the battle unfolded the way they did. I would argue that the dominant factor and primary cause of the American victory was their possession of more timely, accurate, and relevant information. The Americans held no other advantage: the IJN forces were both more numerous, and their aircraft were both more numerous and of higher quality. The Japanese forces were highly disciplined and had highly capable officers. In every single category the Japanese had a clear advantage over the Americans, save one: timely, accurate, and relevant information.

The Americans knew the size of the Japanese forces, their objective, and even their approximate timetable. The Japanese were unaware of the American presence until well after the commencement of fighting. The battle may have had a very different outcome had *Tone*'s float plane not been delayed, or even if it could have avoided the 40-minute delay between discovering the American forces and reporting that a carrier was among them. Forget the all-things-being-equal qualifiers: better information will triumph, even in highly lopsided conflicts.

Back to Business

Game Theory, even when combined with Risk Management, Networking, Gamesman, or Transactional Analysis theory, simply cannot provide a structure for accurately predicting the future, and no amount of brilliance from Thomas Nash nor Isaac Asimov can change that fact. But once we abandon the idea that these theories can produce narratives that can successfully make that leap, from explaining why history unfolded the way it did over to predicting how future events will unfold, we are liberated to evaluate how these theories can describe the efficacy of information. But before these evaluations can take place, we will have to proceed from some assumptions:

- Given timely, accurate, and relevant information, the best managerial decisions become intuitive.
- Information streams can be objectively evaluated for relevance, just as they can be evaluated for accuracy or timeliness.
- Many management trends and fads have their roots in an MIS process that's relevant in one arena being transferred to areas where they are not relevant.
- Management theory is not often advanced in a Kuhn-like manner; such theories make inroads in a manner that more resembles a contagion resulting from competing internal narratives than it does an objective, empirical progression.

In moving along to Part 3, I am going to abandon as fruitless the pursuit of any managerial theory that claims to be able to predict future events or human behavior. We can, however, use these theories to better describe the causal factors behind things that have happened, in the order they occurred, and provide tests for the robustness of our organizations to deal with an unpredictable future.

3 *The Structured Solution*

Luck is the residue of design.

Branch Rickey (1881–1965), *Lecture title, 1950*

Throughout Part 1 of this book we examined the power of Game Theory, and its promise to approach the attainment of a Code of Nature when combined with Risk Management, Network, and organizational archetyping (as in Maccoby's work). Part 1 also reviewed the staggering success enjoyed by Enron during the California energy crisis as they were in a better position to play the de-regulation – of- a- commodity game than the California legislature, and the potential economic success that could be enjoyed by those familiar with the theory of games in management.

Part 2 evaluated the upper limits to the efficacy of these theories, going so far as to a near overturning of the claims of adherents of Game Theory, Risk Management, Organizational Archetyping, and virtually any structure that pretends to accurately depict future events or behaviors. As contentious as it may be, the following is indisputably true: Future events and people's behavior – other players in the game – cannot be predicted with any reliability, no matter how complex the theories purporting to do so may be. But being in possession of timely, accurate, and, most important of all, relevant information *can* position the player to win, and win consistently, even against daunting odds.

But before the executive hands the keys to the boardroom over to the head of corporate computing, we have more analyses to perform. I've posited that the key to successful management is to be in possession of timely, accurate, and relevant information. Timeliness can be measured, as can accuracy. But what about relevance? The difficulty in testing for relevance is that there is a vast array of those who, in pushing the supremacy of their particular information stream way beyond the limits of its efficacy, essentially blur the lines of relevance, clouding the issue with assertions long on passion and short on logic.

As we discussed in the previous chapter, those doing the blurring of the boundaries of information stream relevance, for the most part, are not doing so out of a desire to deceive or confuse. They have built their narratives, structures that seem to explain their past successes and failures in a consistent fashion. These narratives are invariably chock-full of cognitive biases, most centrally the confirmation bias – they know that, say, keeping risk analysts around the project team well past the creation of the baseline was the key difference in bringing the project in on-time, on-budget, and any challenge to this "knowing" can only be brought by the ignorant or incompetent. I discussed at length one of the more prevalent versions of this business-world pathology in my previous book, *Things Your PMO Is Doing Wrong*,[1] (PMI Publishing, 2008) the attempt to leverage organizational power or authority to compel the advancement of a particular capability. Managers with extensive military experience are particularly susceptible to this error, since, in their experience, that's the way things got done, and the failure to get things done in a timely manner is ipso facto evidence of failure. Their narratives are set: deviations on their part represent weakness, and opposition from without must be overcome with any and all resources on hand.

What's needed is an overarching structure, where information streams can be categorized and prioritized, evaluated with respect to their relevance, and tested for robustness and efficiency. Such a structure would also have to compensate for things as disparate as organizational culture and the interaction of the macro organization with an ever-changing, highly dynamic business environment. As we will see in the following chapters, a structure strong enough to place different information streams into their proper place in the overall information scheme – by its ability to test for relevance – while maintaining the flexibility to compensate for multiple organizations, industries, and business environs can not be one-dimensional. In order for this structure to have any relevance, it will have to allow the manager to evaluate its results with respect to all of the other components that contribute to timely, accurate, and relevant management information. And, finally, such a structure will have to account for that most coveted piece of management information: what is going to happen in the future? Or, more precisely, what future events is the organization most vulnerable to? To what events – random, or brought about by my organization's decisions – is the competition most vulnerable?

As testing for robustness or vulnerabilities in our organizations – as well as others' – leads to an ability to forecast likely future interactions, Game Theory reclaims its theoretical capacity to steer business decisions to ensure success. Note that we are completely abandoning the Von Neumann and Nash precepts of Game Theory creating a structure that allows the calculation of the most likely mixed strategies being employed by the other players in the future for a given game. By shifting the focus of Game Theory to testing for robustness or vulnerability, as well as relevance in information streams, we are not calculating Nagumo's most likely strategy: we are discovering his vulnerabilities, and positioning our management decisions to take maximum advantage of those vulnerabilities.

So, without further ado, let's explore this structure.

---

1   Hatfield, Michael, *Things Your PMO Is Doing Wrong*, PMI Publishing, 2008.

10 *Managing to the Corner Cube*

Order is not pressure which is imposed on society from without, but an equilibrium which is set up from within.

Jose Ortega y Gasset (1883–1955)

I came of age as a young Project Manager during the 1980s, when The BDM Corporation sent me on a pair of week-long Earned Value Management System courses, one taught by the Decision Planning Corporation, the other by then-named Martin Marietta Denver Aerospace. I had been assigned to perform the baselining and cost and schedule performance analysis and reporting on several US Department of Defense (DoD) contracts, and the DoD expected their Earned Value reports to be provided under a set of rules called the Cost/Schedule Control System Criterion, or C/SCSC. Most of the data I needed to process into the information that was printed on these reports I generated myself, or could go out and get on my own. There was, however, one key exception: the actual costs incurred, which had to come from the company's general ledger and its keepers, the accountants.

It didn't take me long to realize that the accountants and I belonged to two different universes, and theirs was the one where Spock has a beard.

For my start-up project, I had been told that we would need to collect actual project costs based on a Work Breakdown Structure, or WBS. The WBS is a hierarchical decomposition of the overall project's scope into manageable-sized pieces, and the Earned Value Management system would need to know how much each of these pieces of the project had spent. The company's accountants weren't keen on this, however. Why should we need multiple accounts for the same project? Wouldn't one, project-wide set of accounts do as well?

Well, no, it wouldn't, not if the project was going to be in compliance with the C/SCSC. After what seemed like an eternity of wrangling with the keepers of the general ledger, they finally allowed for multiple accounts.

But the fight wasn't over. Where they were willing to allow multiple accounts, the accountants wanted the demarcation to be centered on the various groups contributing to the project. This line of demarcation, known as an Organizational Breakdown Structure, or OBS, proved to be a far more significant barrier than the previous one, and only fell after executive intervention at the highest levels.

I took away two observations from this conflict: that the keepers of the general ledger do not have anything to do with analyzing a project's cost performance, and that they were more interested in keeping data involving the organization than any other type.

As my career as a project controls specialist continued, this conflict would arise time and again. Different people, different circumstances, different projects, same conflict. It was during this time that I began to realize that this delta between the keepers of the general ledger and the project's Earned Value specialists was inherent, but I didn't have the breadth of knowledge I needed to know why it should be so. When I started to work for Advanced Sciences, Inc., though, they had a very generous tuition reimbursement program, and I took advantage of it and went back to school to get my Master's degree in business. I didn't have long to wait before the nature of the conflict was presented, loud and clear. On the first day of the first class, we were told – without a trace of uncertainty in the instructor's voice, mind you – what the purpose of *all* management was: to maximize shareholder wealth. Whatever else we thought we were doing as managers had to be left by the wayside, for this was the overarching purpose of all management, or so it was presented. At the time I accepted this axiom at face value, confident that between then and graduation two years hence it would be made known how the Project Manager's goals, of meeting customer expectations with respect to scope, cost, and schedule, would fit into the structure that had at its summit the words "maximize shareholder wealth."

Alas, it was not to be. Meanwhile, back at my real-world job with ASI, their Finance and Accounting Department was far more organizationally influential than my pitifully small Project Controls team, and nobody thought that this was odd in the least. Fortunately for me, the Head of Accounting, Rob, was a capable, patient, and very agreeable fellow; but I don't think that even he bought in to the idea that, in a company full of project work, the chart of accounts should reflect the Work Breakdown Structure, and so the conflict continued. But I must admit that my desire to attain an MBA was only partly rooted in the idea that I needed more education to get ahead: what I really wanted was a thorough understanding of where the keepers of the general ledger were coming from, why they believed the things they did, so that I could counter their resistance with irrefutable arguments. Such an understanding, much less presentation of the irrefutable arguments, did not come about in class, or at work.

The actual epiphany came about most unexpectedly, as such epiphanies often do. I was watching a presentation by Professor Tom Peters, he of *In Search of Excellence* fame, where he was recounting a story of his attempts at checking in to a very swanky hotel. He described the décor of the foyer, its Italian marble floors and stylish accoutrement, and how expensive it looked. He approached a young lady behind the check-in desk, and asked about checking in. She looked over at a man also behind the counter – presumably the watch manager – and asked about checking in. Peters relayed, in an angry voice (I'm paraphrasing here), that the son-of-a-b*&^ didn't even look up, and said "Check-in's not until noon."

Peters went on to make the point that all of that Italian marble, all of the fancy décor was, in an instant, rendered useless by the hotel's staff and rules. And that's when it hit me: that manager wasn't saying that to be rude, and he certainly didn't want to lose a customer. It was just that he had been taught to behave that way by his superiors. And why would his superiors come up with rules like "no check-ins before noon?" Because they were managing in a way to maximize shareholder wealth, and some consultant performed an analysis that indicated that, given the size of the room-cleaning staff, expected time from last check-out to first check-in time had to be just so long in order to reach maximum efficiency.

I would hear some of Professor Peters' other stories as well, about the grocery-carrying capacity of his pickup truck, or the success of a gas station that retained pump attendants (in uniform, no less) while charging higher rates for gasoline in the middle of an energy crisis, and they always seemed to turn on the same issue, the very same conflict that I had been encountering in my interactions with the keepers of the general ledger. But the implications were huge, if I was right: not only did Asset Management and Project Management describe two very different *types* of management, but also the point of all management wasn't to "maximize shareholder wealth."

I Have Two Types … Do I Hear Three?

Starting in 1984, the CBS Broadcasting Inc. televised a show entitled "Murder, She Wrote."[1] The series starred Angela Lansbury, and was highly successful for over a decade. In fact, through its 11th season it was never rated lower than #13 overall. But, suddenly, between seasons 11 and 12, it dropped from #8 to #64 overall, and would be cancelled soon thereafter.

What happened in between the 11th and 12th seasons? One possible contributing factor and concurrent event was CBS's loss of its rights to air the games of the National Football League, or NFL, in 1993. CBS had had the rights to broadcast the games of the NFL's National Conference, which included some very popular teams. "Murder, She Wrote" aired immediately after the afternoon game, and the football game's announcers would usually make mention of that fact heading into the fourth quarter of football.

Okay, so why did CBS lose its NFL contract? They were out-bid for that contract by the Fox Network, by around $100 million. One hundred million US dollars is quite a chunk of change today, and it was even more so in 1984. Fox out-bid CBS by a significant amount, to engage in significant understatement. When two organizations are evaluating the same asset, or opportunity, and price it so differently, it simply begs to be evaluated as to why.

I have no way of knowing this, but I would speculate that what happened was that analysts at CBS evaluated the expected revenue that could be gleaned from selling advertising during professional football games, subtracted the costs of personnel, equipment, and all the other costs, such as travel, and recommended a bid amount that would allow CBS to make their target profit from the overall enterprise. And I think that Fox did something very similar, and then performed an additional analysis: the value of acquiring more overall market share, and adjusted their bid accordingly upwards.

If the conflict between the maximize-shareholder-wealth Asset Managers and Project Managers was frustrating and irksome, the loss by CBS of its NFL rights has to be considered a management science Waterloo, with the Asset Managers' analysts on the losing end. But the winner wasn't Project Management – the product, or television shows and programs didn't change significantly. The football games were what they were. There had to be another type of management in play that would explain why these events unfolded the way they did.

---

1   "Murder, She Wrote" (October 17, 2010). In *Wikipedia, The Free Encyclopedia*. Retrieved 22:43, October 18, 2010, from http://en.wikipedia.org/w/index.php?title=Murder,_She_Wrote&oldid=391263345

One Ring to Unite Them All

As these economic and managerial phenomena began to occur that couldn't be explained by the Asset Managers' narrative, the Asset Managers' narrative, in true Kuhnsian fashion, began to take on epicycles on top of their nominal cycles in an attempt to compensate for the disparities. But just as the Asset Managers' narrative relegated to axiom and cliché the unrecognized needs of the Product and Project Managers ("Quality is Job One!," cited by the Ford Motor Company, at a time when it was widely perceived that their cars were of extremely poor quality), the epicycles employed to explain moves in the strategic management realm were clearly inadequate. The Asset Managers' explanation, that the money would be made back "eventually," represents intellectual fraud similar to the Risk Managers' tactic of assigning "unknown–unknown" status to events that they did not anticipate, even as they insist their techniques can anticipate future events. A new theory of the overarching goal of management would need to be introduced, even if it overturned the theories taught by business schools Ph.D.s everywhere. And so, in a fashion that would make Kuhn proud, here it is.

There are three distinct types of management:

- Asset Management is oriented towards maximizing shareholder wealth, and seeks efficiency in the use of the organization's assets. The Return on Investment, or ROI, is a key performance indicator in this realm.
- Project Management, or product management, concentrates on meeting the customers' expectations with respect to scope, cost, and schedule. Cost and schedule performance systems, usually based on Earned Value and Critical Path methodologies, provide the central information streams that make this type of management possible.
- Strategic Management deals with market share, or where the organization stands with respect to its competitors in any given industry. (Incidentally, *none* of my, or my wife's, Strategic Management textbooks defined Strategic Management this way. They usually approached it as if it were some form of high-level Asset Management.)

When I say that these are different types of management, I do mean they differ by type, and not degree. They have different goals, and different information tools used to attain those goals. They also have their own advocates, who have built their own internal narratives based on the structures, goals, and information tools that are inherent to their management types.

Recall the discussions on the manner in which management theories are perpetuated. It closely mirrors the manner in which other types of non-scientific theories are furthered, since business, or management "theories" are highly resistant to empirical testing. The experimental environment is simply too broad: there are too many parameters. The free marketplace is far too complex to test singular parameters with respect to isolating a plausible cause and effect relationship. Therefore, any theory of management that gains widespread acceptance – like the notion that all management's goal is to "maximize shareholder wealth" – is very likely to be chock full of a wide variety of cognitive biases, particularly confirmation bias. As with Ptolemy's theories' supporters in the eighteenth century, when confronted with Kepler's ideas, I fully expect to be discounted by current management theorists; however, my theory explains more of the observed management behavior and observed economic phenomena than their theories can.

For example, consider the hostile takeover. One company buys another, most often in the same industry, and does so at an apparent loss on the acquiring company's general ledger. Why should they do that, if "maximizing shareholder wealth" was the end-all and be-all of management? In fact, since most hostile takeovers involve the purchasing of a majority share of the target company's stock at a price above its current selling level, by the Asset Managers' standards it would always be a bad idea for the acquiring company to even make the attempt, and a great turn of events for the target company. So why would the acquiring company ever seek to perform a hostile takeover, and why should the target company resist? If we remain in the realm of the Asset Manager, we can't hope to know the answer.

Only by placing the Asset Managers' point of view into a larger context can we explain the logic of the hostile takeover. The acquiring company is willing to take a loss – a reversal, if you will – in the Asset Management realm in order to make progress in the Strategic Management arena. By eliminating a competitor, the acquiring company can expect to expand its market share, and an expanded market share can be leveraged later to benefit Asset Management, i.e., to increase shareholder wealth.

Astronaut Alan Shepard was once asked what thoughts he had on the rocket that would take him into space. He replied "The fact that every part of this ship was built by the lowest bidder." It was an astute observation, implying, as it did, that the National Aeronautics and Space Administration (NASA) was more concerned about production efficiency than it was with quality. Shepard also articulated the conflict I encountered as a project controls analyst, all those years later, with the accountants: that Project (or Product) Management has different goals than Asset Management. Both Shepard and Peters were pointing out that the sense of perspective that had overtaken conventional managerial thinking – based, as it was, on the Asset Managers' model – was proving unworkable, and needed to be replaced.

Quantifying the Structure

So, if these three types of management do provide a superior theoretical structure to those currently held commonly, how does that benefit the manager? We'll begin by quantifying them.

First, take a single measurable parameter for each of the three management types, and establish their ranges. For this exercise, these parameters are:

- For Asset Management, we'll use one of their favorite (and often mis- and over-used) information bits, the Return on Investment. In this example, we'll posit the company is in an industry where the typical margin is 4%, where anything below a 2% return means the company should consider bankruptcy, and 6% is considered highly successful.
- Project Management will use the Earned Value information point Cost Performance Index, or CPI. It's calculated by dividing the value of the work accomplished by the amount of money it took to perform the work. In the Widget Project example examined earlier, the project team had completed 1,300 widgets, worth $1 each, for an earned value figure of $1,300. The accountant in that example told us that the actual costs were $1,100. This yields a CPI of 1.1818. For this exercise, we will assume that all of the company's project work has (at least) a rudimentary Earned Value

Management System, and their nominal CPI target is 1.05. Anything below a CPI of 0.85 would indicate serious project problems and endangered customer relations, and a cumulative CPI over 1.15 indicates an unusually advanced PM capability.

- For this hypothetical company, we'll posit that their current market share is 5% for either the region, or the entire industry. Industry dynamics are such that a dip in market share below 4% would represent a serious setback, and market share of 6% would indicate robust expansion.

Based on these captures, the three-dimensional model would look like this (Figure 10.1):

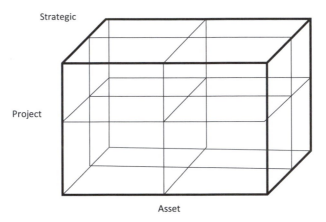

Figure 10.1 A Three Dimensional Model of the Three Types of Management

By placing the lowest acceptable figures at the origins of this XYZ graph, with the targets at the mid-points and high-ends at the extremes of the axes, the graphic of the structure looks like this (Figure 10.2):

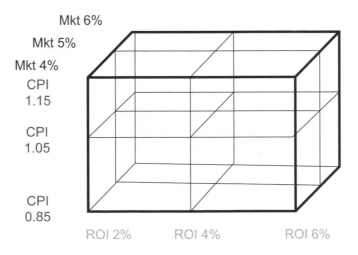

Figure 10.2 The Three Dimensional Model with Lowest Acceptable Figures

In this representation, there are eight possible placements within the model. Numbering them starting with the lowest combination, and moving clockwise, the eight possible scenarios are (Figure 10.3):

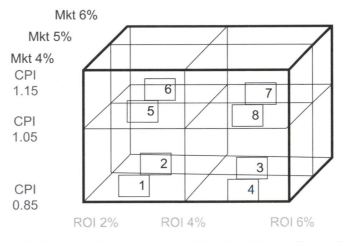

Figure 10.3 The Eight Possible Scenarios within the Three Dimensional Model

As you can see, the model appears to be a cube, made up of eight smaller cubes. The point of our enterprise-managing game, then, is to navigate through this model to the most coveted cube, the one in the corner, number seven. This is where the model gets its name, the Corner Cube model. Let's examine each of the model placement scenarios to see what they can convey with respect to the organization's health, as well as its vulnerabilities. We are assuming, of course, that the management information systems that can measure and relay our key parameters are in place and (at least marginally) operational. The vulnerabilities that are automatically introduced in the face of a lack of any (or all) of these information streams will be examined more closely in Chapter 11.

Block #1: Low Asset, Low Project, Low Strategic

This is the point where virtually all companies begin, as well as where they usually end up immediately before they end – kind of like hospitals to humans. In other words, if your organization is in this scenario, and you are not in the initial formative stages, it's time to consider how to best liquidate your assets and go out of business.

However, if the organization is in its infancy, you should orient management towards improved project/product management, or in getting to Block #5 (Low Asset, High Project/Product, Low Strategic). The vulnerabilities here are the managerial orientation temptations: if you hearken to the siren's song of the Asset Managers, and seek to increase shareholder wealth without paying attention to your customer base, you will almost certainly fail. This is why the script so often associated with new business is that of its principals investing scant savings and putting in long hours with little or no compensation, with a focus on attracting and pleasing clients and customers. Again, it's an economic and management phenomenon that can't be explained within the "maximize shareholder wealth" axiom – in fact, it presents as the exact opposite. New organizations tend to abandon expectations of any return at all in order to gain an advantage in project/product management space. They are often even willing to take short-term losses in order to build a client base. Another way of putting this is to say that they are willing to leverage whatever they can muster in assets in order to gain an edge in project/product management. Different goals, different tools, different management types.

Block #2: Low Asset, Low Project, High Strategic

This is an unusual block. It is rarely encountered by organizations in their ascendancy – what new organization captures large chunks of market share with unhappy customers and sub-par returns?

On the other hand, this is part of the path of organizations that had attained success in the past, but are on their way out. Consider the story of International Business Machines, or IBM®. Prior to the introduction of the personal computer, they were giants in the industry of providing machines – including computers – to organizations in need of automation. However, with Apple®, Microsoft®, and widespread access to non-IBM® personal computers, their product performance suffered, followed by their asset performance. In short order, they had little else than their reputation, which was eroding fast, perceived as it was as representing a moribund and restrictive management style.

This is a highly tentative octant. The organization so situated is highly vulnerable to the organizations in Blocks 5 through 8 (high project/product management scores), since unhappy customers are usually hard to retain. It's even axiomatic that it is far more difficult to attract a new customer than it is to retain an existing one. The most appropriate direction for the organization that finds itself in Block #2 is to cut down on the advertising, and bring in project/product management specialists to immediately and significantly improve the quality of the product or service being provided. From Block #2, scratch and claw your way to Block #5. Block #2 organizations are also extremely vulnerable to hostile takeovers, or other acts of aggression from competitors who are perhaps in a position to enact economic tactics that will speed the Block #2 organization back to Block #1, and thence to oblivion. Again, leverage your advantage in Strategic Management into improvements in project/product management, and do it quickly. Otherwise, well, see the discussion on Block #1 for non-startups.

Block #3: High Asset, Low Project, High Strategic

This is another unusual block, also rarely seen in new private sector organizations. It is the realm of the monopoly, where high returns are realized, large parts (if not all) of the market share are attained, but the product or service rendered is either a necessity, or is perceived to be. It's the exact opposite of a commodity, in that the suppliers are artificially restricted, usually by politics or government.

Either the organization that finds itself in Block #3 is a monopoly, or it isn't. If it is, then you might want to consider throwing a bone to the project/product management side of things. Television cable companies were notorious for treating their customers poorly – until personal satellite dishes became available. Then – wouldn't you know it? – they suddenly became far more customer-friendly. It makes me wonder how much they regretted the squandering of the opportunity to build a strong customer base, and instead created a mass of clients who patiently waited for the first viable alternative, and took it. Besides, monopolies are usually tightly restricted by the government, and in democracies and republics the nature of the government can change with an unpredictable suddenness. Building goodwill among your virtually captured clients will steel your organization against unforeseen future problems.

If your Block #3 organization is not a monopoly, I want to know: what do you have going on? Either you have some sort of artificial barrier that prevents you from encountering the consequences of delivering poor products or services, or some form of deception is in play, or both. Non-monopolistic companies that have struck special deals with governments, as well as organized crime-backed organizations, occupy Block #3. But such arrangements are notorious for being difficult to engineer and, once engineered, maintained. That's why the fictional Michael Corleone, from *The Godfather* series, sought to leverage his "advantage" in being in Block #3 into an asset windfall, and then disengage. There were simply too many threats, too many strategic competitors to keep track of, and they were all dangerous, not only to his organization, but to his family and him personally.

Block #4: High Asset, Low Project, Low Strategic

If you find yourself in Block #4, the short answer is to stop listening to your accountants and others who hold to the maximize-shareholder-wealth meme. There may be several reasons why an organization's executives would seek this block deliberately, but I can only think of two: in those instances where the company is going out of business, and is liquidating its assets, or in those cases where the organization is the target of a hostile takeover, and seeks to make itself a less attractive target.

If your organization has arrived in this sector inadvertently, immediately leverage your assets towards improving the quality or lowering the price of your products or services. The primary vulnerability of the Block #4 organization is that it is prone to being pulled back into Block #1, and from there into non-existence. The goal here is to attain Block #5 as soon as possible. And, if your accountants are telling you that everything is okay, and no change is necessary because your profit-and-loss statement indicates that you are in great shape, ignore them (or else buy them a copy of this book, and highlight this chapter). The Block #4 organization is *not* in good shape; it is, in fact, in desperate straits, and if it does not effect significant change in the near term, it's doomed.

Block #5: Low Asset, High Project, Low Strategic

This is the preferred target block for young organizations, as well as for non-monopolistic or honest organizations that find themselves in Blocks 2, 3, and 4. There is, in fact, a preferred path through this model for virtually all organizations engaged as participants in a free market economy. Assuming start-up organizations begin in Block #1, the preferred path goes through Block 5, then Block 6 (Low Asset, High Project/Product, High Strategic), before arriving at the goal of the preferred Block, the previously-mentioned Corner Cube, Block #7.

Once Block #5 has been attained, the organization is perfectly placed to leverage its strength with respect to its client base to make inroads against its competitors. The Block #5 organization, however, becomes vulnerable in the following areas:

- After having achieved a strong client base, grave difficulties await the organization that subsequently loses those customers. Recall the axiom that it is much harder to attract new customers than it is to keep existing ones; conversely, once you have lost a customer, it is extremely difficult to bring them back.
- Once you have gained a strong client base, or following, the other players in the industry will take note of you, and may engage in strategies aimed at preventing you from taking away their market share, which will tend to happen naturally. My karate instructor, Mr Phil Gilbert of the American Kenpo Karate Academy in Albuquerque, New Mexico, had instructors from other martial arts organizations in the area threaten him with violence if he didn't close his school and leave. That was over 25 years ago, and Mr Gilbert and his school are still there; still, there have been multiple instances of vandalism and break-ins. I'm not saying that all Block #5 organizations should fear for their safety; just that the other players in the industry can be counted on to take note of organizations with a good client base, and may respond in ways designed to keep the Block #5 organization from further success.
- Block #5 organizations are also vulnerable to the gravitational pull of Block #8 (High Asset, High Project, Low Strategic). The options before the Block #5 organization's executives involve leveraging the strength of a good client base to one of two purposes: better strategic standing (Block #6), or better Return on Investment (Block #8). Work towards your strategic goals from Block #5, and ignore your accountant's advice to wring more profit out of the organization. Electing to improve your Asset Management goals, either through efficiencies or pricing decisions, may endanger your client base. As noted in the first bullet, once a customer is lost, it's hard to get them back.

Note that the recommended path through the model is a further rebuke of the maximize-shareholder-wealth approach. Of the three types of management, this model, along with the preferred path, indicate that Project/Product Management should come first, followed by inroads in Strategic Management, with Asset Management's goals coming in dead last. Not only is maximizing shareholder wealth not the ultimate goal of all management, it's not even an equal among the other types' goals. Indeed, the organization that suddenly makes a profound change in emphasis away from Project/Product or Strategic goals and towards Asset Management goals is signaling that it's in decline.

Block #6: Low Asset, High Project, High Strategic

This is the next preferred step in the progression. Most tactics in improving the organization's strategic stance, or where it is in relation to its competition, involves marketing and advertising initiatives, but there are others. Recall the discussion of the Hawk–Dove Game, the 100-bird variant. In that game we have a population of 100 nominal birds, who can either act passively ("doves") or aggressively ("hawks"), with aggressive action defined as devoting energy into preventing the doves from keeping the food they have foraged, or from even foraging in the first place. The payoff for the entire population of birds is maximized when they all act like doves. However, the introduction of just one hawk disrupts the payoff matrix. The Nash Equilibrium in the 100-bird Hawk–Dove game comes out to an approximate 25–75 split, meaning that our nominal birds reach the Nash Equilibrium when they employ a mixed strategy of 25% hawk, 75% dove. In a nominal strategic management scenario, a passive strategy would mean doing little or even nothing to your competitors and, as we have seen, in a two-bird (or few bird) Hawk–Dove game, the doves die out rather quickly.

Of the three management types, Strategic Management most closely resembles the scenarios proposed in Game Theory. In fact, many of the games that are used to evaluate Game Theory precepts are based on problems germane to Strategic Management, such as the variant of Hawk–Dove that pertains to whether or not an established company should actively hinder or remain neutral to a new company attempting to break into the established company's industry. I believe the Game Theory has significant sway in this area because the payoff matrices can be quantified down to the single variable, market share. The invalidating effects of mixed payoffs are significantly lessened, but the possibility of Black Swan events remains. In the next chapter I will cover the efficacy of management techniques and information streams in supporting advances in Strategic Management, and will discuss the utility of Game Theory in those techniques and information streams at that time. For now, suffice to say that positive actions must be taken to improve market share to move to Block #6 from Block #5. And don't bother threatening Mr Gilbert to try and make him abandon his karate school – it won't work.

Block #8: High Asset, High Project, Low Strategic

I've skipped Block #7 for just a moment, because it's the ultimate destination in the Corner Cube model. The organization that finds itself in Block #8 is going to have a more difficult time making it into Block #7 because of the threat of losing customer base, and returning to one of the 1–4 Blocks. The competitor who sought to enter Block #6 from Block #5 did not weaken his commitment to his client base by extracting too large a profit, or by threatening quality by seeking efficiencies in his product or service. If you find yourself in Block #8, and you are confident that your customer base has not been compromised, then by all means put energy into pursuing your strategic goals, and slide into Block #7.

If, however, you did increase your margin by pursuing actions of reducing costs or pricing so as to increase profit, your organization is vulnerable to having customers leave you for your competitors. Seeking to maximize that old shareholder wealth without a thorough understanding of the organization's place in the industry where it does business is short-sighted and foolish. It's being introduced into a Hawk–Dove game and not only failing to know what the most appropriate mixed strategy might be, it's not knowing what strategies are likely to be employed by the other players. Block #8 is very tenuous, but its fragility won't be conveyed to you by your accountant. On the contrary, based on his interpretation of the profit and loss statement, the organization is in fine shape. It's not – it's vulnerable, particularly to Black Swan events. The non-monopolistic organization that finds itself in Block #8 should immediately leverage that coveted advantage in Asset Management space to shore up its (probably short-lived) advantage in project/product management, and then seek to improve its strategic standing. (Theoretically, no organization involved in commodities, or where the supply and demand curve approaches that of the commodities market, could ever be in this Block. Customers in the age of advanced world-wide access to pricing information would not remain happy with a company if the exact same good or service was available from a different supplier with a lower return.)

Block #7: High Asset, High Project, High Strategic – the Corner Cube

Well, you've made it. You are on the high side of each of the management types' goals you had set for yourself. But before you congratulate yourself and relax, you should know that this is not a very stable Block. Organizations that are particularly susceptible to technical advancements (and what industry isn't?) will not stay in Block #7 very long if they are not on the leading edge of innovation in the industry, and innovation is probably the hardest element to anticipate. The very finest organizational (or personal) narratives, devoid of cognitive or confirmation biases, which most accurately describe why past events unfolded the way they did and appear to be highly successful in describing how future events will unfold, are nevertheless completely vulnerable to the uneven advance of technology. Just think of all those risk management consultants who had absolutely no idea that this book, which essentially reveals that certain parts of their management science is fraudulent, would come out. No doubt they will, in hindsight, attribute it to an "Unknown–Unknown" risk event.

It is because of this vulnerability that smart non-commodity organizations leverage their advantage in all three areas of management into pursuing goals in innovation via research and development. It's why the United States Department of Energy spends billions of dollars on their national laboratories, and why pharmaceutical companies spend similar amounts in their research and development efforts.

When I first posited the triple types of management,[2] I wrote that the organization that has successfully made it to the top of the model should re-evaluate its parameters and assumptions that went into the first model, and start over. While I still believe that that's a good idea, I also believe that organizations place insufficient emphasis on innovation at their own risk. To not be a player in the innovation sector of a given industry is to be consigned to the receiving end of whatever innovations are developed by the competition. Only in extraordinary circumstances will your competitor develop technology that is advantageous to anyone but themselves, at least in the short term.

Note also that the whole innovation topic – of bettering existing products or services, or introducing new, novel ones that perform the same job better – lives exclusively in the Product/Project Management realm, since it addresses goals that are oriented towards attracting and keeping customers. I take this as evidence that the assertion that the seeking of Product/Project Management goals over and above the goals of the Asset Managers – particularly in the early stages of the organization's evolution – was valid. I'm not saying that the Asset Managers' notions are completely invalid – obviously no organization can fail to realize any return at all and stay in business for long. But engaging in tactics that maximize shareholder wealth all too often makes the organization vulnerable to competitors and unhappy customers. The only safe way to pursue such tactics would be to have timely, accurate, and relevant management information streams that could

---

2   Hatfield, Michael, "Managing to the Corner Cube," *Project Management Journal*, March 1995.

inform the organization's decision-makers of where they were in the Corner Cube model, so that they could back off the wealth-maximizing tactics the nanosecond the other types' indicators showed trouble.

More on the Overall Model

I believe that there is an inherent conflict between efficiency and robustness. Taleb joked that if an MBA (presumably, the ultimate in Asset Management practitioners) had ownership of a human body, he would want to sell off a kidney, since the human body has four times the kidney capacity it is believed to need.[3] If the Corner Cube model shows anything, it indicates that pursuit of maximized profits leads to efficiency in the organization's assets, but it also introduces vulnerabilities that can be exploited and that can lead to the organization's downfall. Table 10.1 summarizes the advantages and vulnerabilities inherent in the Corner Cube model's positions.

Table 10.1   Corner Cube Model Summary

Corner Cube Position	Advantages	Vulnerabilities
Block #1 (Lo Asset, Lo PM, Lo Strat)	None; this is where organizations begin, and where they end.	Stands to lose just the initial capitalization – there's literally nothing (or not much) to lose.
Block #2 (Lo Asset, Lo PM, Hi Strat)	For young organizations, none. For those on their way out, the high market share can be leveraged to increase liquidation value, particularly as a takeover target.	Retaining high market share with low project/product performance is virtually impossible, except by deceit. This organization is vulnerable to its competitors, even the ones just entering the industry.
Block #3 (Hi Asset, Lo PM, Hi Strat)	If the organization has lived in this Block for any length of time, it is a monopoly, which usually brings many advantages.	Monopolies are not vulnerable to anything, except innovation. A non-monopoly in this octant is vulnerable to any organization – even newcomers – that can out-perform them in PM space.
Block #4 (Hi Asset, Lo PM, Lo Strat)	None, unless you are positioning yourself as the target of an acquisition.	Multiple: these organizations have been heeding the Asset Managers, and are now poised to reap the whirlwind.
Block #5 (Lo Asset, Hi PM, Lo Strat)	Many: these organizations are well placed to leverage their strong client base into strategic advantages.	Two: losing the commitment to the customer base that got you here, and the temptation to begin to glean profits prematurely.
Block #6 (Lo Asset, Hi PM, Hi Strat)	Many: these organizations are finally positioned to increase margin safely.	One: losing the customer base that enabled the move into a strong strategic stance.
Block #7 (Hi Asset, Hi PM, Hi Strat)	Strongest, most robust possible position.	Sudden, unexpected changes in the industry, like a competitor's innovation.
Block #8 (Hi Asset, Hi PM, Lo Strat)	Should be poised to move to Block #7.	Long-term residence in this sector is fatal.

---

3   Taleb, Nassim, *The Black Swan, The Impact of the Highly Improbable*, Random House, 2007.

Recall the discussion from Chapter 8, on how organizations develop narratives that appear to explain how and why events they have encountered unfolded the way they did, and the attempts to flip this narrative from explaining the past into what can be expected in the future. Also, recall the singular deficiencies in Risk Management's techniques to add to or refine such narratives, no matter how many probability-based cycles and epicycles compound the techniques. When combined with the Asset Manager's approach, it creates a perfect storm of organizational vulnerability to Taleb's Black Swan events. Think about it: the Asset Managers are constantly pushing for greater efficiency, greater return from the existing assets. These tactics, as we have seen, are only appropriate when the organization is in a very specific place with regards to the Corner Cube model: in all other instances, it is the exactly wrong approach. Blindly following the maximize-shareholder-wealth approach is to ignore the other types of management. It also introduces vulnerabilities to future events, events that cannot be reasonably anticipated, no matter what the Risk Managers say.

In the arena of managerial theory, the Asset Managers' and Risk Managers' techniques have combined to form an unholy, complimentary alliance. The Asset Managers push relentlessly for efficiency, which introduces layers of Strategic and Project/Product (client base) vulnerabilities. Not to worry, say the Risk Managers: use our techniques, and we can anticipate those future untoward events, enabling you to mitigate, avoid, absorb, blah blah blah. However, as I discussed in Chapter 8, the Risk Management techniques simply cannot perform the predictive capability they claim. And, if you don't accept Chapter 8 as a positive refutation of Risk Management techniques (as currently practiced), then Taleb absolutely nukes the use of Gaussian Curves – the very basis for Risk Management techniques – in his book, *The Black Swan*. Not to put too fine a point on it, but the Kuhnsian cycles posited by the maximize shareholder wealth advocates, layered with the epicycles of the Risk Management "experts," represents an economic theory that has to be considered an obsolete management structure, and an invalid narrative.

Yes, I'm aware that I have, in essence, just accused thousands of business school professors and risk management consultants of being flat-out wrong. No, I do not anticipate that they will be gracious in their attempts to refute my arguments. Yes, I'll stop writing in a manner that implies I'm being asked questions by an unseen person.

Other Model Parallels

When Freud posited his personal internal structure of Id, Ego, and Superego, he theorized that the Id was completely self-contained, oriented solely towards satisfying the needs of the inner person. He also asserted that the Ego was oriented towards relating to other individuals in such a way as to satisfy the base needs of the Id, and that the Superego sought personal perfection.

Eric Berne's structure, as presented in *Games People Play*, is similar.[4] He argued for a Child–Adult–Parent structure, where the child was completely self-absorbed, the adult had advanced to where it could interrelate to others, and the parent sought perfection in the self and in their offspring.

---

4   *Games People Play* (book) (October 15, 2010). In *Wikipedia, The Free Encyclopedia*. Retrieved 01:41, November 1, 2010, from http://en.wikipedia.org/w/index.php?title=Games_People_Play_(book)&oldid=390848556

My assertions are somewhat similar. In my types of management, the Asset Manager's goals are oriented towards the assets already contained within the organization. The Project/Product Manager's orientation is towards the organization's customers, attempting to satisfy the self-centered needs of the Asset Managers by interacting with the customers in the outside world. The Strategic Manager's functions are performed in order to keep up with, if not overtake, competitors.

In Chapters 3 and 7 we also evaluated how the Maccoby and Bartle archetypes resembled each other, but also how they (roughly) mirrored Freud and Berne (Table 10.2).

Table 10.2   Aligning the Archetypes

Freud	Berne	Bartle	Maccoby	Hatfield	Characteristics
Super Ego	Parent	Achiever	Gamesman	Strategic	Overarching; seeks perfection
Ego	Adult	Socializers, Explorers	Craftsmen, Company Men	Project/Product	Focus on Peers, Customers
Id	Child	Killers	Jungle Fighters	Asset	Self, primal, internal focus

We have seen how both the individual and the macro organization create and deploy narratives that attempt to bring a rational structure to three areas:

* Who we are and how we are different from the others we encounter in our environs; why the things that have occurred in the past unfolded the way they did; and
* (Where we often get into trouble) by flipping the narratives from explaining the past across the present-day timeline, and now explaining how future events are likely to unfold.

Notice how the functions of the narratives align with the other triad classifications we are evaluating. The first function of the narratives, explaining who we are to ourselves, is inwardly-focused, just like Freud's Id, Berne's Child, and the Asset Manager. The second function, of placing causal links onto the events that have happened to us in the past, deals with the way we encounter the world around us, external to the person or organization, just like Freud's Ego, Berne's Adult, Bartle's Socializers, and Product/Project Managers. And finally, the third function of the narratives, to provide a structure for anticipating future events, resembles the higher functions of Freud's Superego, Berne's Parent, Bartle's Achievers, and the organization's Strategic Managers. It simply defies common sense that these similarities are coincidental.

Since both the individual and the macro organization employ such narratives, all I have done is to align the experts on how these narratives tend to fall into certain categories as they pertain to the individual, and project them onto how they can manifest in the larger organization's narrative. Like the individual's narrative, the larger organizations can be chock full of cognitive biases, based on the timeliness, accuracy, and (most of all) relevance of the information streams that feed those narratives. And yet it must be noted that the accuracy of the organization's narrative has little to do with its influence over the likely choices of its decision-makers. Have you ever wondered why a political conservative and a liberal can observe the exact same set of historical events, and not only come away with diametrically opposite conclusions on the reasons the events unfolded as they did, but conclusions from which they cannot be dissuaded? The answer lies in the highly personal nature of those narratives. Recall that these narratives' first function is to tell us who we are. Should a significant error exist in that script, it would mean that at least some aspect of who we tell ourselves we are is in error, and recognizing and correcting that error would perhaps lead to some source of pride now becoming a reason to feel ashamed. The Id/Child is powerful and primal, and its response to any perceived attack on its very essence can be counted on to be similarly powerful and primal, which is perhaps the reason that politics and religion are often considered taboo topics of conversation among diverse populations of adults. When marked differences in people's narratives become obvious, the disagreeing parties never say "That's not the way I interpreted those events, nor the causal analysis I overlaid on them as they became part of my narrative." Rather, denigrating the other person's intelligence becomes a particularly tempting tactic, since we are almost always certain that *our* narratives have been picked clean of any cognitive or confirmation biases. Our sense of perspective simply *has* to be accurate. World views and narratives that contradict our own *must* be the result of sub-standard mental faculties, or nefarious motives, or both – otherwise, we would have to take a long, and, more importantly, hard look at the possible faults in the way we constructed our personal narrative, which would very likely lead to a realization that our decisions have been influenced by an error-filled narrative.

The so-called theories of management science, coming as they do from the narratives of the macro organization, can be just as powerful, and just as prone a primal backlash when they are challenged (as I found out the first time I wrote a column that challenged the underpinnings of the Risk Management crowd's practices).

Since I have been arguing that many of the theories in the current management science codex have far outstripped their boundaries of relevancy, you can imagine the level of disservice these management theorems' advocates have wrought on the organizations that have accepted their ideas as insightful. It's simply astonishing – recall the fair coin flipping discussion in Chapter 8, how the risk analysis techniques, by their own definitions, can contribute absolutely nothing to the narrative on why things that have happened, happened the way they did. And we are supposed to believe that these same risk analysis techniques suddenly acquire accuracy and relevancy when they are used across the timeline, into the future?

Yet the allure of knowing what's in the organization's (and individual's) future is so powerful that managers are not only willing, but eager, to employ whatever so-called management theory that gives the slightest hint of being able to do so. In Dante's *Divine Comedy*, soothsayers are damned to walk around with their heads on backwards, never being able to see even the ground in front of them. We laugh at what primitive peoples did in order to get some idea of future events and the consequences of their decisions, from teenaged girls inhaling volcanic gasses (the Oracle at Delphi), to reading tea leaves, staring at crystal balls, dealing out tarot cards, even analyzing the look and feel of animal entrails. An old management science axiom is that which is measured, is managed. To measure the future is to manage it, and to manage the future is to master the universe. At last check, there's room for only one master of the universe.

One of my all-time favorite karate instructors (and people), the late, great James Joseph Dwyer, had a constant mantra during training for kumite:[5] "Don't anticipate!" Why not? Because if the opponent does not behave in a manner highly consistent with what you are expecting, you become extremely vulnerable to what he actually does. Robustness in response is a far superior approach in kumite than attempting to accurately anticipate your opponent's next attack, or response to your attack. The same holds true for the organization engaged in the free marketplace.

On Ingesting a Corner Cube

If all of what I am positing is true, the combination of these assertions would provide some very stark challenges to the narratives behind much of what passes for current management science. The good news is that I'm not asking anybody to change their organization's narrative, or even their own personal one. It's axiomatic that change in the macro organization is painful – why should that be so? Could it be because challenging the organization's familiar script, and seeking to re-write major sections of it, is as painful as the kind of life-changing event that leads to individuals re-writing their own narratives? (Think George Bailey in *A Wonderful Life*.)

This is where Game Theory in management becomes most relevant. Forget about Game Theory's ability (or lack thereof) to predict the likely strategies and choices of others for any given "game." As we reviewed in Chapter 6, it can't. But … what if it could be used to signal vulnerabilities in the organization? The integration of Game Theory into management science could become very powerful indeed.

But, vulnerabilities against what, exactly? Why, the very vulnerabilities documented in Table 10.1, which can be expected to occur at very specific times in the organization's maturation cycle, and under very identifiable circumstances. And that's the beauty of it: we don't have to push any changes onto the organization, pain and all. We don't have to attempt to persuade others of the efficacy of our logic, the validity of a new narrative that may challenge both the organizational and personal scripts of all who are affected. All that's required is that we accumulate some very relevant (and, of course, timely and accurate) information, and, just like Spruance at Midway, the best decisions will become clear.

The use of relevant information streams to identify (and, hopefully, remediate) weaknesses in the organization is not confined to those organizations that take what I have argued to be the optimal path through the Corner Cube model, 1 to 5 to 6 to 7. For example, if it is the manager's decision to have her organization immediately seek to capture market share, and then leverage that into a cash windfall through, say, allowing a buy-out, then the use of the Corner Cube model, along with certain key information streams, can help make that happen, too, as we will see in the next chapter. If the unread parts of Senor Eco's library represent the information the manager needs to deal with future events in a robust fashion, but a whole lot of information that the manager does not need to know as well, then the Corner Cube model is analogous to the card catalogue, pointing out where the needed unknown information resides, and how to get to it.

---

5   Kumite is where opponents actually line up across from each other, and fight.

Tom Siegfried wrote in *A Beautiful Math* that "Game theory was created to provide a mathematical language for describing social interaction."[6] I hold this defining statement to be as hopelessly broad as Webster's definition of economics. I mean, seriously, by this definition "Veronica visited her mother seven times in September" would qualify as being part of Game Theory. To be fair, Siegfried's assertion of why Game Theory was created may very well be accurate, but it is not accurate to say that that's what Game Theory brings to the table. In keeping with the practice of returning types of information streams to their original banks, where they were relevant prior to hitting advocacy-backed flood stages, we will be confining Game Theory to its point of maximum relevance and utility, that of testing for strengths and vulnerabilities within the organization as it strives for its next target in the Corner Cube model.

Certainly there will be opposition to the adoption of the Corner Cube model. As was previously discussed, the advocates of Generally Accepted Accounting Principles, Risk Management, Six Sigma Quality management, Game Theory, Agile, Scrum, Project Management, Capability Maturity, Critical Chain, and a myriad of other so-called management theories cannot be considered ready and willing to take that long, hard look at their narratives, weed out the cognitive and confirmation biases that have led them to promote their theories well outside their nominal relevancy range, and accept a new (or, perhaps, former) role in the overarching structure of all things managerial. After all, people have made fortunes off the idea that it is perfectly appropriate for, say, Six Sigma techniques to leave the production room and invade business processes that have nothing to do with producing manufactured goods. And, taking a step back from even that, the notion that the role of management has far more to do with making the most appropriate decisions, as opposed to enacting behavioral change within the macro organization, must be considered radically outside current managerial science thinking. Corner Cube theory cuts to a circular, chicken-or-the-egg type argument: does the current management science meme center on changing the behavior of the macro organization because the Asset Managers have held sway in the arena for so long, or have the Asset Managers been considered the most insightful because of the popularity of the idea that changing behavior is the primary focus of management? I frankly do not know, but I do know that superior information streams – that is, information streams that are aligned with their areas of relevancy – lead to superior decision-making, and superior outcomes. When the maximize-shareholder-wealth zeitgeist dominated business schools, the only way to improve organizational performance was to eek better performance out of assets, and those assets most able to suddenly improve performance happened to be the organization's personnel. That improvement usually had to be accompanied by some change in the human resources' personal narratives, at the very least the addition of the epicycle that suggested that failure to adopt the new, improved management science idea would lead to negative personal consequences, and/or positive results, should the new idea be embraced.

Then Project Management came along, offering the notion that meeting the customers' expectations had, at the very least, some sway in the overall scheme of how to improve the economic performance of organizations. Even though the Project Management Institute® was founded in 1969, and its famed credential, the Project Management Professional®,

---

6   Siegfried, Tom, *A Beautiful Math, John Nash, Game Theory, and the Quest for a Code of Nature*, Joseph Henry Press, 2006, p. 175.

was launched in 1984,[7] business schools are, as of this writing, still teaching the maximize-shareholder-wealth supremacy theory. But then, Nobel Prizes in economics are still being handed out to Keynesians, creating a perfect storm of generations of MBAs walking out of academia and into the marketplace with a full suite of profoundly flawed theories and tools of inference. No wonder they, and the organizations that hire them, are afflicted by Black Swan events – completely unexpected, and of significant consequence, usually negative.

The ideas of Project Management were dramatically furthered, interestingly enough, by the United States Government, when it issued the Cost/Schedule Control System Criterion guidelines in 1967.[8] I suppose the government got tired of its contractors failing to focus on the expectations of the agencies doing business with them, and responded by mandating such a change in orientation. Even so, many of the organizations that were forced to comply with the C/SCSC did so, for the most part, unwillingly. To this day, many organizations, both inside and outside the US Government contractor industry, view Project Management as an optional approach to executing their business goals. As discussed in Chapter 5, the Project Management Institute even went so far as to commission and publish a book, *Quantifying the Value of Project Management*,[9] which attempted to demonstrate the value of implementing Project Management precepts. This "value," of course, was "demonstrated" by attempting to prove that the creation of Project Management Offices, or PMOs, had a positive Return on Investment (ROI). However, the ROI is an Asset Managers' tool. In essence, PMI was attempting to establish that its advocates should be considered more vital members of the decision-makers' team based on the parameters of the Asset Managers. As a long-time member of PMI®, and one of its early PMP®s, I found this approach highly disconcerting. I felt then – and do now – that PMI®'s approach should have been one of strongly asserting the Project Management technical approach to management, and seek to overturn the Asset Managers' narrative. When was the last time anybody saw an article on why the maximize-shareholder-wealth theory was justified using the Project Managers' tools of Earned Value or Critical Path analysis? The very fact that such an analysis is impossible should be taken as evidence that the Asset Managers' and Project Managers' *types* of management are profoundly different, with different goals and tools. And yet, there was the Project Management world's biggest and most widely-recognized advocate, trying to gain traction for their ideas using the other team's metrics. Disappointing, to say the least.

One has to wonder if an identical tome would have been written by the advocates of Asset Management. My guess would be, umm, no. Just imagine the organizational power that would flow to the person who delivered the information stream considered most vital to the organization's decision-makers. Such a one could punch their own proverbial ticket.

Ironic, isn't it? The Asset Managers' technical approach is to enact initiatives that maximize the return on the organization's assets, i.e., change the behavior of the personnel. But they want nothing more than to be considered the ultimate source and residence

7   Project Management Institute (October 4, 2010). In *Wikipedia, The Free Encyclopedia*. Retrieved 04:50, November 7, 2010, from http://en.wikipedia.org/w/index.php?title=Project_Management_Institute&oldid=388684936

8   Earned value management (October 11, 2010). In *Wikipedia, The Free Encyclopedia*. Retrieved 04:55, November 7, 2010, from http://en.wikipedia.org/w/index.php?title=Earned_value_management&oldid=390018364

9   Ibbs, William, and Reginato, Justin, *Quantifying the Value of Project Management*, Project Management Institute, 2009.

of the information streams that most profoundly influence executive decisions. Are we seeking to change behavior, or provide information? It can't be had both ways – unless nobody is looking at the underlying narratives, and testing them for their relevance.

Parallels with Crossing the Chasm

In 1991, HarperCollins published Geoffrey A. Moore's book *Crossing the Chasm, Marketing and Selling High-Tech Products to Mainstream Customers*. This book came to be known as a classic business book, and was described as "still the bible for entrepreneurial marketing 15 years later" by Tom Byers, Faculty Director of Stanford Technology Ventures Program.[10] Moore discusses how many business plans are based on a traditional Technology Adoption Life Cycle, portrayed as a bell curve of customers who are classified as Innovators, Early Adopters, Early Majority, Late Majority, and Laggards, representing, left-to-right, areas under the bell curve. The nominal approach to marketing products is to capture each of these classifications of customers, in the specified order. However, Moore posits that there are "chasms" in between the customer classifications, particularly between the Early Adopters and the Early Majority. To attract the Early Majority customers, and cross the chasm, Moore argues that the organization focus on a single market, called a *beachhead*, and dominate it so that it can be used as a springboard to expand into adjacent extended markets.[11] He also argues pointedly for niche marketing as the most effective, disciplined way of capturing the customer classifications to the right of the Early Adopters. Once these have been captured – the Early and Late Majorities, and the Laggards – the product can then be priced in such a way as to produce maximum revenue before it ends its product life cycle.

There are several parallels between Corner Cube theory and the ideas set forth in *Crossing the Chasm*. While Moore does not posit a clear distinction between Asset, Product/Project, and Strategic management, his recommendations are very similar to my suggested optimal path through the Corner Cube model. The optimal path through the model, 1 to 5 to 6 to 7, represents a focus on Product/Project Management first, in order to create a satisfied customer base – the Early Adopters. Then, I wrote that the organization should focus on Strategic Management, and not Asset Management (yet). The pivot in focus from Project Management to Strategic Management involves taking actions with respect to competitors, while maintaining the Product/Project Management strength that attracted your client base in the first place. What I'm calling a pivot in focus is identical, I believe, to Moore's Chasm-Crossing. However, where Moore calls for a modification of the organization's behavior (which, presumably, would represent a modification of their internal narratives, and all the hazards accompanying such modifications), I am advocating for the creation of specialized information streams that would provide the basis for more informed and intelligent decision-making.

One of the analogies Moore uses in his book has to do with the Allied invasion of Europe during World War II, at Normandy (what's with these management theory writers and their fixation on World War II battles?):

---

10   Crossing the Chasm (June 30, 2010). In *Wikipedia, The Free Encyclopedia*. Retrieved 21:48, November 11, 2010, from http://en.wikipedia.org/w/index.php?title=Crossing_the_Chasm&oldid=370934080

11   Linowes, Jonathan S., "A Summary of 'Crossing the Chasm,'" Parker Hill Technology.

Our long-term goal is to enter and take control of a mainstream market (Eisenhower's Europe) that is currently dominated by an entrenched competitor (the Axis). For our product to wrest the mainstream market from this competitor, we must assemble an invasion force comprising other products and companies (the Allies). By way of entry into this market, our immediate goal is to transition from an early market base (England) to a strategic market segment in the mainstream (the beaches of Normandy). Separating us from our goal is the chasm (the English Channel). We are going to cross that chasm as fast as we can with an invasion force focused directly and exclusively on the point of attack (D-Day). Once we force the competitor out of our targeted niche markets (secure the beachhead), then we will move out to take over additional market segments (districts of France) on the way toward overall market domination (liberation of Europe).[12]

I like the analogy, but I believe it supports my argument of creating change through the use of relevant information systems, as opposed to modifying organizational behavior or changing the internal narrative. In the lead-up to D-Day, Eisenhower was, of course, concerned about the morale of his troops, the size of his armies, and the quality or number of his weaponry. But his overriding concern was that the Germans be kept ignorant of the specific times and places the Allies would land their invasion craft. He knew that if the Axis armies had accurate intelligence of the specific beaches, or even the general area (Normandy), his invasion would be repulsed into the English Channel. Eisenhower spent considerable energy keeping that information secret, and providing misleading information. Papier-mâché tanks and aircraft were parked in airfields north of the intended invasion zones, to give the impression that materiel was being amassed for an invasion of Calais. George Patton, widely (and rightly) considered by the Germans to be the Allies' best general, conspicuously stayed in hotels in London to convey the notion that the invasion was not happening any time soon.

Another parallel in *Crossing the Chasm* has to do with the recommended post-crossing behavior of the organization. Note the sequence of targets: Innovators to Early Adopters, across the chasm to the Early and then Late Majorities, and, finally, the Laggards. This is very similar to the optimal path through the Corner Cube: first, the Product/Project Management focus on the early customer base (Cube 1 to Cube 5); then, the pivot to increase market share (Cube 5 to Cube 6); and then (and only then), with the majorities captured, a focus on maximizing revenue, or shareholder wealth. Recall also the discussion earlier in this chapter of the vulnerabilities of the organization that has actually attained the Corner Cube, Cube 7 – innovation. *Crossing the Chasm* goes ahead and makes the assumption that the product will follow the nominal product life-cycle curve, which may very well be the case in product management. Corner Cube theory addresses organizations, which may or may not follow a particular maturity model, but are more ongoing concerns than specific products. Different structures, but almost identical paths to success.

And, finally, probably the best, most appropriate use of Game Theory – in any model or context, really – has more to do with becoming informed as soon as possible of the selected strategy of the other players, instead of computing odds and predicting the most likely selection of known strategies from the other players. The Germans believed that the odds were that Eisenhower would land in Calais, and positioned their forces

---

12   Moore, Geoffrey, *Crossing the Chasm*, (Second edition), HarperCollins Publishers, New York, 1999, p. 66.

accordingly. Because that was not the strategy the Allies adopted, the German response to the real landing site was insufficiently robust to prevent it from happening. Two pieces of information – June 6, 1944, and Normandy – were far more valuable than all the analysis and all the estimated odds before the fact put together. An informed response is a robust response – as long as that information is timely, accurate, and relevant.

The Wrap-Up

This is the first chapter of this book to exceed 10,000 words. We've covered a lot of territory, and I felt the number of new ideas being introduced needed to be covered to a certain depth, since they do appear to fly in the face of much of what passes for modern management science. So, let's recap.

The long-held meme that management's ultimate and all-encompassing purpose is to maximize shareholder wealth is singularly flawed. As a testable theory, it simply can't explain why many economic and business events and phenomena have occurred the way they did. As with Ptolemy's theory of the ordering of the cosmos, additional cycles and epicycles have been proposed to try and support the current widely-held theory, but there are obviously other things going on that can't be explained, even with the expanded versions of the theory. But, according to Kuhn, the existing theory can't be simply dropped – it has to be replaced by one that seems to better explain the wider data set.

I have dubbed that replacement Corner Cube theory, and it is predicated on the idea that there are three different types of management, each with its own goals and information tools used to achieve those goals. These three types are Asset, Product or Project, and Strategic Management. Since these three types of management are so different from each other, it follows that the use of an information tool from one type in another arena will provide irrelevant information, and yet such mis-application is fairly common (more on this in Chapter 11).

Since there are relevant information systems for each of the three management types, it is possible to quantify parameters for each that represents unacceptable performance, target performance, and exceptional performance levels. These three scales can then be assembled into an XYZ-style performance model, one that truly measures the performance of the entire enterprise. This model resembles a cube, made up of eight smaller cubes representing a specific placement of the organization's performance with respect to its expected performance.

The specific scoring, or placement within the model, provides crucial information with respect to the vulnerabilities of the organization. In *The Black Swan*, Taleb argues for improved robustness for the organization, in order to better deal with unexpected, high-impact events, and points to Senor Eco's library of unread books to make the point that it is the unknown information that constitutes the greatest danger to the organization. By clearly defining the three different types of management, measuring their performance with timely, accurate, and relevant information streams, and then combining these information streams into a single model, those vulnerabilities can be known and managed.

The Corner Cube model resembles other models of psychology and organizational behavior and performance, which also posit three distinct modes of thinking, orientation, or behaving. From Eric Berne's Transactional Analysis theory, we learn that individuals maintain a script, or a narrative, that tells them who they are. I believe that this narrative has two other functions: (1) explaining to ourselves why historical events unfolded the way they did, via causality analysis, and (2) to predict what will happen to us in the future, based both on what we experienced in the past, but, more importantly, the causal analysis we assigned to events from the past. This narrative can be very difficult to change, even in light of direct evidence that singularly refutes part of the narrative.

Organizations also maintain narratives, for the same reasons individuals do, and overturning parts of the macro-narrative can also be very difficult to do, even in the face of direct refuting evidence. Feelings follow attitude, and attitude follows belief. Our beliefs drive the narratives we maintain, so that implementing change within the organization that requires identifying a particular flawed inference, tracking down which parts of the narrative are based on it, and then replacing the affected parts of the narrative with a more accurate version is difficult in the extreme.

A superior alternative to effecting change in the manner described in the previous paragraph is to create and maintain the information streams that allow far more robust responses to events as they occur in real time, rather than attempt to use information systems that appear to quantify future occurrences, and then press for efficiencies. The informed decision, or response, is a robust decision, as long as the information is timely, accurate, and relevant. It must be all three of these things; otherwise, the organization becomes vulnerable to devastating, or even fatal, Black Swan events.

So, how, exactly, can all of these ideas taken together improve the organization and its performance? This is what we will take up in the next chapter.

11 *Corner Cubes and Robustness*

The wise are instructed by reason; ordinary minds by experience; the stupid, by necessity; and brutes by instinct.

Cicero (106 BC–43 BC)

The main obstacle to creating and implementing the information streams that will allow for both tests of robustness within the organization and for optimally-informed decisions is the mis-application of management information systems into areas where they are no longer relevant. But advocates of these systems further their techniques and practices beyond their nominal boundaries of relevancy because such furthering is consistent with their internal (or organizational) narratives, and the very worst thing one can do in trying to influence others is to imply that their internal narratives are, in any way or in any part, irrelevant.

But the brutal fact is that management information systems require resources and time to set up and maintain, and pursuing information streams that are not timely, accurate, and relevant is to waste that time and those resources, as well as to remain ignorant of the very information required to achieve success in any even remotely competitive environment.

When confronted with evidence that their technique or MIS is woefully inadequate for the job it was intended, defenders of the irrelevant MIS will inevitably resort to the argument that, for this particular information need, there was nothing in place previously, and the current system, no matter how flawed, is certainly better than nothing. This is sophistry of Cecil B. DeMille proportions. An untimely, inaccurate, or irrelevant information stream is worse than useless, since it both provides a facade of validity while actually being misleading. It's the equivalent of the World War II German high command going over the data and analysis that showed why the Allies would most likely land at Calais, and confidently basing their decisions on that analysis. There is an old Turkish saying: it's never too late to turn back from the wrong road. I would adapt that to: it's never too late to abandon or dramatically modify an irrelevant information stream.

Another disingenuous dodge that often comes up when an information stream is shown to be irrelevant presents as the question, "Well, why wouldn't you want to know that information?" The answer, of course, is that information takes time and resources to collect the data, process the data into information, and deliver the information in a timely and accurate fashion, and in a manner that the receivers can readily digest. Wasting time and resources on irrelevant information streams is, well, a waste. Nagumo needed to know the whereabouts of the American aircraft carriers; the number of barnacles on the bottoms of their hulls was irrelevant, and, therefore, a waste of time and resources should he have sought it. And it was his not knowing this most relevant information, while Spruance was in command of the information on the Japanese's disposition that spelled doom for the Imperial Japanese Navy fleet at Midway.

On Useless MBAs

There apparently is a whole generation of market analysts known as "quants," short for quantitative analysts, who are gifted mathematicians and statisticians. Their job is, generally, to go over massive amounts of data in order to tease out a causal link between observable trends in market behavior. So coveted and prevalent have the quants become, that traditional Masters of Business Administration degrees, with their emphasis on finance, accounting, and micro- and macro-economics, are increasingly viewed as undesirable in the field of advanced market analysis. This is, of course, ironic in the extreme. For starters, the very first lesson in every initial statistics class I've ever had was the notion that correlation is not causation. And yet, here are these analysts, poring over vast amounts of data in order to ascertain some sort of correlation, and immediately overlaying a causal loop onto them in order to provide a narrative that can be flipped from explaining how history unfolded over to how future events will unfold. The negating factors of our personal narratives, and our organizational narratives, of cognitive or confirmation bias have been replaced by the invalidating influences of the fact that correlation is not causation. It's as if thousands of modus ponens arguments have been unleashed onto millions of points of data, looking to capture them in their logical structure and produce a valid conclusion, or even a truth. Wall Street firms think it's great, but Karl Popper is rolling his eyes.

In *The Black Swan*, Nassim Taleb likened this business behavior to snatching nickels from the near path of oncoming steamrollers, and I think he has a point. Without knowing the performance of the organization along the three types of management, or even acknowledging the different types, a certain organizational myopia sets in, and leads to vulnerabilities that invite Black Swan events. As Taleb asserted, we tend to view Black Swan events as having been predictable after the fact, even though, by definition, they are not. Now consider how that happens on a micro basis. The asset managers observe what transpires, and, with the gift of perfect hindsight, point out how the organization could have handled the situation more efficiently. Their confirmation bias sets in and, when combined with the tendency to view Black Swan events as having been predictable, this aspect of management pseudo-science becomes even more entrenched in their narrative. In their 1975 book *The People's Almanac*, Irving Wallace and David Wallechinsky included an article entitled "The Trillion Dollar Rat Hole."[1] The article listed a series of public works and construction projects that could have been performed for $1,000,000,000,000 (one trillion US dollars), while still leaving a significant amount of money for defense – an amount that the author clearly believed to have been sufficient. Look how the effects of after-the-fact analysis twist the author's logic. The modus tollens structure is:

---

1   Wallachensky, David, and Wallace, Irving, *The People's Almanac*, Doubleday, 1975, p. 652.

- If the United States military is too weak, the nation will be attacked.
- The United States has not been directly attacked since World War II.
- Therefore, the military was not too weak.

This represents a valid argument (though the initial premise may not be completely sound). But the additional assertions point to a perspective that the United States had spent far too much on defense since the end of World War II, assumed to be true because the United States had not been directly attacked. The validity of the initial premise evaporates, since there was absolutely no way of knowing which ship, airplane, missile, or even bullet represented the point at which potential attackers went from planning a direct attack to being dissuaded from doing so. For example, the last full year of peace prior to the United States being pulled into World War II, 1940, defense spending was a suicidally low 1.7% of Gross Domestic Product (GDP). As discussed in Chapter 2, even Yamamoto knew that if more of America's industry was devoted to defense, it would become a "giant" on the world stage. But, at 1.7%, America was clearly vulnerable in a rapidly militarizing world, with some pretty bad players coming to power overseas. By 1941 defense spending had increased to a still inadequate 5.7%, with sharp increases during the war years. It never dropped below 5% again, and the United States did not endure a similar sneak-attack until September 11, 2001. However, had the United States followed the advice of this article's silly author,[2] defense spending between 1946 and 1975 would have remained below 7%, with many years below 5% and even 2%. This *Almanac* contributing editor looked at the (relatively) peaceful years following World War II, and lamented the allegedly wasted resources devoted to defense. He or she elected to not make the connection, the causal loop of a strong military dissuading potential enemies from attack, and integrated this non-connection into their narrative, leading to a conclusion that the United States could have spent more on social programs (automatically assuming such spending is beneficial, thereby committing the syllogism of Begging the Question) without recognizing the concurrent lapse of robustness.

Similarly, asset managers watch how their organizations interact with outside market events and forces, and assume that the outcome would have been identical had the organization been less robust, and more efficient. It's profoundly illogical, but it's a meme that appears time and again in modern management science teaching.

The quants suffer from the same problem that the asset managers do, at the point where they attempt to flip their narratives from explaining the past over into predicting the future. And, on occasion, they'll even admit it. Check this discussion on sensitivity analysis from *Quantitative Models for Management*:

SENSITIVITY ANALYSIS

One of the assumptions we have made in our discussion of linear programming is that the values of the parameters of the problem are known with certainty. We assumed, for example, that in the extended Argo-Tech problem the objective function coefficients were 18.5, 20, and 14.5, respectively … But the values of these parameters are not always known with certainty. For example, changes in the cost of materials, cost of labor, or price of a product would cause

---

2   The authors of articles are usually identified in *The People's Almanac* by their initials, but no initials appear on this article (though there is a mention that the piece was written "Based on material by Vince Copeland").

changes in the coefficients. On the resource side, delayed shipments from suppliers, strikes, spoilage, and other factors all lead to changes in the supply of resources. Each of these changes could affect the optimal solution to the original LP problem.[3]

"But the values of these parameters are not always known with certainty."[4] It would be more accurate to say that the values of all of the relevant parameters is *never* known with certainty, and yet the entire field of quantitative analysis in management is predicated on the idea that in most instances, the values of all the parameters can be known with certainty and, in those instances where they can't, some sort of "sensitivity analysis" can be invoked to save the analysis. I would argue that this is a myth, and I would project that Taleb and Popper would agree with me.

Another trend that erodes the effectiveness of traditional MBAs has to do with the lack of boundaries to the knowledge and the techniques being taught. It's as if the epistemology of management specialties has never even been considered. Recall the discussion on my classmates while I was pursuing my MBA, and how, after becoming familiar with a particular aspect of business, they would peel away to pursue that specialty, convinced of its primacy in the management world. Of course, we expected each of our professors to be a specialist in their field, and to be enthusiastic about their expertise. But never – not even once – did any of them step up, and tell the class "This is where on the management science map these ideas hold sway, *and this is where they don't add a thing to the decision-making process.*" Newly-minted MBAs come off the assembly line knowing, say, how to read a balance sheet, but (probably) with no idea that Generally Accepted Accounting Principles bring next to nothing to the realm of project management. This ignorance is both bad for the MBA, and the organizations they are attempting to support. Recall also the struggles I recounted, about being a young project controls specialist and having to fight the accountants excessively to get my project's actual costs collected by Work Breakdown Structure, instead of by Organizational Breakdown Structure. The accountants were simply so enamored of their knowledge and expertise that they could not be easily persuaded to accommodate the project managers' most basic business information needs.

To be intellectually honest, though, I must now admit that I don't perceive an outer boundary to Corner Cube theory as it pertains to management science, but there's a difference here. When the Asset Managers assert that the whole point of management is to maximize shareholder wealth, they are actually reducing the realm of management to a certain set of confines – kind of like what happens in the whole Game Theory realm. When successful organizations make decisions that do not appear to have anything to do with maximizing shareholder wealth, the Asset Managers' narrative cannot plausibly explain them. What Corner Cube theory does is to argue against such confines, and posit an almost infinite realm on the outside of the organization, one where the organization interacts with that wide-open realm in one of three ways. These ways mirror psychological models, with the several parallels noted in the previous chapter. Just as Game Theory sought to engineer circumstances so that options available to the players were reduced to a quantifiable amount, with the rewards and punishments also reduced via quantification in order to arrive at valid conclusions and truth, so, too, do the various specialties in

3   Davis, K. Roscoe, and McKeown, Patrick G., *Quantitative Models for Management*, Kent Publishing Company, Boston, MA, 1981.
4   Ibid.

management science seek to reduce that world by excluding the events and occurrences that cannot be reconciled via their theories. Recall also the results of the Ultimatum Game, when it was tried out with real people and real money. The actual outcomes virtually never matched the mathematically calculated predictions and, when they didn't, the reason was ascribed to "cultural" differences that the model hadn't taken into account. In short, the model was not sufficiently expansive to adequately reflect reality, just as much of today's management science is insufficiently broad to reflect what goes on in the free marketplace. And yet management school graduates – and their professors – have profound confidence that not only do their techniques and knowledge exhibit high degrees of effectiveness, these people do not appear to have ever sought to discover the limits to the arenas where their ideas hold sway. This is what makes the proposition of doing exactly that so unattractive: these people's livelihoods and future income streams are predicated on the perception that their knowledge and techniques are valuable across broad applications, and any assertion to the contrary isn't going to be welcomed. Ah, well, let's just plunge in, and see how much trouble we can get in to, shall we?

Limits of Asset Management Information Streams

The title of this section alone was fun to type. Here are the areas where Generally Accepted Accounting Principles, or GAAP, contribute to overall management information:

- Number, amount, and value of the macro organization's assets.
- Amount and nature of the organization's liabilities.
- Value of the organization's equity, and who holds it.
- Amount of money coming in to the organization.
- Amount of money spent by the organization.
- When the organization is likely to have states of higher or lower liquidity.
- The profitability (or lack thereof) of the organization.

But unless GAAP information is combined with information from the other management types, *that's it.*

Of course, much insightful management information can be gleaned from combining these elements. There's no denying that these elements, both singular and combined, can be essential to such decisions as to whether or when an organization should issue an initial public offering (IPO), or decisions on whether, when, or even how to expand or contract. But without input from the project or strategic management, asset management information can't perform many of the functions it claims to cover completely, like how much inventory the organization should have. Without some notion of Product/Project Management and Strategic Management, there's no way to accurately anticipate demand for the organization's products or services, and without knowing approximate demand, the inventory decision must be made with woefully incomplete information. Don't misunderstand – I'm fully aware that many (if not most, or even all) of the decisions that managers make are made with incomplete information. But the use of untimely, inaccurate, or irrelevant information returns us to the problem of maintaining a facade of an informed basis of decision. The issue here is that techniques exclusive to GAAP have been asserted far beyond their most appropriate range of relevancy. Consider this quote from *Introduction to Management Accounting (Fourth Edition)*:

> *The accounting system is the major quantitative information system in almost every organization. An effective accounting system provides information for three broad purposes: (1) internal reporting to managers, for use in planning and controlling routine operations; (2) internal reporting to managers, for use in strategic planning, that is, the making of special decisions and the formulating of overall policies and long-range plans; and (3) external reporting to stockholders, government, and other outside parties.*

****

> *Management accounting is concerned with the accumulation, classification, and interpretation of information that assists individual executives to fulfill organizational objectives as revealed explicitly or implicitly by top management.*[5]

The first quote reveals that, like Corner Cube theory, Management Accounting believes it has three target customers. But, unlike Corner Cube's triad, Management Accounting's information customers are all internal to the organization – a highly limited grouping. The second quote contains the assertion that Management Accounting is "concerned with the *interpretation* of information that assists ... executives to fulfill organizational objectives ..." (italics mine). The collection and interpretation of the information streams that the organization's decision-makers need and use to attain their objectives is certainly not confined to the internal domain of the organization. This is indisputable (using logic, anyway), and yet asset management techniques are often invoked outside of the asset realm.

For example, consider the Return on Investment, or ROI. For reasons that elude me, this calculation has been used to assess the value of things that have nothing to do with assets in-hand. As discussed earlier, PMI® has used it to support the creation and maintenance of Project Management Offices, or PMOs. In my view, to invoke the ROI calculation in the Project Management realm is to cede the intellectual high ground to the Asset Managers, at the very time Project Management specialists ought to be dominating the management science debate.

There are many derivative formulas to calculate the ROI, but common to them all is the central parameter of the most basic version: expected return. What is the expected return? On an asset like corporate bonds, it's the stated return minus the impact involved in the odds of default. For government bonds, it's the stated return, minus the odds of default plus the inflation rate, since governments are in a position to print more money and thereby default on their creditors. What are the odds of those things happening? Who knows? The Risk Managers? They can't possibly know, but they will never admit as such. Consider commercial paper traders who become rich on so-called junk bonds. What's the definition of a junk bond? That's a corporate bond that offers a high rate of return, but is considered risky. Again, considered by whom? Risk analysts, of course, so that if anyone should become adept at identifying high-yield bonds where these risk analysts erred in classifying them as being at high-risk for default, then that person is almost guaranteed to become rich. It's unfortunate that such insightful ones are somehow considered devious

---

5   Horngren, Charles T., *Introduction to Management Accounting, (Fourth Edition)*, Prentice-Hall, Inc., 1978.

at best, and criminal at worst. Why the negative connotation? Because they profited from betting against those who derive bond default risk classifications, and won? What you have, in essence, are two scenarios: one where the expected value is known (the stated rate of return on the bond), but the odds of it being realized are uncertain; and the other most often involved in the ROI calculation, where the expected value can't be known, but the odds of it being realized (whatever "it" is), are pretty predictable. The junk bond dealer is excoriated, but the everyday ROI calculator is considered insightful. Amazing. Once again, there are simply too many parameters involved (and only one has to be mis-cast to utterly invalidate the entire analysis) to accurately calculate an expected value or odds of default that would enable a precise and accurate (read: usable) Return on Investment calculation, which would lead to truly informed decision-making.

And yet, the ROI calculation has somehow achieved Litmus Test status, the key arbiter for all efforts undertaken by the organization (a Yahoo! search on "ROI" and "Project Management" returned 1.62 million hits in November 2010). This is a highly dubious meme perpetrated by Asset Management advocates throughout organizations. That is, organizations poised to be stricken by Black Swan events. I would love to attend a debate between the ROI advocates, and the Six Sigma proponents, both of whom believe they should be the final arbiters of which business processes deserve consideration, and those that don't. What are the top executives to make of information from the Asset Managers, who claim that a certain project or acquisition has a negative Return on Investment, when the Six Sigma guys are simultaneously asserting that the exact same project requires an infusion of resources in order to bring about a favorable end, from a Quality Management point of view? It would come down to whose input is considered more valuable and, based on traditional management science, the fall-back position always goes to the Asset Managers. Without the perspective provided by the Corner Cube model, what other choice can be expected?

The "expected future revenue" parameter makes a comeback when Asset Managers are calculating opportunity costs, except, in this instance, they are compared to "expected future costs." It's unfortunate that when politicians spend tax monies, they obviously have absolutely no concept of opportunity costs, which are defined as "… the *maximum* available contribution foregone by using limited resources for a particular purpose."[6] Otherwise they may be less inclined to advertise how those taxes are being spent. But, with no alternative to the new federal office building offered up, the new federal office building just looks like a gift – provided by the politician, of course. Nobody need know that the same amount of money spent at, say, the Center for Disease Control could have brought about a breakthrough that made everybody's life a few pennies better every day.

But in the business world, managers are (usually) acutely aware of opportunity costs, and this piece of information is often used in making decisions about the organization's future. But should it? The whole concept of "expected return" and "expected costs" bear a striking resemblance to the Drake Equation analyzed earlier, which supposedly provided a positive value of the odds of extraterrestrial intelligence in the universe. As with the Drake Equation, both expected future revenue and expected future costs depend on little more than rank speculation. And rank speculation does not suddenly assume prescience just because it's CPAs who are engaged in it.

---

6   Ibid, p. 116.

Look at how expected future costs are assessed – they are estimated. But, according to AACE (the predecessor to AACEI), the best possible estimate, performed by a professional estimator with off-the-shelf software, is accurate to within 15% of the final project's costs. Decisions made using ROI or with considerations of expected costs often turn on far more precise parameters – a swing of a percentage point, or two. Even if one concedes that the expected cost data point is not rank speculation, a la the Drake Equation, the *very best* it could hope to return is 15% accuracy, and that's with a considerable investment in resources and expertise. Leaving aside the scarcity of professional estimators in the typical organization's accounting department, the use of these tools in an attempt to quantify future market conditions or events is far riskier than is generally accepted. They simply don't work as advertised, and, when they do, they are not nearly as precise or accurate as they purport to be.

Another highly irksome intrusion of the Asset Managers has to do with their interactions with the Product/Project Management folks. As discussed previously, when asked what the final costs will be of a particular project, they will employ devices such as performing regression analysis on the project's actual cumulative costs, compare original budgets to actual costs on a detailed basis, or try to re-estimate the remaining work, add that figure to the cumulative actual costs, and pretend to present relevant information. All three of these analyses are profoundly flawed, and yet continue to be incorporated in organizations even today.

Take a look at performing regression analysis on actual costs. This is as questionable a technique as it is popular. The script here would appear to be one of equating a given project team's spending behavior with their performance against project objectives, and I would argue that such a script is utterly bereft of logic or reasonable causality. And yet the Asset Managers will confidently take this flawed structure for explaining how observed events have unfolded the way they did, and take that step of flipping over the time-now line, and pretend that the resulting data takes on the mantle of valid information. The data derived from performing a statistical regression analysis on a project's cumulative actual costs provides two symptoms of uselessness: one, it's an asset management technique trying to perform in the project management realm, meaning it's irrelevant; and, two, the narrative being projected going forward includes fatal flaws in its function to explain how past events unfolded, meaning it's invalid. In addition to these two shortcomings, this technique shares the unattractive characteristics of appearing to provide usable information, while it is actually misleading, as well as taking time and energy to collect the data and perform the analysis, time and energy which would have been better spent on truly usable information.

As for comparing budgets to actual costs, this technique actually does have a relevant function: that of evaluating the accuracy of the budgets. It's also part of the equation to calculate depreciation. But, again, this technique has been extended far beyond its areas of relevancy. The aforementioned *Introduction to Management Accounting (Fourth Edition)* can't get seven pages into the first chapter without asserting that this is the method for evaluating cost performance.[7] As discussed using the Widget Project example, comparing budgets to actual costs simply can't provide relevant information regarding cost performance. The Earned Value information is central to this piece of management information. Without Earned Value, there is no way to capture cost performance, as the

---

7   Ibid, p. 7.

Widget Project example showed so clearly. And yet the asset managers persist. *Introduction to Management Accounting (Fourth Edition)* was written by Charles T. Horngren, who is both a Ph.D. and a C.P.A., and is associated with Stanford University.[8] It's hard to get more mainstream in the arena of management science principles than that. And yet, in my opinion, he's simply wrong.

Misapplication of the estimators' skills makes another appearance here, though it could have easily been placed in the project management section. As we have seen, the Return on Investment and the calculation of opportunity costs require an evaluation of expected value or expected return which, in turn, relies on some form of estimate. These estimates are often inaccurate, even when performed by professionals using top-notch software, which, in my experience, is a rarity. Most often they are performed by low-to-mid-range analysts, using spreadsheets, meaning that their accuracy rate rarely approaches the 15% level. The next-level estimate, known as a budget estimate, has an accuracy range of 25% to 40%, which means that it borders on useless. Recall that an information stream must have all three characteristics of validity: timely, accurate, and relevant, and the estimators' product often fails to be accurate. And, harsh as this may be, it is, therefore, often invalid – except in some very specific areas, which we will come to.

Memory, the Mirror, and Anticipation

Management Information Systems are usually predominantly feed-back or feed-forward, but can sometime manifest characteristics of both. Feed-back systems have the following attributes:

- The data elements are matters of historical fact – they've already happened, and can be quantified.
- Data so collected can be processed into information using known methods (though, as we have seen, these methods are often expanded well beyond their nominal ranges of relevancy or accuracy).
- Feed-back systems are based on objective data.

Conversely, feed-forward systems have the following characteristics:

- The data elements are comprised of projections.
- Data so collected cannot be processed into information using trustable methods.
- Feed-forward systems are based on subjective data.

Another way of defining feed-back and feed-forward systems is that feed-back systems help to construct the narrative that describes why history unfolded the way it did, while feed-forward systems attempt to provide the narrative of how things can be expected to unfold in the future. Asset management systems are based on feed-back, meaning that they are singularly ill-suited to predict the future. It falls to reason, then, that any attempt from asset management information streams, based on GAAP, to predict the future are probably going to fail the accuracy test.

---

8   Ibid.

Consider how feed-forward and feed-back systems mirror the Berne archetypes. Feed-back data points are used as fodder for piecing together how history unfolded, and are assembled into narratives that tell the macro organization who it is. Based on the narrative supported by feed-back information streams, the attempt to flip it forward, to describe the most likely future scenarios, supported by the subjective, feed-forward information streams, becomes the basis that serves as the foundation for decisions that determine the organization's future direction. Feed-back systems create the narrative, and feed-forward systems anticipate when similar circumstances and scenarios appear, and how the ensuing events will unfold.

However, only in the realm of Project Management does past performance provide a strong and reliable indicator of future performance. In all other areas the ability to flip the narrative from accurately describing why past events occurred the way they did over to providing a model for anticipating how the future will come at us is highly suspect, and defies a usable and consistent quantitative structure. Caleb, from *East of Eden*, may have recognized that investing in beans as the First World War breaks out was a good (if fictional) investment, and I have a friend who benefited greatly by adjusting his investment portfolio towards Northrop-Grumman and Halliburton at the onset of the Gulf War. But, as they say, you can get away with these things now and then, but you can't make a living off of them. Such insights do not lend themselves to all-encompassing economic truths: speculating in commodities is one of the riskiest acts in all of free-market participation. And, most importantly, these insights do not and cannot come from analyses completely rooted in Generally Accepted Accounting Principles. They must be fed from other types of management.

Which brings us to: what happens when we look at ourselves in the mirror? Do the biases behind our internal narratives keep us from seeing the evidence and facts that might lead us to seriously examine those parts of the narrative that may be invalid, or obsolete? And, if that is happening on a personal basis – as it almost certainly is – what does that mean for the macro organization, with all of those individual biases coming together in large teams?

Generally speaking, GAAP provides relevant and accurate information when using its feed-back type information streams to tell the organization about its internal characteristics. As soon as the asset management analyst attempts to use those techniques (like Return on Investment or Opportunity Costs) that rely on a feed-forward element, they suddenly swerve into irrelevancy or inaccuracy. This inaccuracy and irrelevancy becomes all the more acute when feed-forward-based GAAP techniques are used to provide information streams on subject areas external to the organization, such as Product/Project Management or Strategic Management (Table 11.1).

Table 11.1   Asset Management Information System Efficacy

Asset Management MISs	Internal	External – Customer	External – Competition
Berne Archetype	Child	Adult	Parent
Corner Cube Type	Asset	Product/Project	Strategic
GAAP – feedback	Relevant, Accurate	Irrelevant, Inaccurate	Irrelevant, Inaccurate
GAAP – feed-forward	Relevant, Inaccurate	Irrelevant, Inaccurate	Irrelevant, Inaccurate

Referring to Table 11.1, note that the sole area where GAAP provides both relevant and accurate information is when the techniques used are based on feed-back type systems with the purpose of providing information internal to the organization. When attempting to provide information internal to the organization based on feed-forward type systems, the information is still relevant, but the difficulties involved in predicting the future (or "flipping the narrative") makes such information more suspect. Past these areas, though, Generally Accepted Accounting Principle techniques take on enough irrelevancy and inaccuracy aspects as to render their output unusable.

Again and again, it comes down to information. Relevant, timely, accurate information. All things being equal on the information front, the organization with the most bias-free narrative will win most of the time. But, if things are not equal on the narrative front, the organization with the most timely, accurate, and relevant information will win every time.

Limitations to Project Management Information Streams

Project Management is not without its limitations. Compared to the asset managers, though, they have had approximately 500 fewer years to assert their supremacy in the arena of management science ideas. The Project Management Institute® was founded in 1969, and its first certification, the Project Management Professional®, was initially issued in 1984.[9] They now boast over 350,000 PMP®s.[10] These PMP®s must pass an examination that covers the nine (formerly eight) sections of the *Guide to the Project Management Body of Knowledge*, or *PMBOK® Guide*. These areas include:

- Scope.
- Cost.
- Schedule.
- Risk.
- Communications.
- Human Resources.
- Procurement.
- Quality.
- Implementation/Integration.

I do not know who came up with these areas of management as the building blocks of Project Management. Knowing PMI® as I do, my bet would be that it was done by committee. I do not agree that all of these topics should be considered the essentials of Project Management. I want to examine each of these nine areas, to evaluate if and where PMI®'s technical approach has been extended past its boundaries of relevance. And, in the arena of Project Management, it all begins with scope.

---

9   Project Management Institute (October 4, 2010). In *Wikipedia, The Free Encyclopedia*. Retrieved 06:24, November 27, 2010, from http://en.wikipedia.org/w/index.php?title=Project_Management_Institute&oldid=388684936

10   Ibid.

Scope

Scope Management is entirely predicated on the ability to fully and clearly define the product, project, or service being undertaken by the organization. Without a clear definition of the organization's intended output, it's impossible to assess how much the output will cost, or when it can be delivered. All project management-based information streams depend on the scope management piece being performed adequately.

Work that should be managed as a project has the following characteristics:

- It has distinct scope, i.e., an independent observer can ascertain if the intended work has been completed (as distinct from a function, or an asset).
- It has ascertainable beginning and ending dates.
- Resources are dedicated to the work.
- A single person (or organizational entity) is responsible for the work.

Often work that does not meet all four of these characteristics should still be managed as a project, but work that does meet all four is best managed as such.

The main technique involved in scope management is the decomposition of the overall project into smaller pieces in a hierarchical structure known as a Work Breakdown Structure, or WBS. The WBS is usually documented in the following formats:

- A graphic chart, resembling an organization's line management relationships, except instead of indicating which departments report to which executives, the graphics indicate the parent–children relationship of the decomposed project work.
- A WBS Index, which lists the number and title of each WBS element.
- A WBS Dictionary, which is a WBS Index with a relatively short description of each element in the WBS Index.
- Work Packages and Planning Packages, documents that describe in detail the work associated with the most detailed (or lowest) level of the WBS. Work Packages and Planning Packages belonging to the same parent are often combined to form Control Accounts.

Based on the detailed description of the scope, cost and schedule, estimators can create their respective baselines that allow for control of the project.

Outside of project scope management, the technique of decomposing work into smaller, more easily evaluated pieces is common among quality analysts and industrial engineers, most often with the goal of making a given function or organization either safer or more efficient, or both. However, once a technique's given goal is no longer oriented towards improving performance from the customer's point of view, it's a sure sign that we're no longer talking about project management. In this case, since the decomposition technique is being used on functions or organizations in order to improve aspects that are internal to the organization, we have stepped back into the realm of the Asset Managers. That's okay, just as long as everybody's clear on the topic of which Corner Cube area is being addressed or evaluated.

Schedule

Much information system chicanery occurs in attempting to manage a project's schedule. The only valid manner to manage all but the very simplest project's schedule is through the Critical Path Method, and there are no exceptions. Critical Path involves estimating the duration of accomplishing the scope detailed in the Work Packages, and then establishing which pieces of work must be accomplished before other pieces can begin. When these pieces of work have been linked in sequential order, they are said to have *schedule logic*, and a critical path network can be established to calculate total planned project duration. There are many off-the-shelf software packages that can accommodate and calculate these networks, varying in degree in ease of use and robustness.

The Critical Path Methodology is particularly powerful in its ability to tell the future. There's no narrative flipping, either – CPM does it with (mostly) objective data. For example, suppose an activity for pouring a building's foundation was originally estimated to take 30 days. On day 15, the scheduler contacts that activity's manager and asks for an estimate of how much progress has been made. The manager measures how much concrete has actually been poured, and informs the scheduler that the activity is 30% complete. The scheduler dutifully enters this piece of data into the CPM software, re-calculates the schedule, and, voila!, the building's foundation will not be completed on day 31. Rather, at the current rate of performance, the foundation will not be done until day 50, so that all of those activities' managers who were planning on showing up on day 31 assuming they could start their activities because the foundation would be finished need to be contacted and told to wait an additional 20 days.

Of course, there are limits to this predictive power. Rates of performance can and do change (though, as we saw earlier, no more than 10% in either direction once the activity is 20% complete), and Critical Path can only provide this information within the project management realm. The acid test here is the ability to assess an activity's percent complete. Obviously one can't glean percent complete on the engineers' department, or from an asset. But as long as we recognize where CPM is relevant and accurate, the fact that it uses mostly objective data in a feed-back-type system means that its ability to accurately depict the timing of future completion dates is matched by no other information stream or technique.

But that certainly doesn't mean that simpler, but invalid, techniques won't give it a try. Recall that all legitimate information streams' architecture can be reduced to the following model:

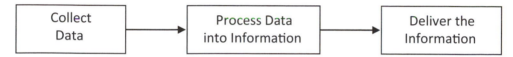

Figure 11.1 Valid MIS Architecture

Probably the most common invalid MIS structure is a poll. Mapped out, it looks like this (Figure 11.2):

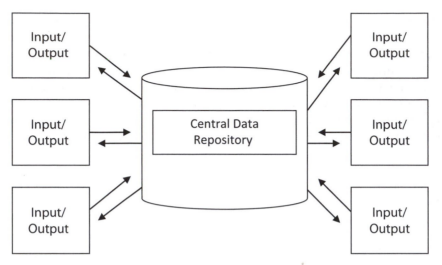

Figure 11.2 Invalid MIS Structure

This poll-type structure is the basis for uncounted milestone lists and action item trackers. There are several problems with this structure, including:

- Note that no actual processing of the data into information is taking place. It's simply a raw data repository.
- There's rarely any discipline involved in the data being entered. In the case of milestone lists, "updates" are invariably a given manager's opinion about whether or not she will meet her deadline. Even if said manager is aware of a problem, it's a rarity for her to self-identify early, preferring to believe that the problem(s) can be addressed and corrected before a deadline is missed.
- It's very difficult to evaluate the data with respect to its timeliness. One of the problems with the so-called information coming out of a poll is that there's always someone with better, more recent data, and they may or may not have entered (much less superseded) the obsolete data in such a system.

The use of poll-type structures in an attempt to manage a project's schedule has a particular consistent, almost comical, manifestation. The milestones are set up at the beginning of the macro reporting cycle, usually an organization's fiscal year. Since these milestones are for the whole year, most of them come due towards the end of that time. At the end of each micro/reporting cycle (usually monthly), the owning managers are contacted to gauge their opinion if they will meet their deadlines or not. Almost always they will answer that the milestones will be met on time under the following circumstances:

- They honestly believe that the milestone will be met on time.
- They recognize problems exist, but believe these problems are too minor to impact completion dates.
- They recognize deadline-threatening problems exist, but believe they can be remedied in time.

In fact, the usual case is that the owning manager will not readily self-reveal a schedule problem unless and until a delay cannot be avoided or covered up. This leads to the output of the poll-structure system indicating that all is well up until the closing reporting cycles of the milestones' baseline, when early trouble signs begin showing up in the reports. Finally, in the closing cycle of the reporting baseline, all of the problems surface simultaneously, essentially negating the organization's ability to effectively deal with the problems until after they have completely manifest. The system that pretended to anticipate problems can only point to where the problems were after the fact.

Now, if these systems function as a sort of broad-based to-do list, I have absolutely no problem with that. It's only when this type of structure moves to displace a Critical Path-style system in order to "manage" project or program milestones or activities that they should be considered irrelevant and inaccurate. CPM systems are populated with mostly objective data elements – not so polls, which are often populated with subjective data elements. And when I say "displace," I do not mean that a CPM system has to already be in place on a given project. The previously-discussed ruse of "There was nothing there before, and this system is better than nothing" should never be allowed to serve as the basis for installing a poll on a project when a CPM is the appropriate system.

Cost

The next in our cavalcade of counterintuitive but inescapably true challenges to current management science that will draw the ire of business professors everywhere is this gem: the techniques contained in the GAAP codex do not provide the information needed to manage costs. The closest they come is in managing spending, which is something different altogether. In addition to the amount spent by members of the organization and the amounts planned to be spent, one more critical piece of information is needed: Earned Value. As discussed in Chapter 9, there is no cost management without Earned Value. Chapter 9 also discussed the calculated Estimate at Completion, or EAC – in other words, Earned Value can accurately predict future project costs in the same fashion that Critical Path can accurately predict the timing of future project completion dates.

But, like the polls that attempt to elbow aside legitimate CPM systems, GAAP techniques are often (mistakenly) employed in place of Earned Value systems when trying to predict future costs from project work. Ironically, Earned Value was originally a GAAP concept, which was adopted by the Project Management realm much as English readily steals words from other languages. It's easy to see why – Earned Value has limited value when removed from the project realm, particularly when it is tried in the Asset Management world. But, in the project management arena, it is clearly indispensable. Similarly, when GAAP tools make an appearance in project management, they simply don't work as advertised. This is because (a) the narrative is no longer about the characteristics of the internal organization – it's now about why things unfolded the way they did, and how they are likely to occur in the future; and (b) the attempt to flip the narrative is based on the "expected value" parameter which, as we have seen, is highly suspect.

One of the most powerful characteristics of Earned Value Methodology (EVM) is its self-correcting capability. If a GAAP analysis contains a profoundly flawed expected value figure, the whole analysis is rendered inaccurate and misleading, and will remain as such unless until the offending parameter is discovered and corrected. However, a poor initial assumption, such as planned budget, is almost automatically exposed and corrected in an EVM system. Say a project is originally estimated to cost $100,000, but a perfectly prescient estimator would have known that the final costs will really turn out to be twice that. The project gets underway. At the end of an early reporting period, the EVM analysts learn from the project manager that the project is 25% complete; however, the accountants have dutifully been collecting costs based on the Work Breakdown Structure, and total project costs are $50,000. The EVM analysts know instantly (and, if they don't know instantly, any EVM software would tell them) that the project's EAC is going to be $200,000, even though a completely flawed assumption served as the basis for the original budget creation.

Risk

I think I did a fairly thorough job of deconstructing the Risk Managers' narrative in Chapter 8, and do not wish to revisit it here. However, I would like to point out that Risk Management is commonly considered an essential part of project management, both in the public and the private sectors, as evidenced by its being required by many government agencies and mega-corporations, as well as its continued presence in the *PMBOK® Guide*. There's an interesting rumor floating around the blogosphere, that there is not a single solitary major project that can point to Risk Management techniques as being responsible for attaining project objectives on time and under-budget, but I don't know how that assertion could be proven (or disproven) empirically. I do know (from experience) that publicly asserting that Risk Management is little more than institutionalized worrying expressed in mind-numbing statistical jargon is almost sure to draw a plethora of angry responses, many of them unhinged.

Risk Management suffers from both problems of relevancy and accuracy. Chapter 8 mostly focused on accuracy, especially with respect to Black Swan events. The relevancy issue can be settled with one simple question: did the accurate prediction of the contingency event change the response from the project team in any substantial fashion? If the answer is "no," then there can be no question – the risk analysis was irrelevant. In fact, the only time after the establishment of the project's cost and schedule baselines that risk analysis techniques can be said to add any value whatsoever is when the analysis is both accurate and substantially changed the project team's response. Consider a payoff matrix based on the risk analysts' information stream (Table 11.2).

Note that only in the instances where the information is relevant AND accurate does the outcome have any possibility of justifying the time and expense of pursuing a robust Risk Management system. But it has been my experience that, rather than seek

Table 11.2   Risk Management Information Stream Payoff Matrix

	Irrelevant	Relevant
Inaccurate	Wasted effort producing misleading information	Misleading information
Accurate	Waste of effort	Usable information, lending credence to the system

augmentations to the accuracy rate of Risk Management techniques, combined with an identification where risk analysis is and is not relevant, the Risk Management community has instead sought the expansion of their techniques into the so-called "upside risk," or opportunities management.

Ironically, the Risk Managers' greatest contribution comes when they abandon the idea that they can predict the project's future, and embrace the notion that they can process valuable insight into the narrative of why the organization's history unfolded the way it did – but they would have to embrace CPM and EVM to do so. For example, when an organization encounters a project management disaster, the forensic analysis that can provide a clear script as to what went wrong, and why, can be elusive. However, by using a Responsibility/Accountability Matrix, or RAM, which cross-connects the project's Work Packages with the specific team or organizational units that perform the work, past cost and schedule performance can be gleaned and analyzed. Can you imagine the value of the information that indicated, say, that those Work Packages that performed the poorest in the Big Dig project disaster were those with the highest union participation? (To be clear, I'm not saying such information exists. But can you imagine the value of such information?) Besides the explosive political implications, those contractors most concerned with success in the Project Management realm (unfettered by forced union participation) would work to avoid the characteristic associated with project failure. Because correlation is not causation, Risk Analysts could test for confidence intervals that would indicate which characteristics were most probably the proximate cause of the project encountering the negative event.

But eliminating cognitive bias errors from the organization's internal narrative is not what these guys are about. It's really too bad, too.

Communications

Check the definition of project communications management from the *PMBOK® Guide*:

> *Project Communications Management includes the processes required to ensure timely and appropriate generation, collection, dissemination, storage, and ultimate disposition of project information. It provides the critical links among people, ideas, and information that are necessary for success.*[11]

If one accepts, as I do, that information is the lifeblood of any organization, then this definition is so broad as to not exclude virtually any aspect of management science. As with the overly broad definition of Risk Management, this definition, by failing to establish that which clearly falls outside the realm of Communication Management, also fails to give a usable definition of what it actually is. This section of the *PMBOK® Guide* actually goes on to define a variance as the difference between the plan and the actual costs, and claims Earned Value analysis as belonging in the Communications Management purview. It's as if the PMI Standards Committee provided distinct lines mapping out the subject areas they believed comprised project management proper,

---

11   Duncan, William R., and the PMI Standards Committee, *A Guide to the Project Management Body of Knowledge*, Project Management Institute, 1996.

coloring-book style, and then allowed the various contributing writers and editors to color not only their own areas, but to cross the lines into other contributing writers' areas, without coming back afterwards to comment on the transgressions. The result is an intellectual blur, a series of overlapping management science theories and hypotheses competing for supremacy within the vaguely-defined realm of "Project Management." And here, ironically, we have "Communications Management," as poorly defined as any of them, apparently overlapping virtually all others. I hope that I am up to the task of reining in the communications management aficionados, and placing appropriate limits on where their theories contribute to the narratives and, more importantly, where they do not.

I readily concede that any miscommunication that leads to misunderstandings, conflicts, and poor decisions should be avoided, but I am not ready to concede that they should be avoided at all costs. Communication Management advocates, in my experience, are extremely fond of depicting enhanced communication techniques as the key to complete understanding, harmony, and good decision-making, and I'm just not buying it. Most conflicts – perhaps a strong majority – have nothing to do with a breakdown of communications. The belligerents are perfectly clear where they stand with respect to their opponents, and discussing the nature of the conflict does not help resolve it. It's true in politics, it's true in military affairs, and it's true in management.

Indeed, none of the text in the *PMBOK® Guide*'s section on Communications Management addresses the concept of deceit – the writers act as if all communications are genuine representations of the communicators' true intentions and positions. However, as we saw in Part 1, deception is a key component of communications in games – perhaps *the* key component in games such as Chicken, Poker, or Diplomacy. And, to the extent that these games model aspects of managerial interactions in the free marketplace, it must be conceded that deceit plays a significant role in management science in general, and Communications Management in particular. Information must be timely, relevant, and accurate; but, if your organization can't get sufficient information that passes all three of these criteria, then injecting inaccuracy into your competitors' information stream becomes a tempting alternative. In these instances, attempting to ratchet up the communications would not only fail to lead to an acceptable resolution, they would do the exact opposite, by providing greater opportunities for deceitful and inaccurate information to taint the organizations' MIS streams.

It's hard to make clear distinctions where the Communications Managers' techniques begin to lose efficacy, because the assertions of where they do hold sway are so poorly defined in most cases. I did learn of one Communications Management approach from the brilliant Fred Tarantino, currently the President and CEO of the University Space Research Association. At the time, Fred was Principal Associate Director for Nuclear Weapons Programs at a national laboratory, and I was his Director of Program Controls. Our customer was the US National Nuclear Security Administration, and (obviously) incomplete, inconsistent, or inappropriate communications could have led to severe organizational setbacks. Dr Tarantino set up something he called a "zipper plan," where each of his management team members knew their specific customer contacts (Fred did not invent this approach – he merely taught it to me as he implemented it in his organization). These lines of communications were exclusive – like the interlocking teeth on a zipper. In matters concerning cost and schedule performance reporting, I was responsible for managing that relationship on behalf of the Laboratory. I knew my point of contact within the NNSA, and the Program Directors who reported to Dr Tarantino knew these things as well. Similarly, on matters of science or engineering I knew which Program Directors were responsible for managing those areas, and would defer to them in all instances where there was a possibility that I would receive a request for information outside my purview. We sought to avoid the appearance of "stovepiping," or limiting the functionality of the program team to specific organizational units, while at the same time respecting the other team members' areas of expertise. I think the zipper plan worked great, though I have to admit that it's impossible to differentiate the contribution to the excellent customer relations we enjoyed during that time between the utility of the plan and Dr Tarantino's (and his team's) personal charisma.

Much of the current scholarship on Communications Management (including the *PMBOK® Guide*) is oriented towards delivering information among project team members and others, without much consideration of the accuracy, relevance, or appropriateness of that information. I would argue that, much as information must be timely, accurate, and relevant, so too the communication of that information must ensure that it is done in an appropriate way. Communications designed for consumption within the organization are rarely appropriate for customers, and almost never good for transmission to competitors, and vice versa. The transmission of information must be managed – but primarily to ensure its security, not its broadest and quickest dissemination. The pop management culture idea that any and all who can make even the most tenuous claim to being a project "stakeholder" ought to have ready access to a wide variety of organizational and project information is seriously flawed, and should be rejected.

Human Resources

I have never been associated with, nor become aware of, an organization where the Human Resources department is contained within the Project Management Office, or PM Organization. This managerial area's name alone, Human *Resources*, gives a clear indication that it belongs with the management of other resources, and not within Project Management.

What, exactly, are we talking about when we reference "Project Human Resource Management?"[12] As could be expected, the cavalcade of overly-broad definitions of management science techniques or theories continues unabated. Again referring to the *PMBOK Guide*, it "… includes the processes required to make the most effective use of the people involved with the project."[13] This definition appears to encompass every other section of the *Guide*, save Procurement – and, if we're talking about hiring consultants or subcontractors, not even the buyers are safe from being claimed as falling under the purview of the Project Human Resource Management experts.

I would like to offer a more narrow definition of Project Human Resource Management: Project Human Resource Management is confined to acquiring the personnel that are best able to accomplish the project's scope, within the project's constraints of time and budget. Whether or not they are already part of the organization is not a *Project* Management concern – that variable belongs to the Asset Managers. Similarly, whether

---

12   Ibid.

13   Ibid, p. 93.

or not luring the person(s) involved away from a key competitor, and thereby inflicting a setback on such a competitor, is not a Project Management concern – it's a Strategic Management issue.

Granted, it's far less sexy than making "the most effective use of … people …" but I believe it's much more defensible in the realm of management science. Many a dramatic project failure made very effective use of their people, and many projects have seen amazing success with arguably poor use of people. And what, exactly, constitutes effective or ineffective use of people? Isn't it the outcome of the endeavor? What Human Resources expert worthy of the name would have counseled the Biblical King Saul to send the diminutive shepherd boy David – who was too small even to wear any of the available armor – up against Goliath?

Assigning the role of arbitrating what constitutes an "effective use of people" to the Human Resources crowd is similar to giving the Quality Management-types the power to define which business processes are valid, and which are not, and is similarly misguided.

Procurement

What's being procured? Assets.

No, I'm not being deliberately obtuse. I'm well aware that there's a lot more to procurement than accounts payable, and a good chunk of that does fall legitimately into the realm of Project Management. But only to the extent of the project manager judging of fit and meet with respect to attaining the project's (or task's) scope, within the parameters of cost and schedule. In this area the *PMBOK® Guide*'s discussion of vendor and bid evaluation is highly valuable.

There are two aspects of procurement management that I would like to examine: how procurement behavior adds to the narrative that explains how history unfolded, and how it may broadcast to customers and competitors alike what is likely to happen in the future.

I was a complete geek in High School (if you couldn't tell by my Part 1 discourse about being First Board on the Chess Team). I actually spent the night of my Senior Prom studying chess openings for an upcoming USCF tournament, since I couldn't get a date. Then, in the Summer before I started attending the University of New Mexico, my parents bought me a 1963 Cadillac Sedan de Ville (at the onset of the late 1970's energy crisis, cars with terrible gas mileage were fairly cheap). It was painted gold, with a cream-colored interior, and I never wanted for dates thereafter. Girls practically jumped into the thing. Now, I hadn't changed significantly in the intervening weeks between missing prom and bearing a striking resemblance to the subjects of the old Hai Karate commercials – the Cadillac was clearly the dependent variable. The things we procure and hold do not necessarily define us, but they do convey information about us, both accurate and relevant, and not.

An organization's assets – its offices, location(s), even company cars – transmit information to customers, competitors, and itself. And what this information tells the organization about itself is highly vulnerable to the cognitive and confirmation biases of those who assemble the interior narrative. I have often wondered why such a large percentage of high-value lottery jackpot winners return to their previous economic conditions within five years, and I think it has to do with cognitive or confirmation biases in their internal narrative. The cold, hard truth that winning a large amount of money in a lottery is both (a) incredibly rare, and (b) has absolutely nothing to do with the relative merit of the recipient does not make for comfortable incorporation into the internal narrative, leaving recipients vulnerable to a script that pushes them towards future failure.

In many areas of management, a significant procurement can transmit information to customers, competitors, and the procuring organization on likely future pursuits. In the (American) National Football League, a team that expends significant resources on, say, a wide receiver is telegraphing to the other teams in its Division that it intends to pursue an enhanced capability in its aerial game. Transactions such as corporate takeovers are virtually impossible to keep secret, and can be very telling about the acquiring organization's future plans.

In both of these two instances, procurement behavior generates an information stream, the output of which can be consumed by employees, customers, and competitors. As we will see in the next chapter, combinations of information streams can be highly enlightening when used by the owning organization, but highly dangerous when competitors are in possession of their output.

And one more thing: I have never encountered an organization where the folks doing procurement report to the Project Management Office.

Quality

Like the Risk Management supporters, I've already done significant deconstruction of the Quality Management script. To reiterate, the techniques employed by Quality Management experts are highly valuable in the production world. They are also valuable in the service industry, but less so than in production. But once you get a bunch of Six Sigma guys crawling over your business processes, there's no end to the mayhem they can cause.

I am, nevertheless, sympathetic to their situation. Many (if not most) areas of management can and do hinge on the ability to make the best decisions, which, in turn, is often predicated on having the best information in hand. This is only partially true of the quality guys. Measurements of tolerances and other parameters may indicate which products are likely to fail prior to their expected lifespan, but to make significant improvements in the organization's willingness to significantly improve the quality of a given product, you need to be able to change people's narratives, which can be difficult in the extreme – just ask any clergy. While in graduate school one of my professors passed along a story about a quality consultant who had been hired by General Motors. This expert came to a board meeting with a forged and polished Honda piston, along with a comparable GM piston, at a time when GM tended to cast their pistons. The visual difference in the quality of the two pistons was striking, so GM responded by firing the consultant and forbidding him from ever entering another GM plant. I have no idea if the story is true or not, but it does help illustrate that in order for the Quality Management specialists to have a positive influence, they must change organizations' internal narratives. As discussed earlier, changing an individual's internal narrative is usually painful, and can be expected to be for the organization, as well.

Integration

This part of the *PMBOK® Guide* ostensibly deals with the coordination of each of the other areas. But there is no narrowing of definitions, no lines of demarcation where each of the other eight areas can claim efficacy, and where they cannot. Imagine the processing of management information as if it happened on a conveyor belt. Along the sides of the conveyor belt are taped-off areas indicating where each employee works, adding to or processing the information stream as it comes into their taped-off area. The information stream, like a manufactured item, is incomplete as it enters their area, and the expectation is that the worker will change the item to a state that is acceptable to the next person down-line prior to the information item leaving their own area. At some point in the process the next person to receive the information is its ultimate consumer, the manager/decision-maker.

Now imagine that a provocateur sneaks in during the night, and moves the tape that represents the information stream's integrated components. Some areas now overlap, others have gaps. Obviously, chaos ensues, severely damaging the timeliness and accuracy of the information, even assuming its relevancy is already established.

Any document or analysis that presumes to represent project management integration would have, in this analogy, to serve the function of being able to go in to the information processing assembly line, and putting the tape back into its appropriate place, whether or not the previous map of the lines was archived and retrievable. The *PMBOK® Guide* section on integration does not attempt this, and, in my opinion, that is unfortunate. Such an effort would send a clear signal that at least some thought had gone into analyzing the limits of project management science efficacy, the limits of PM epistemology.

Don't misunderstand – I'm not assigning blame. As has been previously discussed, the Asset Management crowd has so oversold their techniques that any competitor to them almost has to do some overselling themselves. To self-limit or self-contain is tantamount to ceding the argument at the outset. But if we are to evaluate the three types of management and their information streams, the only even-handed approach is to identify their logical limits, apart from the political or pop management implications, leading us to the following table (Table 11.3).

I'm maintaining that, via the Responsibility/Accountability Matrix, or RAM, cost and schedule information can be isolated to the specific teams or groups that contributed to the project. That being the case, valuable information can be obtained concerning the

Table 11.3 Logical Limits of Management and Information

Project Management MISs	Internal	External – Customer	External – Competition
Berne Archetype	Child	Adult	Parent
Corner Cube Type	Asset	Product/Project	Strategic
EVM/CPM– feedback	Relevant, Accurate	Relevant, Accurate	Irrelevant, Accurate
EVM/CPM – feedforward	Relevant, Accurate	Relevant, Accurate	Somewhat relevant, Accurate

performance of the various parts of the internal organization. Of course, performing an Earned Value analysis on non-project work is futile, and yields no usable information. However, knowing which sub-organizations are the optimal performers, and which are not, must be considered key internal management feedback. Cost and schedule performance information assigned to specific sub-organizations also provides a powerful basis for flipping the narrative forward, and using the ensuing projection for anticipating future events. NFL teams have command of the statistics concerning their place kickers. If a given place kicker is inaccurate outside the 40-yard line, that team is more likely to go for a first down in fourth-and-short situations outside the kicker's limits of accuracy. Similarly, organizations that know which of their sub-organizations are likely to perform poorly will approach real-time situations forewarned with a usable knowledge of their vulnerabilities, and can make informed decisions based on that knowledge. Hence, I'm giving the Internal Management/Feed Forward block a green light.

Of course, Earned Value and Critical Path Methodologies are the only source of relevant and accurate cost and schedule performance information in the project management realm. That's why they get the green light in the PM blocks.

In the strategic management realm, EVM has powerful predictive abilities, but its ability to add to the narrative of why an organization lost ground to a competitor is limited. While customer satisfaction is a usable variable in market share analysis, there are too many other variables to declare PM techniques viable. I would like to remind the reader of the discussion of calculating a project's Estimate at Completion from Chapter 9. Both Critical Path and Earned Value Methodologies have powerful predictive capabilities that are not possessed by any of the techniques from GAAP that depend upon the variable "expected value." The ability to accurately quantify performance germane to Earned Value and Critical Path is key to this ability to flip the narrative forward and (somewhat) accurately predict the future. Nothing in GAAP has this ability, and is therefore pretty much helpless when Asset Management techniques are pressed into this sort of duty. It is this ability to project likely future *performance* outcomes that leads me to assert that project management information systems can provide accurate information in the strategic realm. Those capabilities are limited, however, because project management information streams are centered on the cost and schedule performance of products and projects, which are oriented towards customers, not competitors, bringing about questions of relevancy.

Conclusion

There is absolutely no doubt in my mind that the Project Management Institute® has had an extremely powerful, positive impact on management science as currently practiced. That having been said, its problem, like that of a myriad of other sciences and scientists, is that they have not displayed the ability to get to a point where they are comfortable asserting what they don't know, that their ability to provide a meaningful contribution to certain parts of the management science arena loses efficacy.

But, if that is true of the Project Management supporters, what is to be said of the Asset Management aficionados? How far outside their legitimate realm must they be when PMI® commissions a book that attempts to justify the PM function in GAAP terms, i.e., return on investment? All of the attempts to quantify the value of Project Management

– and there are many – mis-state the problem from the beginning. Project Management as a type of management (like Asset or Strategic Management) can't be quantified as a constant variable. What's the value of completing a project successfully versus failing to do so? It depends on the project, the customer, the size of the project, its scope, and thousands of other parameters that can't be accurately captured, or even conflated and then glossed over by substituting the expected value data point. Even if we reduce the question to evaluating the value of the Project Management information stream, that can only be known in retrospect, if at all. The information of the Imperial Japanese Navy's order of battle for Midway – could that be valued at four aircraft carriers, one heavy cruiser, 248 aircraft, and 3,057 lives? Or was that the value of Spruance's decisions, while the intelligence simply supported those decisions? It's impossible to say one way or the other. Similarly, it's impossible to quantify the value of the three types of management, or their information streams. The only conclusion that can be drawn with any certitude is that the lack of these information streams represents a profound vulnerability within the organization. If these vulnerabilities, to both competitors and Black Swan events, are not exploited, then the information is useless. If the vulnerabilities are exploited, then the information streams that could have provided sufficient warning are as valuable as the damage done, up to and including the total value of the organization and its assets.

CHAPTER 12 *Strategic Management and the Rehabilitation of Game Theory and Risk Management*

Truly successful decision making relies on a balance between deliberate and instinctive thinking.

Malcolm Gladwell, *Blink: The Power of Thinking Without Thinking*, 2005

Of the three types of management, Strategic Management has the greatest potential of having its best tactics and approaches discoverable through Game Theory and Risk Management theory. This is because most of the games used in Game Theory analysis resemble the Strategic Management environment: the payoff can be reduced to a single or very few parameters (money or prison time in Game Theory, market share in Strategic Management), the other participants are almost exclusively either adversaries or potential adversaries, and which players receive which payoffs is known (or knowable) by all of the participants. But, before we can evaluate Game Theory's efficacy in the Strategic Management environment, we'll have to turn our attention to the management information streams that support the Strategic Management world.

The information that supports the narrative of how and why things unfolded in the organization's strategic management past – how market share ebbs and flows – is usually known or knowable. For example, the number of cars Ford has sold versus Chrysler or GM, or the outside-the-United States manufacturers, is public knowledge. All a competitor has to do is own a single share of stock, and such intelligence must be disclosed by law. In the case of small businesses, market share information may be more anecdotal or subjective, but it's still discoverable. A local Chamber of Commerce, for example, will probably publish the number of, say, advertising agencies in a given locale, and the total amount of money spent on media promotions is also discoverable, meaning that a quick comparison of a given agency's project backlog divided by the total amount of media sold in that particular market yields the percent of that agency's market share.

So, where the organization stands with respect to current or historical market share can be known. What of future Strategic Management parameters? Like the brokers' advertisements constantly remind us, past performance is no indication of future returns (which is their more succinct way of admitting one of my recurring points, that flipping the narrative forward is highly dangerous, even though we do it all the time). But while placing an entire investment portfolio into a single mutual fund is a highly risky strategy, past performance can be highly useful in making lower-level tactical decisions en route to the creation of a more robust organization.

Project-oriented organizations – those with a nominal business cycle of bidding on project work, winning the work, performing the work, closing out the project, and looking for the next project – can employ a Strategic Management information system capable of predicting future revenue streams with a fair degree of accuracy. The formula used is pretty simple – the difficulty is in securing a key variable. The formula is:

$$\sum [(\text{oP}n * \text{P}n\text{V}) / \text{P}n\text{per}]$$

where oPn is the odds of winning project n, PnV is the value of project n, and P$n$per is the number of accounting cycles (usually months) in the project's period of performance. Sum these for all of the projects in the organization's proposal backlog, and the time-phased revenue streams from expected future work can be known.

Ah, but there's that red-flag word again, *expected*, pointing directly to the difficult-to-secure key variable, the odds of submitting the winning proposal for any given project work. Leave this variable to the proposal managers, and the results will be timely, and obviously extremely relevant – they just won't be accurate.

The answer is to use the objective evidence in feedback information systems to bind the odds-of-winning parameter. This can be done in several ways, including:

• Ratio of wins to losses for proposals for work by sub-organization;
• Or by type (or size) of work;
• Or from this customer.

At this point the analyst who advises that the odds of winning parameter should be the average of these three ratios should have a Talebian rat put down his back (and I'm not talking *Star Trek* here). Your strategic management software must be able to vary the weight given to each of the three tracked ratios, and adjusted based on (finally! A role for …) regression analysis, to see which factor is a stronger indicator of future performance.

Let's posit an organization has records of multiple proposals, along with their outcomes. Prior to the submission of those proposals, this organization would also know the winning percentage of the performing team, for that type of work, and from that customer, and they are (presumably) three different ratios. If the proposal being analyzed ended up winning, then the ratio with the highest value would be considered the strongest indicator of future performance, with the lowest ratio being the weakest. Conversely, should that proposal have lost, the highest ratio would be the weakest; the lowest, the strongest.

Repeat this analysis for every proposal the organization has ever issued, and a genuine trend will emerge that will point to the stronger of the historical performance ratios. Note that we will not abandon the weaker – we'll just assign them a smaller role.

Unless your organization is highly schizophrenic, the variables that predict the winners and the losers most accurately will tend to be the same ones. Pro-rate the three as percentages, and weight them accordingly.

For example, consider the following table, a sort-of strategic management report card (Table 12.1):

Table 12.1 Proposal/Contract Backlog Example

Proposal #	Division's Win Rate	Customer Win Rate	Type/Size of Work Win Rate	Eventual Outcome
1	20%	50%	10%	Won
2	10%	5%	5%	Won
3	15%	20%	50%	Lost
4	30%	25%	10%	Lost
5	20%	5%	25%	Won
6	5%	10%	30%	Lost
7	30%	20%	5%	Lost
8	10%	5%	20%	Won
9	20%	10%	25%	Lost

Based on this completely made-up data, the best predictor in the winning proposals was the percentage of proposals in that particular type of work, with the customer and division tying at one each. The strongest predictor of losers was also by type of work, with three, followed by Division performance (two), and weakest was by customer.

So, we now have a new Request for Proposal. It's the same type of work as proposal #5, but with the customer from proposal #3, and performing division as proposal #9. Our (correctly designed) strategic information system yields the following suggested odds of winning the new proposal:

- 25% for this type of work;
- 20% from this (type of) customer; and
- 20% from this performing division.

By norming the data to 100%, the weights become:

- 38.4% for this type of work;
- 30.8% for this customer; and
- 30.8% for this performing division.

Okay, so is everybody ready for the answer? Multiply the winning percentage for this type of work (25%) by the weight (38.4%), yielding 9.6%. Do the same for the two 20% winning ratios – multiply them by the two 30.8% weights, yielding 6.1% each. Total them, and the usable odds of winning the proposed work is 21.9%. Multiply this number by the value of the work, and time-phase it over the period of performance.

The obvious downside to this analysis is that, in the end, project work is either won, or it is not. What sense does it make to make an assumption that the organization will win 21.9% of the work? The answer lies in the (previously derided) device of conflation. For a single proposal, this analysis is clearly irrelevant. However, like Harry Seldon's plan, when this analysis is performed for the aggregate of the whole proposal backlog, it provides a remarkably accurate picture of the future revenue streams from new work.

I would like to reiterate some of the key characteristics of this approach, and contrast them with other managerial approaches to the same problem, that of projecting future revenue streams. This approach – let's call it the Strategic Past Performance (SPP) approach – does not rely on the accuracy of anybody's (or any group's) internal narrative. You could have an organization full of people convinced they are descendants of the Romanov dynasty and it would not damage such a system's capability in the least. (If you would like to set up an SPP-based system, go to www.austintechpubs.com, where such a system is already available.)

Conversely, from the Generally Accepted Accounting Principles side, formulas for predicting future revenue streams depend on one of two approaches: either the efficiency rate of the current facilities or assets is assessed, and projected into the future based on planned facility or asset procurements, or else they need the elusive "expected value" data point which, as we have seen, is weak and prone to unreliability. The futility of the former approach was placed on full display for me 20 years ago, when I was working for the now-defunct Advanced Sciences, Incorporated, or ASI. My boss, the head of the Project Controls Department, had left abruptly, and I was catapulted at age 31 into that office. At a board meeting (where I was the youngest person in the room by a good two decades) the far-flung satellite offices were represented via conference telephone call, and one of them was discussing their revenue projection for the next fiscal year. They stated that, since their contract backlog was x, and the number of engineers they had on hand was y, that, with the addition of additional engineers, their future revenue could be calculated on that basis.

That's not the way you calculate future revenue [I stated flatly].

The august heads turned and looked at me as if they truly regretted that anybody under the age of 45 was allowed in the executive board room.

You have to multiply the odds of winning each proposal in the backlog by that proposal's value, and time-phase the information over the period of performance.

I don't want to proscribe a specific formula for this … [the president began].

Okay, fine. You could also take the historical win rate for this type of work, or this customer, and multiply that by the proposals' value.

ASI's president at the time – I'll call him "Don," because that was his name – had this ability to take his glasses off of his face in such a dramatic fashion that everybody in the room instantly knew to shut up, because he was going to say something emphatic.

Again [he sighed] I don't want to proscribe a specific formula for these revenue projections, but we need them by mid-month. The next order of business is …

And that was that. After the meeting, I approached him, and said:

Listen, Don, if I can code a system for you that will do this revenue projection, easier and better than the current system, will you at least give it a look?

Knock yourself out.

I practically lived in my office for the next week. At the end I had compiled enough code to begin alpha testing. An administrative assistant from the proposal-writing team, Anna, performed the initial data input, and we started sending the first reports to the printer to check for errors. I fixed a few formatting problems, and re-ran the reports. It was getting late, so Anna and I left for the day, intending to finish up the initial tests the next day. The next morning, Anna came in just after 8:00, breathless:

> Michael! Sometimes I stop at IHOP (American restaurant chain, International House of Pancakes) before coming here, and I'll run into Ed (ASI's owner). He was there this morning, with the reports from your system in hand! He was poring over them!

My first response was to panic.

> *Those reports weren't supposed to go upstairs! We're still de-bugging!*

> Yeah, I know [Anna replied] But I think this is going to work!

Indeed it did. After some more testing and debugging, the program was copied and dispatched to the various satellite offices, where it became the primary source of ASI's revenue projections. However, the head of the Finance and Accounting Department was a particularly unpleasant fellow, who never forgave me for usurping his vital information stream with something far easier and more accurate than he had put forth. Since he was a Jungle Fighter, my days at ASI were numbered. But it turned out okay, since ASI's days were also numbered.

Other Differences

Current Risk Management approaches to projecting future revenue don't work either. The most robust of their techniques, the Monte Carlo analysis, is predicated on so-called Subject Matter Experts positing future events, and estimating (guessing?) their future impact and odds of occurrence. These Subject Matter Experts (SMEs) attained their "expert" status, usually, because of their experience. Okay, so what is "experience?" Isn't it being exposed to many different events over a (presumably) extended period of time, and linking those events via the experts' command of causality into some sort of structure, or narrative? How is anybody to know the extent of these experts' grasp of legitimate causality analysis, or that it is free of invalidating factors? The tendency to link events that happened sequentially in time as the predecessor causing the successor is common to human intelligence, and is vulnerable to confirmation and cognition biases in the extreme (one of my favorites was from the movie *Conspiracy Theory*, when Mel Gibson's character asserts that every time a Space Shuttle is launched in Florida, within a few days an earthquake hits Turkey). All Monte Carlo Analysis does in these instances is to collect, distill, and then magnify the influence of these errors into the information stream being generated. If that was the extent of the damage, it would be severe; unfortunately, it goes far beyond that. Dressed as it is with the trappings of advanced, sophisticated analysis, the (mis-) information is granted a level of respect that it absolutely does not deserve.

Indeed, I would go so far as to say that any information stream that depends on feed-forward data, or allows for the injection of "expected values," or data elements that are predicated on the flipping of individuals' (or whole organizations') narratives into the future, should be considered largely unreliable, and eschewed. They should all be replaced with MISs that are based on objective, performance-based data, using processes that are confined to their appropriate areas of Asset, Product/Project, or Strategic Management.

The Other MIS Stream Strategic Managers Need to Know About

Which products to produce? Which projects to bid? Which customers to pursue? Knowing the correct answers to these questions is a virtual guarantor of success, and any who believe they have swerved into a formulaic approach to discovering these answers are either rich themselves, or else are becoming rich by presenting seminars.

I remember my Strategic Management professors' use of material that evaluated the executive decisions of the United States' main retail chains. In those days, K-Mart and Woolco owned the low-price spectrum, with JCPenney, Montgomery Ward, and Sears one notch up. Nieman-Marcus, Bloomingdale's, and Saks Fifth Avenue dominated the upper end. I was taking these classes in the early 1990s. By the latter part of that decade, Walmart had ominously surpassed Toys 'R' Us in toy sales[1] en route to becoming the largest retailer in the world.

How did they do it? A lot has been written about it, but a common thread has to do with a particular information stream. A computer is notified every time a Walmart item is sold. This manner of inventory control, with only shrinkage rates introducing inaccuracies, was pioneered by Walmart, and it provided an extremely powerful information stream. When I was a teenager, I worked in the JCPenney store in Albuquerque's Winrock Mall, mostly in the Men's Suits department, but with stints in Hardware, Photography, and Shoes. We went around counting the inventory once per year. Knowledge of what products are selling, and which are not, and what inventory needs to be replaced live-time is an extremely powerful information stream, and allowed Walmart's decision-makers to streamline their processes so effectively that they became "the low-price leader," and by wide margins. Montgomery Ward, once one of the largest retailers in the United States, closed all of its stores in 2001,[2] no doubt due at least in part to Walmart's ascendancy. By leveraging strong advances in customer satisfaction (Project/Product Management), Walmart could (and would) score significant strategic victories, as competitors began to fall by the wayside.

Okay, so how do non-retail-giant organizations capture that kind of information? Referring back to Chapters 10 and 11, using legitimate information systems (timely, accurate, relevant) for each of the three types of management (Asset, Project/Product, Strategic) enables the organization to identify which octant it occupies in the Corner Cube model, which, in turn, reveals both the organization's vulnerabilities as well as its

1   Wal-Mart (December 13, 2010). In *Wikipedia, The Free Encyclopedia*. Retrieved 05:07, December 19, 2010, from http://en.wikipedia.org/w/index.php?title=Wal-Mart&oldid=402215959

2   Montgomery Ward (December 13, 2010). In *Wikipedia, The Free Encyclopedia*. Retrieved 22:49, December 19, 2010, from http://en.wikipedia.org/w/index.php?title=Montgomery_Ward&oldid=402221008

strengths. Like Raymond Spruance prior to the Battle of Midway, being in possession of this kind of information can easily change the fortunes of the organization.

In evaluating which new markets or proposals to pursue, the key factors have to do with the ability to capture a given strategy's impact on the organization's assets, project/product portfolio, and strategic position within the Corner Cube model. For example, assume a fifth octant organization (low Asset, high Project, low Strategic management scores). Such an organization would nominally look to improve its Strategic Management position prior to looking to directly increasing its shareholders' wealth. Two large Requests for Proposals (RFPs) have come up, large enough so that our sample organization can't do both of them. Let's further posit that our sample organization is in this particular market for the long term, and is not looking to cash in and leave the market.

RFP A is from a new customer, but in a very familiar field. The organization has performed well on this type of work previously, and this particular project is so simple that there is every expectation that it will be brought in on time, on budget. The work will pay for the salaries ("cover") 100% of the performing division – in fact, they may have to hire one or two more people.

RFP B is from a familiar customer, but in a somewhat new, innovative field. The organization has performed well on similar types of work, but never with the technology that makes up a portion of this RFP. The work will only cover 90% of the performing division, and it may even be necessary to hire one or two new people while releasing two or three existing personnel. A key competitor is currently engaged in another project that includes this RFP's new technology.

To the Asset Manager, this decision is simple: of course the organization should pursue Request for Proposal A, and eschew B. RFP A is clearly more profitable. The Project Managers are divided; one sees A as an easy job, while the other perceives B as a desirable challenge. Finally, the Strategic Manager wants the organization to bid on RFP B; as a fallback, she recommends that the organization bid on both. If one or the other bid wins, or if they both lose, then no further decision is required. If both bids win, then the organization should perform Project B's scope, and subcontract out Project A.

Fortunately, our sample organization's Chief Executive Officer read Managing to the Corner Cube in the *Project Management Journal*®.[3] He knows that the best direction from the fifth octant is towards the sixth (low Asset, high Project, high Strategic), and not the eighth (high Asset, high Project, low Strategic) and, over the howls of protest from his head of Finance and Accounting, proceeds as the Strategic Manager has recommended.

In practical terms, the way this type of decision is supported by an MIS tool is by evaluating all future proposed work in terms of its impact to the strategic, project/product, and asset management realms of the owning organization, and norming this data to 1.00. When evaluating competing proposals to pursue, the following data should be collected and evaluated:

- The Asset Management data point is the percentage of the organization's personnel covered by the proposed work, should it be won. Contrary to (probably) every management book ever written that discusses this topic, this data point should NOT be the Return on Investment.

3   Hatfield, Michael, *Managing to the Corner Cube*, Project Management Journal, 1995.

- The Project Management parameter is the cumulative Cost Performance Index of similar work performed in the past (it's relevant to know which work the organization does well, and which it performs not-so-well).
- The Strategic Management component is more subjective. It is the rating of the proposals in the proposal backlog of "highly desirable" (1.2), "desirable" (1.1), "neutral" (1.00), "undesirable" (0.90), or "highly undesirable" (0.80) from the point of view of what is the projected impact of the won work on the organization's market share.[4]

After each proposal in the backlog has these three parameters, multiply them by each other for a composite score, and sort on that score. This is the information stream that will point your organization towards the customers and market(s) most likely to ensure future long-term success.

I was once involved in a large environmental program, where the number of projects planned far exceeded the number that could be funded in any given year. A scoring system was developed, but it was one-dimensional. There was a maximum score assigned, based on different factors, many of which were subjective. As could be predicted, the meetings of the various projects' advocates could become contentious, as each attempted to leverage their personal and professional influence to get their projects' score above the funding cut line.

The Corner Cube model eliminates such contentiousness in the project/proposal selection process. Or, at least it has the potential to, by confining the selection process to a given formula that reduces subjective elements. Of course, the subjective elements can only be reduced, never eliminated, which is why an additional analysis overlay should be employed. As with the norming and weighting of the factors that serve as predictors in the odds-of-winning formula, the asset-project-strategic scores can be weighted based on the amount of emphasis the ultimate decision-makers wish to place on the analysis.

For example, here is a nominal table of proposals, with their scores (Table 12.2):

Table 12.2   Sample Proposal Evaluation

Proposal	Asset Score	Project Score	Strategic Score	Nominal Score
A	0.90	1.00	0.90	0.81
B	1.00	0.90	1.10	0.99
C	1.00	1.00	0.90	0.90
D	1.10	0.90	1.00	0.99
E	1.10	1.00	1.10	1.21
F	1.10	0.90	1.10	1.09
G	0.90	1.10	0.90	0.89

However, when the proposals are weighted with the level of emphasis for each of the three different types of management, a different ordering presents itself. If, for example, an

4   The only way to ensure that this parameter is calculated "fairly" is to make sure the overall average (finally! A use for the average of something!) of the Strategic Management score is 1.00.

organization in the fifth octant wishes to place 50% emphasis on Strategic Management, 30% emphasis on Project Management, and 20% emphasis on Asset Management, the weights calculate out to (Table 12.3):

Table 12.3   Proposal Evaluation Table with Weights

Proposal	Asset Score	Project Score	Strategic Score	Nominal Score	Composite Score
E	1.10	1.00	1.10	1.21	1.05
F	1.10	0.90	1.10	1.09	1.00
B	1.00	0.90	1.10	0.99	1.00
G	0.90	1.10	0.90	0.89	1.00
D	1.10	0.90	1.00	0.99	0.95
C	1.00	1.00	0.90	0.90	0.95
A	0.90	1.00	0.90	0.81	0.95

Note how Proposal D had been considered more desirable than Proposal G until the emphasis weights had been taken into account. Also note how, even though the strategic score has been given the highest emphasis value, that does not necessarily mean they get their way in all cases: the strategic score for Proposal D is higher than for Proposal G, and yet G's score from the other two areas gives it a higher composite.

The actual formula for this analysis is:

$$CS = (SMs * Sw) + (PMs * PMw) + (AMs * AMw)$$

Where CS is the Composite Score, SMs is the Strategic Management score, Sw is the Strategic Management weight, PMs is the Project Management score, PMw is the Project Management weight, AMs is the Asset Management score, and AMw is the Asset Management Weight. (All of this is included in the aforementioned software package available from www.austintechpubs.com.)

A Critical Combination

When the information stream that identifies the optimal targets for future work is combined with the system that accurately reflects the odds and impacts of winning that future work, this combination provides for an extraordinarily powerful information stream, one that gives the organization that uses it an automatic advantage over those that do not. And, when *that* stream is combined with the ability of a properly-functioning Earned Value Management System to predict future project revenue streams, the advantage becomes even more profound.

The sheer value of this kind of information is difficult to understate, which is why, once developed, every effort must be made to keep it from falling into the hands of the organization's competitors. As discussed earlier, parts of the information stream supporting the model are impossible to keep secret. Owning just one share of a publicly-traded company's stock provides information on its assets, holdings, and key projects. But the information streams concerning Project and Strategic Management that are not typically disseminated widely must be considered sensitive, and treated accordingly by the organization.

Conversely, if this sort of information on competitors is available, it ought to be collected with the ultimate goal of generating a Corner Cube analysis that would point directly to the competitor organization's vulnerabilities. For example, if your organization is in the sixth octant of the Corner Cube (High Project, High Strategic, Low Asset performance), and you were in possession of information that a key competitor was in the eighth octant (High Project, Low Strategic, High Asset performance), your organization may have been considering ways of leveraging the advantages in Project and Strategic management in order to maximize shareholder wealth. But, with the knowledge of your competitor's position, and knowing they were vulnerable with respect to your shared customers, the better decision would be to devote even more energy into the Project/ Product Management realm, making it that much more difficult for the competitor to get out of their vulnerable octant. At the same time a shrewd maneuver would be to work on advances in the Strategic Management arena, such as bidding on proposals that represent larger market share performance (for engineering/service contractors), or spending money on marketing and advertising (for manufacturers). These tactics will go a long way towards increasing the odds of the competitor's future failure(s).

Of course, if these positions were reversed, and it's your organization that finds itself in the eighth octant while a key competitor is in the sixth, you are vulnerable to their implementing the tactics discussed in the previous paragraph. The most robust response that an organization in the eighth octant can select would involve implementing the previous paragraph's tactics of pouring more energy into Project/Product Management, followed by an increased emphasis on Strategic Management, and to do so more quickly and effectively than the competition.

All of this presumes that the players in this game, like the players of Game Theory games, have perfect knowledge of the options and payoffs of all of the other players. Without timely, accurate, and relevant information streams supporting the organization's placement within the Corner Cube model, the player(s) don't even know that about themselves, much less about the other players. They are figuratively flying blind, with all of the vulnerabilities that implies.

The True Nature of The Game

What emerges, then, is a game where the players are comprised of all of the organizations participating in efforts to make money within a specific market. But, unlike Von Neumann's work, it is possible to articulate a game structure that acknowledges the nature of Black Swan events. In contrast to Nash, we're not seeking to be able to anticipate the most likely strategies – mixed or pure – to be undertaken by the other players. We are seeking to create the most robust organization possible, strong enough to endure unexpected damaging future events, and able to nimbly respond to positive ones, as well as being able to respond quickly and effectively to competitors' vulnerabilities. This response, however, is predicated on the availability of timely, accurate, and relevant information streams that inform us not only of our organization's place in the Corner Cube model, but, to the extent possible, of our competitors' place, as well. This information points out our vulnerabilities and weaknesses, and allows for a latitude of management action that lessens or eliminates them, allowing for a stronger positioning of the organization.

The goal of the Corner Cube Game is to attain and remain in octant seven (high Asset, Project/Product, and Strategic Management performance). The players are limited to the following broad strategies:

- Leverage assets to make advances in project/product management.
- Leverage assets to make advances in strategic management.
- Leverage advances in project/product management to make advances in asset management.
- Leverage advances in project/product management to make advances in strategic management.
- Leverage market share to increase shareholder wealth.

And that's it.[5]

Recall the discussion on the Ultimatum Game, from Chapter 2. For those who have slept since reading Chapter 2, the Ultimatum Game involves two participants, Player A and Player B. Player A is offered a sum of money (usually $100), and must propose how it is to be split among him and Player B. If Player B agrees to Player A's money-split proposal, the money is divided as proposed. However, if Player B rejects Player A's plan, neither player receives anything. Game Theory experts supposed that Player A's maximum payoff would come from proposing a $99/$1 split, since Player B would more likely accept $1 than nothing at all. In actual trials, though, the $99/$1 was almost always rejected, for a variety of reasons. These reasons were often attributed to "cultural influences." In other words, when participants did not respond as expected, it was attributed to either irrationality on their parts, or else factors outside the stated parameters of the game. But these two explanations vividly demonstrate the futility of employing Game Theory outside its relatively confined area of efficacy. Von Neumann posited that most or all of the participants would employ strategies that maximized their payoff, if only they were all clear on what was the relationship between the selected strategy and ensuing payoff. But this is not so, as was demonstrated by experiments using the Ultimatum Game. As for the strategy – mixed or pure – employed by the game's participants being influenced by factors outside of the game's nominal structure, there's a universe of factors that are outside of the free market game's nominal structure, and these factors cannot all be identified, much less quantified.

That's the beauty of using Game Theory within the confines of the Corner Cube game. The Corner Cube game just so happens to have the following characteristics:

- Most (if not all) of the players within a specific market can be known;
- Their tactics are limited to those listed in the previous paragraph;
- The standing of most of the participants can be known, at least generally; and
- The payoff for the long-term participants – gaining octant seven – is universal to all of them.

---

5   It's impossible to use an advantage in market share to make customers happier. The closest you could get would be a two-step process, of leveraging market share to increase assets, and then spending those assets to improve project/product capability.

That having been said, the Corner Cube's model of real-life management is susceptible to some of the same vulnerabilities of other games', specifically anything that constitutes a game-changing event, including:

- The introduction of new technologies, and the eventual obsolescence of existing ones;
- Players who are not in for the long term, and adjust their strategies accordingly;
- Changes in the political or regulatory environment (which is why governments with far-reaching power are highly detrimental to their respective nation's macro economy);
- Upheaval in nearby markets (including suppliers).

However, those organizations whose place in the Corner Cube model is supported by timely, accurate, and relevant information streams have an advantage in their ability to spot these endangering trends far earlier than their benighted competitors, and, presumably, respond in far more robust ways.

In the next chapter, I want to try to review all of the territory covered thus far, and try to put it into a perspective that allows the most effective use of these strategies, tactics, and models.

13 *Life, the Universe, and Everything*[1]

One's first step in wisdom is to question everything – and one's last is to come to terms with everything.

Georg Christoph Lichtenberg (1742–1799)

We've covered an awful lot of ground in the preceding chapters, and so I'd like to spend some time summarizing and synopsizing, leaving the reader with the key concepts that will (hopefully!) lead to their organizations' making the mild course corrections that will, in turn, lead them to greater robustness in response, and thence to greater success.

In a way, I began researching this book 40 years ago, while reading Asimov's *Foundation* trilogy. But, while the ability to provide insight into future events via calculation is obviously extremely valuable, the very impossibility of creating or arriving at such a formula, a Code of Nature, is not as easily grasped, much less embraced. From Von Neumann's time to the present, it seemed as if Game Theory could provide the framework for just such a Code of Nature; where it fell short, perhaps others theories of information efficacy, such as Risk Management and Network Theory, could fill in the epistemological gaps.

In the meantime, management science was advancing in a most helter-skelter fashion, as if its adherents were unaware of the difficulties involved in reducing the parameters involved in economic activity to the few needed to objectively evaluate the cause-and-effect sequences empirically. Game Theory seemed to be the perfect answer, reducing, as it did, the parameters (available strategies, available payoffs) involved in intelligent interactions. If Game Theory couldn't explain the Universe, then perhaps it could help explain why macroeconomic schemes could advance or deter the creation of wealth; at the very least, Game Theory should be able to help anticipate individual or organizational strategy selection in a given market, right?

As Maccoby turned his gaze inwards, inside the organization, and realized that its personnel tended to behave in ways consistent with his *Gamesman* archetypes, John Adams (from East Carolina University, not the second President of the United States) and his colleagues were formulating the basis for the study of the management techniques and precepts that would lead to the formation of the Project Management Institute. In 1962, Thomas Kuhn published *The Structure of Scientific Revolution*.[2] If the physical

---

1   With apologies to the late Douglas Adams.

2   The Structure of Scientific Revolutions (December 16, 2010). In *Wikipedia, The Free Encyclopedia*. Retrieved 23:45, December 26, 2010, from http://en.wikipedia.org/w/index.php?title=The_Structure_of_Scientific_Revolutions&oldid=402652611

sciences advanced the way Kuhn posited, would management science's advancements behave in a similar fashion? As project management gained in popularity, it certainly seemed a possibility, since traditional (read: asset) management techniques first appeared to be inadequate in explaining observed events in the management world. I can't help but to wonder if, in PMI®'s early days, any of its founders were familiar with Kuhn's work, and had asked aloud, "Do project management precepts represent epicycles to the existing meme of 'maximizing shareholder wealth,' or does it represent a whole new theory, as Kepler was to Ptolemy?"

The notion that project management was different by type, and not by degree, from Generally Accepted Accounting Principles, and therefore not an epicycle, was known by PMI members by 1995, as it was published in their refereed journal, the *Project Management Journal®*. Some unknown wise-guy named Michael Hatfield had submitted a manuscript that detailed the idea that Asset, Project, and Strategic management were fundamentally different.[3] The reviewers approved it, and it was published with not only the different-management ideas, but the notion that the three could (and should) be captured in a three-dimensional model. Had any of PMI®'s Board of Directors been savvy enough to engage the model for PMI® itself, they would have realized that the main standard-bearing organization for project management was probably in the fourth octant (high Asset, low Project [irony knows no bounds], low Strategic), and, if it were to advance at all, more likely to enter the eighth octant (high Asset, low Project, high Strategic) than the sixth (high Asset, high Project, low Strategic).

To put this into perspective, at one point the governing council of PMI® was in a position to choose between championing an alternate view of the management science world, where project management and asset management were fundamentally different, but reconcilable at a higher level; or else, to accede to the traditional, asset managers' narrative, that the objective of all management was to maximize shareholder wealth, and to posit that project management, as a discipline, had a place – a subservient place, to be sure, but a place – at the decision makers' table. Either deliberately, or through inaction, the latter position prevailed. The winner should have been the former.

While Project Management's true place in the overarching scheme of management science was being explored, other events were transpiring that seemed to be outside either narrative. Hostile takeovers were happening left and right, but they could not be explained through either the Asset or the Project Management memes. As discussed earlier, in the Asset Managers' world, no acquiring company would ever attempt a hostile takeover, and no targeted company would ever resist. But there it was, takeover after takeover, many of them quite hostile. It made no sense in the Project Management world either – they were simply not equipped to quantitatively capture the advantages or disadvantages to such goings-on. The nature of economics in general, and business in particular, was far too complex to capture in any all-encompassing theorem, or Code of Nature, that could accurately piece together a narrative that explained why events unfolded the way they did, much less predict the future.

---

3   Hatfield, Michael, Managing to the Corner Cube; Three-Dimensional Management in a Three-Dimensional World, *Project Management Journal*, PMI Publishing, 1995.

On Miniaturizing the Universe

While chess became widespread during the 1500s, the game it was based on, shantraj, has been around since the early Christian era.[4] In a way, chess is a model of life, a miniaturization of the universe. It's not strictly martial in nature – the pieces called bishops have about the same value as knights. Chess is also not considered a standard war game, and is not generally used to train warriors. Nor is it entirely political – the queen is worth a little less than two rooks, or castles, and has greater latitude of movement than any other piece, which is obviously not true of historical female monarchs. Pawns, relatively helpless on their own, become much more powerful when they come together in a winning structure, much like individuals then and now. Chess is also deceptively and astonishingly complex, like the real universe. So, if a computer can be programmed to beat the best human players, does that not argue in favor of a discoverable process that can lead to the creation of mathematical formulas that, taken together, produce the coveted Code of Nature?

In a sense, the entire field of quantitative analysis in business is a similar attempt to miniaturize the world, to create a framework that can be used to categorize perceptions, events, and information, which can lead to a better understanding of why the things that have happened happened the way they did, and why, how, and when events will unfold in the future. Much of the epistemological energy for this galactic shrink-ray comes from the Gaussian Distribution, which is the basis for Risk Management as it is currently practiced.

There's simply no disputing that games often closely resemble analogous interactions in the real, unbounded world. This is true not only of the games that are modeled after real-world events and interactions, such as war games or massive multi-player online role-playing games, but of games that do not seem to have been created as an analogy to anything, such as poker. Poker provides an intriguing example because, like chess (and life), it's deceptively complex. Hoyle's description of the game is confined to a discussion of the combinations of playing cards that represent winning hands, and which such combinations are considered superior to others. But the player whose expertise is confined to knowing how many and which cards to give back to the dealer when drawing is not likely to be successful. An entire additional layer of tactics is involved, including if and how much to bet, when to bluff, how to recognize other players' bluffs, and so on. Indeed, the bluff/don't bluff/good hand/bad hand decisions can be considered to be their own game, with a discernible payoff matrix and calculable Nash equilibrium.

Once the object and rules of a game are established and known, and the players identified, various actions can be assembled into tactics, tactics combined into strategies, and strategies can be evaluated as to their effectiveness. The same sequence of events transpires when cartage schemes are being developed, where the object of the game is to acquire wealth, the rules are established and published by a government, and the players identify themselves by incorporating, obtaining licenses and permits, or performing whatever tasks the respective government requires of them. In both games and in business, tactics and strategies tend to clump together in identifiable patterns, or archetypes, as Bartle and Maccoby, respectively, discovered.

---

4   Shatranj (December 10, 2010). In *Wikipedia, The Free Encyclopedia*. Retrieved 20:04, December 27, 2010, from http://en.wikipedia.org/w/index.php?title=Shatranj&oldid=401648486

As Metcalfe's Law shows, once some basic Network Theory is brought into the mix, the ability of these miniaturized universes to accurately create the structure, or narrative, that explains why history unfolded the way it did becomes more powerful. At the same time, Network Theory seems to argue against the flipping of these narratives into the function of predicting the future, demonstrating, as it does, that the narratives would have to become dizzyingly complex in order to explain the dizzyingly complex future. In a sense, Metcalfe's Law brings Black Swan Theory down to the everyday level. The number of things that happen to us in life that are completely unpredictable, or at least unpredicted, and yet happen, only to have us believe after the fact that they were perfectly predictable, is terrifyingly immense. The conceit that leads us to believe otherwise, that our narratives are certainly capable of providing a reasonable facsimile of how our futures will unfold, is perhaps a defense mechanism. The realization that our worlds are completely dominated by random or unforeseeably complex events is disquieting as best, madness-inducing at worst. And, when we discuss the parts of the narrative pertaining to defense mechanisms, are we not talking about Berne's Child, or Freud's Id? The discussion has taken a sudden and (wouldn't you know it?) unexpected turn into the realm of the irrational, but extremely powerful, inner-self.

If it's true of the individual, it's also true of the macro organization, which is nothing more than a combination of the individuals (and their narratives) in its employ. In the transition from micro to macro organizations, though, the narratives shift structure, from feelings follow attitudes, and attitudes follow beliefs, over to assets are used to achieve project/product goals, and project/product goals follow the strategic path laid out for the organization.

While much of the two preceding paragraphs must present as naked assertions, some of them are, and some aren't. As I read Berne (*Games People Play*), I couldn't help but be struck by the similarities between his assertions on the three components of the persona and my ideas about the three types of management. Berne's ideas about the individual narratives also closely mirrored what I had observed from various management techniques' advocates, particularly when those narratives were adjusted to compensate for which type of management they were consistent with, and attempting to further.

As far as I know, I'm the first person to make the connection of the three types of management, the three narratives, and the roles they play in the macro organizations' persona, particularly with regard to the narratives' functions of explaining the organization to itself (Id, Child, Asset), explaining why external events unfolded the way they did (Ego, Adult, Project/Product), and being flipped forward to predict the future (Superego, Parent, Strategic). Even here, I'm simply connecting the dots, but it did lead to the inevitable question: if the Child's (or Id's) narrative is irrelevant in the Adult's world, would the same be true of the Asset Manager's narrative in the Project Manager's realm? By employing the two tests of management information systems – valid or invalid structure, and, is the information timely, accurate, and relevant? – it became clear which information streams were relevant, and where; and, perhaps more importantly, where they were not.

Revisiting the Upper Limit

After reading *Theory of Games in Economics*, *A Beautiful Math*, and *The Black Swan* in quick succession (just for the record, I do recommend these books, just not in quick succession. It's the intellectual equivalent of drinking a diet Pepsi® after having consumed a ColdEze® tablet), it became clear that some brilliant thinkers had strongly contrasting ideas about the efficacy limits to our knowledge and the information systems that guide our business decisions being furthered by various so-called experts. The question of how to evaluate the efficacy of the information streams within their nominal boundaries, but especially when they go beyond those boundaries, then presented itself. The answer to this problem came, as so many others do, from Aristotle. Evaluating these information streams logically, and eliminating any *pathos* or *ethos* from the equation, represented the best way of uncovering the truth behind their claims.[5]

First under my microscope was Game Theory. Tom Siegfried, in *A Beautiful Math*, mostly argued for the ability of an as yet undiscovered, more sophisticated version of Game Theory's ability to serve as the foundation (no pun intended) for a Code of Nature, similar to Hari Seldon's psychohistory.[6] I say mostly because, in moments of grounded clarity, Siegfried would concede that such a code was virtually impossible:

> *Real life isn't quite that simple, of course. There are usually complicating factors. A bulldozer can push the rock back up the hill; you can add chemicals to spark new chemistry in a batch of molecules. When people are involved, all sorts of new sources of unpredictability complicate the game theory playing field. (Imagine how much trickier chemistry would become if molecules could think.)[7]*

But in the very next pair of sentences, he returns to his main theme:

> *Nevertheless, Nash's notion of equilibrium captures a critical feature of the social world. Using Nash's math, you can figure out how people could reach stability in a social situation by comparing that situation to an appropriate game.[8]*

However, while Von Neumann, Nash, and Friedman discussed and evaluated the notion of mixed strategies at length, I did not see where any of them discussed the concept of a mixed payoff. Central to their ideas of Game Theory's strength of analogy to real-life was that the sought-after ends, or the payoff, could be reduced to one or two parameters.

When Game Theory's tenets were empirically tested, however, a very different outcome than that which was theorized manifested. The Ultimatum Game's predicted maximized payoff scenario for Player A, for example, of a split of $99 for Player A, and $1 for Player B, failed virtually every single time it was tried. The explanations offered for this failure are fascinating by themselves. The game theorists tended to place these reasons into two categories: either there were "cultural" influences that prevented the expected outcome from coming about, or else the players (in this case, specifically, Player B) were acting "irrationally." Taking a closer look at the latter category, it was revealed that those Player Bs who were thought to be acting irrationally offered up as a reason for their decision to forgo the $1 in favor of nothing at all was due to their sense of injustice

---

5   Aristotle, *Rhetoric*, in Patricia P. Matsen, Philip B. Rollinson, and Marion Sousa, *Readings from Classical Rhetoric*, SIU Press, 1990, p. 120.

6   Siegfried, Tom, *A Beautiful Math; John Nash, Game Theory, and the Modern Quest for a Code of Nature*, Joseph Henry Press, 2006.

7   Ibid, pp. 60–61.

8   Ibid, p. 61.

at Player A's proposed split. Presumably, had the game administrator simply walked up to Player B and offered them $1, versus zero dollars, they would have accepted the former. Why, then, did their sense of fair play enter in when the Ultimatum Game was played as designed? Could it be that the $99 to $1 split was inconsistent with their inner narrative, the one that told them who they were to themselves? That some sort of comparative evaluation was underway, and it was worth it to eschew the single dollar in order to keep the internal narrative from having to deal with the assertion that Player A is 99 times more deserving of unearned largesse than Player B? Similarly, for those who rejected the $99 to $1 split for "cultural" reasons – could it be that that split ran contrary to their narrative that explains the hows and whys history unfolded the way it did, and how they would most appropriately interact with their peers?

If the answer to the previous rhetorical questions is "yes," it follows that even when the game being used to model real-life can reduce the nominal payout to a single parameter, that single parameter is being evaluated by three different narratives within the individual, the three narratives that align with Berne's Child–Adult–Parent, and Freud's Id–Ego–Superego. Games like the Prisoner's Dilemma are more successful at calculating the optimal strategies because there is no longer a mixed payoff: it is highly likely that all three Bernesian components of the persona want to get out of jail.

So, far from being able to serve as the basis for Isaac Asimov's psychohistory, or a Code of Nature, Game Theory's ability to calculate or predict future events, or most likely strategies, mixed or pure, from participants in any one "game" falls apart when the payoffs cannot be confined to a single (or very few) parameters. And in real-life, the number of game-like interactions where the payoff can be so confined are extremely rare, so rare as to render Game Theory's insights next to useless outside of those circumstances where:

- The rules of the game are known by all of the participants;
- The participants' range of actions or strategies are limited;
- The payoff is a single parameter, equally coveted by all of the participants; and
- Of course, all of the participants are known, or knowable.

Game Theory does have its area of relevance and efficacy, in the realm of testing for robustness. It's not usable, however, in the arena of accurately predicting the behavior of the other participants.

But what of Maccoby's archetypes from *The Gamesman*? If the participants' selected strategies, or behaviors, are observed to repeat patterns characterized by one of four categories, does that not offer up insights into how and why the various players select their strategies, both mixed and pure, moving ahead into the future?

The central problem in introducing the Maccoby archetypes into the gaps and shortcomings of Game Theory in attempting to predict the players' most likely selected strategies is that we can't know the various comparative strengths of any individual's narratives, much less the precise characteristics of those narratives. An experienced observer of human nature can usually come close to adequately assessing the comparative narrative's strengths question, but even here significant error can creep in. The fellow who appears to be dominated by his Child's narrative, at the expense of the Adult, or Parent – is he immature, or creative? The lady who poses no threat to her peers, and thereby gets along well with them – is she one of Maccoby's Company Men, or does she lack ambition? But even if we concede that the exact drivers of the players' strategy selection behaviors cannot be known, their patterns of strategy selections can be noted and catalogued. The problem remains, though, of the introduction of mixed payoffs. Just as the amount of Ultimatum Game money presented as three different payoffs to the three different aspects of the Berne persona, the same event that occurs to the organization will present as four different payoff values to the Gamesman, Company Man, Craftsman, and Jungle Fighter, and perhaps even 12 different payoff values for each of the three narratives maintained by the four Maccoby archetypes. Rather than enhance Game Theory's ability to project the most probable selection of players' strategies into the future, Maccoby's archetypes illuminate the reasons behind Game Theory's inability to do so: the pieces on this chessboard don't move the way we expect.

I must admit, though, that I was intrigued by how closely the Bartle categorizations of the players in massive multi-player online role-playing games matched the types of workers described in *The Gamesman*. (Interestingly, there is at least one other type-sorting that mirrors both Bartle and Maccoby, an online quiz that determines which House at Hogwarts School of Magic from the Harry Potter series the player should be assigned. I have no idea if the writer(s) of these quizzes, or even J.K. Rowling herself, are familiar with Maccoby or Bartle: it's just that the similarities are striking.) While foreknowledge of the Bartle categories of the people controlling the other avatars in your MMORPG team can be useful from time to time, it's far better to know them personally if being surprised by the actions within the team is considered detrimental. And knowing the Bartle categorization of the members of opposing teams is virtually useless.

The Starkest Boundary of All

The use of Gaussian curves in quantitative business analysis is so prevalent that very few of management science's techniques that pretend to quantify any future event or occurrence – like a return on investment – are free of them. Indeed, the definition of Risk Management offered by the Project Management Institute® is so hopelessly broad that virtually no aspect of management – or any kind of business interaction, for that matter – is beyond its purview.[9] A Google® search of the term "Risk Management" conducted on December 29, 2010 yielded 78,000,000 results. And yet it has to be said: current Risk Management theory, like Game Theory, has its areas of relevance and efficacy; but accurately predicting the behavior of other players in the game, or the occurrence of non-player-related events, is not among them.

There are several reasons for this. One is that the most popular theorem for identifying and quantifying risk events, Monte Carlo and Decision Tree Analysis, retain characteristics consistent with the fraudulent Drake Equation. As discussed in Chapter 8, the Drake Equation is:

---

9   Wideman, R. Max, et.al., *Project and Program RISK MANAGEMENT; A Guide to Managing Project Risks and Opportunities*, The PMBOK Handbook Series, Volume No. 6, PMI Publishing, 1992, pp. 1–2: "In short, the purpose of project risk management is to:

- Specifically identify factors that are likely to impact the project objectives of Scope, Quality, Time and Cost
- Quantify the likely impact of each factor
- Give a baseline for Project Noncontrollables
- Mitigate impacts by exercising influence of Project Controllables."

$$N = R^* \, fp \, ne \, fl \, fi \, fc \, fL$$

where: N = the number of civilizations in our galaxy with which communication might be possible; and R* = the average rate of star formation per year in our galaxy, fp = the fraction of those stars that have planets, ne = the average number of planets that can potentially support life per star that has planets, fl = the fraction of the above that actually go on to develop life at some point, fi = the fraction of the above that actually go on to develop intelligent life, fc = the fraction of civilizations that develop a technology that releases detectable signs of their existence into space, and L = the length of time for which such civilizations release detectable signals into space.[10]

I believe Michael Crichton said it best:

> *The problem, of course, is that none of the terms can be known, and most cannot even be estimated. The only way to work the equation is to fill in with guesses. [...] As a result, the Drake equation can have any value from "billions and billions" to zero. An expression that can mean anything means nothing. Speaking precisely, the Drake equation is literally meaningless.*[11]

Similarly, the process by which future risk events are identified and quantified, while not identical to the Drake Equation, retain some of its speculative nature. Monte Carlo and Decision Tree analysis, as used in modern risk management, are little more than invitations to structured speculation on the parts of the risk analyst and subject matter experts being interviewed to create the risk baseline and contingency plans.

The second central problem to current Risk Management's inability to predict future events or players' strategy selection has to do with the fact that risk analysis adds absolutely nothing to the narrative – individuals', or organizations' – that helps explain why history unfolded the way it did. If it adds nothing to the historical narrative, why should risk management techniques suddenly assume relevancy when that narrative is flipped forward, to try to anticipate future events or players' behavior? The simple answer is, it shouldn't.

Finally, there's the lack of empirical evidence that Risk Management ever significantly contributed to a project being completed early, or under budget (or even on time, on budget). The problem with asserting that Risk Management does add to the overall management of a project is that it must be established that the project team would have responded differently to the project-impacting event had it not been foreseen and quantified, and that the difference in response was detrimental to the successful completion of the project. Again, these are highly speculative and subjective assertions, and are probably not empirically provable, no matter how much probability-and-statistics-related jargon is drawn into the conversation.

I don't mean to just pick on the Game Theory and Risk Management types. Many management science disciplines and quantitative techniques (and their advocates) have overstepped their limits of relevancy and accuracy, including quality, communications, procurement, implementation, integration, and Generally Accepted Accounting

---

10   "PBS NOVA: Origins – The Drake Equation." Pbs.org. Retrieved March 7, 2010, from http://www.pbs.org/wgbh/nova/origins/drake.html

11   Crichton, Michael, "Aliens cause Global Warming," a speech given at CalTech, 1993.

Principles. But by drawing the distinction between these management techniques and their supporting management information systems, it is possible to evaluate the most objective and logically reducible components against each other, with respect to the type of management they represent.

On the Maturation Process

Again referring to the Berne archetypes, it can be argued that an individual's maturation process occurs as their Child's narrative becomes less dominant at the same time as their Adult narrative expands, and then as the Parent narrative becomes dominant as the Adult narrative recedes somewhat, and the Child's is next to eliminated. For the macro organization, the maturation process was (in my opinion) accurately and presciently captured by Carnegie Mellon University's Software Engineering Institute (SEI), in the technical report "Capability Maturity Model® for Software, Version 1.2."[12] This report posited that as software engineering organizations advanced their capabilities, they tended to exhibit characteristics consistent with five Levels®, paraphrased here:

- Level 1, Initial, is characterized by chaos. Everybody is performing the desired capability their own way, or no way at all.
- Level 2, Managed, shows signs of consistency across the organization, albeit at a basic level.
- At Level 3, Defined, the capability is repeatable. Should the "heroes" who led the organization to this capability maturity level be hit by the proverbial beer truck, the capability would not be set back, due to the existence of procedures and training materials.
- Level 4, Quantitatively Managed, capability is attained when the organization can perform so well as to be able to export its expertise to other organizations.
- Level 5, Optimized, is characterized by a level of expertise so advanced that innovations or solutions to long-standing problems in the industry are presented somewhat regularly.

One of the aspects of the Capability Maturity Model®, or CMM®, that I found attractive was that it did not attempt to identify the drivers behind advancing capability maturity within the organization; rather, it used feedback information to identify the interim characteristics of those organizations that were actually advancing in a given capability. The combination of the CMM® and insights from the Tit-for-Tat program's success in the Prisoner's Dilemma game made up a major part of my first book, *Things Your PMO Is Doing Wrong* (PMI Publishing, 2008).

In 2002, the CMM® was succeeded by the Capability Maturity Model Integration, or CMMI.[13] Unlike its predecessor, the CMMI did seek to identify a process by which advances in capability could be realized. According to a presentation from Sally Godfrey,

---

12   Carnegie Mellon University, Software Engineering Institute, "Capability Maturity Model for Software, Version 1.2," CMU/SEI-93-TR-024, ESC-TR-93-177, copyright 1993 by Carnegie Mellon University, used with permission.

13   Capability Maturity Model Integration (December 27, 2010). In *Wikipedia, The Free Encyclopedia*. Retrieved 23:26, December 29, 2010, from http://en.wikipedia.org/w/index.php?title=Capability_Maturity_Model_Integration &oldid=404403588

"CMMI models provide guidance for developing or improving processes that meet the business goals of an organization."[14]

Note the parallels between the CMM® cycle and the maturation of the individual using the Berne categories. CMM® Level 1 is entirely contained within the organization, and is chaotic; Berne's Child category is entirely self-centered, and is chaotic. CMM® Level 2 is still basic, but is moving towards an orderliness evidenced by consistency; as Berne's Adult piece of the persona is developed, it begins to understand the mores of the society in which it exists. CMM® Level 3, repeatable, is consistent with the beginning of the ascendency of Berne's Adult in that the rules for interaction with others is widely disseminated and are usually observed. CMM® Level 4, where the organization exports its capability to others, represents the ultimate achievement of Berne's Adult, not only interacting with peers and customers, but doing so from an advanced position relative to them both. Finally, CMM® Level 5 represents for the organization a level of competency that leads to solutions and ways of doing business that are emulated by younger, less mature organizations, similar to Berne's Parent part of the persona.

I was intrigued by these parallels because of the similarity they held to my previously asserted idea that the advances from Child to Adult to Parent were reminiscent of the management science advance from Asset to Project/Product management, and thence to Strategic Management, and how those parallels, in turn, mirrored the suggested path the organization ought to take through the Corner Cube model.

However, I also drew some distinctions in the areas of how the organization is motivated to make advances in a capability, how it becomes more mature. The key distinction I made in this regard dealt with the difference between attempting to change the internal narratives of the people in the organization, versus obtaining the timely, accurate, and relevant information that would allow for optimal decision-making by those same unchanged-narrative personnel. I prefer the latter approach, but will concede that there will be times when some narrative-changing is in order. But this must be done with the utmost caution, with the following warnings in mind.

Remember that with the individual, as with the macro organization, we're talking about three different (but related) narratives here; or, if you prefer, one narrative that serves three purposes. That part of the narrative that serves to tell the individual (or organization) who it is and what it is like to itself is both extremely powerful and (in all probability) highly irrational. Short of a so-called life-changing event, this narrative will not change in any significant way, and attempts to do so are, in all probability, futile.

The other two narratives are different. The script that uses causality links to explain why observed events in the past unfolded in the manner that they did runs up against evidence provided by interactions with the outside world, with peers and customers. Due to the availability of this feedback, those aspects of the narrative that are out-and-out delusional are usually quickly discovered and rooted out; else, the organization soon loses customers, and is eliminated from the game – it goes out of business. The strategic part of the narrative is similar. Direct evidence of the organization's market share can be ignored, but only at the organization's peril. It follows, then, that if any script-changing needs to occur in order to make the organization more advanced, more robust, or more profitable, the bringer of change needs to specifically avoid the appearance of altering the

---

14   Sally Godfrey (2008) What is CMMI ?. NASA presentation. Retrieved December 8, 2008.

Child's this-is-who-I (we)-am script, and focus on the Adult's and Parent's (Project and Strategist's) narratives.

I still prefer the approach of providing the most timely, accurate, and relative information to the decision-makers. The bringer of change (hopefully, advancement) need not enter the fevered swamps of what people think of themselves, how the organization views itself, what cognitive or confirmation biases may have entered into which narrative, and so on. Such bringers of change need only have a superior handle on which information streams are relevant and accurate in a given management sphere, and focus on getting those systems to provide their output in a timely fashion. The pieces will then begin to fall into place all by themselves.

The Path to Robustness

Efficiency is the enemy of robustness, much as perfection is the enemy of good enough. Given any series of past events, the Asset Manager/analyst can always find areas where time, energy, or material were supposedly wasted, and the result of such so-called analysis is used to bludgeon those who do not hold their world view into compliance via appeals to "the bottom line." I have seen this disingenuous rhetorical device used time and again, in widely different industries, so that I can't help but assume that it is widespread. But disingenuous it is, being, as it is, chocked full of cognitive biases, riddled with lapses in logic and legitimate causal analysis, and replete with attempts to isolate a few parameters to draw pre-determined conclusions while ignoring thousands or even millions of pertinent data points.

The executive perspective dominated by the Asset Managers'/analysts' meme is doomed to fail. Far more likely to succeed is the perspective centered on the customer, on Project/Product Management, followed by an added consideration for the organization's relation to its competitors in the strategic realm. Only a three-dimensional model, like the Corner Cube, can provide the information that supports this overall perspective; but it must be void of irrelevant and inaccurate information streams to be effective.

One of the central problems associated with removing irrelevant information streams is that they will almost invariably have advocates for their use, and the whole relevancy question strikes directly at the Child narrative. Telling a person that the function they perform or the information they provide is irrelevant is one of the most professionally threatening assertions that can be made. I believe this is the reason for the level of vitriol that was injected into the responses I received from any column or blog posting that dared to question the Risk Management-types' claim to the widespread and profound relevancy of their techniques. Many of their missives were positively juvenile.

When implementing the changes to the overall MIS architecture, then, it is important to systematically replace irrelevant or inaccurate streams with their relevant and accurate counterparts, so as to avoid incurring the level of organizational resistance that will doom your implementation efforts. That having been said, the following information systems must be eliminated:

- Polls (unless you're running a political effort).
- Feed-forward systems (except from Strategic Management, and there their use is minimized).

- Any system that contains any parameter that is rank speculation.
- Any system that uses Gaussian curves to predict future events, with the exclusive exception of systems used to create cost or schedule baselines.
- Systems transplanted across management-type boundaries. For example, computing the Return on Investment, a GAAP technique, on the value of a Project Management Office is as irrelevant as computing the Cost Performance Index on the accounting staff.
- Any system with output that is already not timely, accurate, AND relevant, or cannot be improved to become so. Any personnel who defend such systems with the argument that there was nothing in place to satisfy the demand for this information previously and, while the existing system may flunk the timely-accurate-relevance test, it's better than nothing, should be considered a barrier to advancement and change.

The systems that ought to be in place include:

- The General Ledger is a no-brainer, since it's required by law. However, GAAP techniques should be confined to generating information covering the acquisition, holding, and dissemination of assets.
- All project work should, at the very least, be captured in at least a basic Earned Value Management System, or EVMS. The relevancy of these systems in project work is indisputable; the level of sophistication needed will be determined by the amount of time and energy required to make the system timely and accurate.
- For many (if not most) organizations involved in project work, a Critical Path Methodology-capable scheduling system is extremely valuable. As with the EVMS, do not attempt to capture non-project work with these systems – the output would be irrelevant.
- For organizations involved in producing products, a quality control system is a must. However, the quality management information streams should confine coverage to the actual products.
- A strategic management information system, like the one described in the previous chapter. It should have a complete record of all of the company's contracts and proposals, their value, customers, project team, proposal team, periods of performance, etc. Also, this system should be able to predict future revenue streams based on the adjusted data on historical win rates and the existing proposal backlog.
- Finally, a system that can graphically represent the information from the preceding systems in an XYZ-graph format, indicating where the organization is in a Corner Cube model.

The previous six bulleted paragraphs are obviously very high level. There will be myriad supporting information streams feeding these six, and that is as it should be. However, the basic tests of fitness ought to apply to those feeder systems, as well. For example, using risk management techniques, like Monte Carlo, to help estimate a project's cost baseline, or even an appropriate contingency reserve, is perfectly appropriate. Having the risk analysts stick around the project after it is underway, performing multiple Monte Carlo analyses on an ongoing basis, as the *PMBOK® Guide* seems to suggest, is a bad idea, and should be avoided, since the information produced by such ongoing "analysis" is both irrelevant and, usually, inaccurate.

The six MIS streams listed should be able to produce information not only on the overall macro organization, but for each appropriate sub-division in the organizational breakdown structure, or OBS. I add "appropriate" because in some instances the information fails to pass the relevance test. How the Finance and Accounting department is performing strategically is irrelevant – they have no competition, unless the organization is considering out-sourcing some or all of the accountants' function. But the information concerning how Project Team A performs with respect to all the other project teams is extremely relevant, and ought to be made available.

Combining the information provided by the recommended streams can provide intelligence as powerful as Rochefort informing Nimitz of the Japanese order of battle at Midway in 1942. While they can't predict the future, they can indicate the organization's strengths and vulnerabilities, what type of work it should pursue and which it should avoid, and the myriad other relevant bits of information that can provide a significant advantage over the organizations that have been fooled by the various management technique advocates, who have oversold their pet systems' capabilities for years.

That's how this game is played. That's how this game is won.

Index

Pattern Making, Pattern Breaking
Using Past Experience and New Behaviour in Training,
Education and Change Management
Ann Alder
Hardback: 978-0-566-08853-7
e-book: 978-1-4094-1911-2

Project Politics
A Systematic Approach to Managing Complex Relationships
Nita A. Martin
Hardback: 978-0-566-08895-7
e-book: 978-1-4094-1261-8

Project Success
Critical Factors and Behaviours
Emanuel Camilleri
Hardback: 978-0-566-09228-2
e-book: 978-0-566-09229-9

Tame, Messy and Wicked Risk Leadership
David Hancock
Paperback: 978-0-566-09242-8
e-book: 978-1-4094-0873-4

Working Together
Organizational Transactional Analysis and Business Performance
Anita Mountain and Chris Davidson
Hardback: 978-0-566-08846-9
e-book: 978-1-4094-3156-5

Visit **www.gowerpublishing.com** and

- search the entire catalogue of Gower books in print
- order titles online at 10% discount
- take advantage of special offers
- sign up for our monthly e-mail update service
- download free sample chapters from all recent titles
- download or order our catalogue